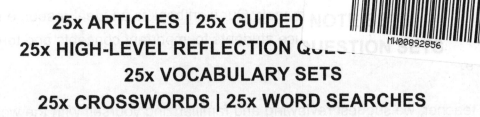

25x ARTICLES | 25x GUIDED
25x HIGH-LEVEL REFLECTION QUESTION SETS
25x VOCABULARY SETS
25x CROSSWORDS | 25x WORD SEARCHES

25x
25x: Biology

Copyright 2024 | 3andB Inc. | All Rights Reserved.
3andB Inc. | Pocatello, Idaho

version 2.0 - October 1, 2024

For more information: 3andB.com | email: info@3andB.com

Welcome & Instructions

Welcome to 3andB's *25x: Biology* workbook. Our workbook is an ideal resource for parents and educators who are looking to introduce students to important concepts and terminology related to Biology.

As a parent or teacher, we suggest reviewing and familiarizing yourself with the workbook content to facilitate a more engaging learning experience. We recommend assigning a designated time each week for the student to complete the assigned reading, guided notes, reflection questions, and term definitions, followed by word search and crossword activities.

Our workbook is strategically structured with 25+ topics that offer a comprehensive overview of important Biology concepts, terminology, and best practices. Each section includes a short and engaging article followed by guided notes and thought-provoking reflection questions, allowing students to internalize the material and apply it to their daily lives.

To enhance the learning experience, we suggest discussing the concepts with the students and encouraging them to brainstorm real-life scenarios where they can apply the concepts learned. This approach brings theoretical concepts to life, leading to a more meaningful and engaging experience for the students.

The workbook also includes 10 terms per section that the students are encouraged to define. We recommend that educators reinforce the importance of finding the best answer when defining these terms, as it will aid the students in understanding and internalizing the concepts.

As a career-oriented and professional organization, 3andB recognizes the importance of a high-quality education that prepares students for future success. Our workbook seeks to introduce Biology concepts that empower students to navigate real-life situations with confidence and a greater understanding of their capabilities.

Finally, we encourage feedback from our users to better understand how we can improve our products and services. Thank you for choosing 3andB's *25x: Biology* workbook. We believe our workbook offers a great foundation for a fulfilling, successful future for our youth.

Very truly yours,
The 3andB Team

TABLE OF CONTENTS
25x: Biology

A Gateway to Understanding
Life Around You

As students, you are about to embark on a journey to explore the science of life. Biology is the study of living organisms, from the smallest bacteria to the largest whales. Let's guide you through some of the basic concepts of biology, helping you understand the incredible diversity of life on Earth.

What is Biology?

Biology is a branch of science that deals with the study of living organisms and their interactions with the environment. It encompasses a wide range of topics, including genetics, evolution, ecology, and physiology. By understanding biology, you can learn how living things grow, reproduce, and adapt to their surroundings.

The Building Blocks of Life: Cells

At the heart of biology is the cell, the basic unit of life. All living organisms are made up of cells. Some organisms, like bacteria, are single-celled, while others, like humans, are made up of trillions of cells. Cells come in various shapes and sizes, but they all have some common features:

Cell Membrane: A protective barrier that surrounds the cell and controls what enters and exits.

Nucleus: The control center of the cell, containing genetic material (DNA).

Cytoplasm: A jelly-like substance where various cell activities occur.

Genetics:
The Blueprint of Life

Genetics is the study of how traits are passed from parents to offspring. Your genetic information is stored in your DNA, which is organized into structures called chromosomes. Genes are segments of DNA that determine specific traits, such as eye color or height.

Biology can give you an appreciation for life and insights to preserve that life.

Understanding genetics helps us comprehend how characteristics are inherited and why you might look similar to your parents. It also explains genetic disorders and how they can be passed down through generations.

Evolution: The Story of Life

Evolution is the process through which species of organisms change over time through natural selection. It explains the diversity of life on Earth. Charles Darwin, a famous biologist, proposed the theory of natural selection, which suggests that organisms with favorable traits are more likely to survive and reproduce.

Over millions of years, these small changes accumulate, leading to the development of new species. Evolution helps us understand the relationships between different organisms and their adaptations to the environment.

Ecology: Interactions in Nature

Ecology is the study of how organisms interact with each other and their environment. It looks at how living things depend on one another for survival. Ecosystems, such as forests, oceans, and deserts, are communities of living organisms interacting with their physical surroundings.

Biology is the study of living things and their interactions with the environment.

Ecologists study food chains and food webs to understand how energy flows through an ecosystem. They also investigate how human activities, like deforestation and pollution, impact the environment and the organisms living in it.

Physiology: How Living Things Function

Physiology is the study of how living organisms function. It examines the physical and chemical processes that occur within organisms to keep them alive.

For example, human physiology looks at how organs like the heart, lungs, and brain work together to sustain life.

By understanding physiology, you can learn how your body responds to different stimuli, how it maintains homeostasis (a stable internal environment), and how it heals from injuries.

The Importance of Biology

Biology is essential for understanding the natural world and addressing global challenges. It plays a crucial role in medicine, agriculture, and environmental conservation. For instance, biologists work to develop new medical treatments, enhance crop production, and protect endangered species. Studying biology can also inspire you to pursue careers in science, healthcare, and environmental management. It opens up opportunities to make significant contributions to society by solving real-world problems.

Biology is a diverse and dynamic field that offers insights into the complexities of life. By studying biology, you can gain a deeper appreciation for the natural world and the intricate processes that sustain it. Whether you aspire to be a scientist, doctor, or simply a well-informed citizen, the knowledge you gain from biology will be invaluable.

I. What is Biology?

Define biology in your own words: _____

_____

II. Key Areas of Biology

Match each area of biology with its description:

_____ Genetics   A. Study of how organisms interact with each other and their environment

_____ Evolution   B. Study of how living organisms function

_____ Ecology   C. Study of how traits are passed from parents to offspring

_____ Physiology   D. Process through which species change over time through natural selection

III. The Building Blocks of Life: Cells

List three common features of cells:

1. _____   2. _____

3. _____

IV. Genetics

Explain what genes are and their importance:

_____

_____

V. Evolution

Who proposed the theory of natural selection? _____

Briefly explain the concept of natural selection:

_____

_____

VI. Ecology

What is an ecosystem? Provide an example:

_____

_____

VII. Physiology

What does physiology study? Give an example:

_____

_____

_____

VIII. True or False

_____ All living organisms are made up of cells.

_____ DNA is stored in the cell membrane.

_____ Ecology only studies plants and animals, not their environment.

_____ Evolution explains the diversity of life on Earth.

IX. Short Answer

Name two ways biology is important in the real world:

1. _____

2. _____

X. Reflection

In your own words, explain why studying biology is valuable:

_____

_____

_____

#1

What is one way understanding genetics can help you in everyday life?

Think about how knowing your genetic traits can help you understand your health, family history, or even personal interests.

#2

How do you think the theory of evolution affects our understanding of the diversity of life on Earth?

Consider how different species have adapted to their environments over time and how this explains the variety of living organisms we see today.

#3

Why is it important to study the interactions between organisms and their environment in ecology?

Reflect on how living things depend on each other for survival and how human activities might impact these relationships.

#4

How can knowledge of physiology help you maintain a healthy lifestyle?

Think about how understanding the functions of your body systems can guide you in making healthier choices and recognizing signs of illness.

#5

What role does the cell play as the basic unit of life in all living organisms?

Reflect on the different functions of the cell structures like the cell membrane, nucleus, and cytoplasm, and how they work together to keep the organism alive.

#6

In what ways can studying biology inspire you to pursue a career in science or healthcare?

Consider the various fields within biology, such as medicine, environmental conservation, and research, and how they contribute to solving important real-world problems.

TERM	DEFINITION
Biology	
Cell	
Cell membrane	
Nucleus	
Cytoplasm	
Genetics	
DNA	

TERM	DEFINITION
Chromosomes	
Genes	
Evolution	
Natural selection	
Ecology	
Ecosystem	
Physiology	

What Is Biology?

```
X A G U N C I Y N V Q V M Y T Q M L D B K P Q G
C G T D U Y U W W U F O T L M E Q U S E O X B J
E R C H C T O S K L B N S J O Y P B W V D F K S
L H T Y L O J P U T V C U W O E C O L O G Y R S
L V J X E P B A Y H R D M M V S S Z C L T M K G
G S C Z U L T L F N U M V A S X F B C U H D C R
E Q W O S A S R V W N A Z T Q S B X O T I T H C
N K S F X S E V A E I I S V N V Q I U I H R W
E Q F X R M J P U L K W K F L Y Y N E O Z K O K
T B J C E L L M E M B R A N E Y D E C N L Q M X
I R N J T Q T V M D C F V F H A M T O D N G O P
C U Q X Q M P D O H J D K R G P A T S Q U M S F
S R U G D J R Z I B X R T X O J C B Y V J U O P
F Z O X M C L B X S G Q L Y G T C I S S D U M N
L Z P U A X V U F Q R Y E H Y F L O T E K M E C
Z D H A F W T X C Y J N L B G V F L E E S E S D
E P Y D S O Z G I V J F U J T U N O M J L Z T M
K H S M O G R U F D D G E N E S H G F E Q W C O
Y W I C L Y D O Y V S T C T I C Y Y V S N U G
S V O M O G J U F T Y G Z L P H M I G E R Z O G
C E L N W Q M U F N U C R O T T U Q X V G W D C
H R O T M Z V D N A T U R A L S E L E C T I O N
H G G T G B U N K H N G Q A M U R G Y T L V O L
X E Y I V F H A G G U A G T N R O I J Z S A P P
```

Natural selection

Ecosystem

Genes

Genetics

Cell

Cell membrane

Ecology

Chromosomes

Cytoplasm

Biology

Physiology

Evolution

DNA

Nucleus

What Is Biology?

Across

5. Segments of DNA that determine specific traits, such as eye color or height.

8. The protective barrier that surrounds a cell and controls what enters and exits the cell. Cell _____

9. The study of how traits are passed from parents to offspring through genes.

10. The study of how organisms interact with each other and their environment.

12. A community of living organisms interacting with their physical surroundings, such as a forest, ocean, or desert.

13. The process through which species of organisms change over time through natural selection.

14. The jelly-like substance inside a cell where various cell activities occur.

Down

1. The control center of a cell that contains genetic material (DNA).

2. The theory proposed by Charles Darwin that suggests organisms with favorable traits are more likely to survive and reproduce. Natural _____

3. The study of how living organisms function, including the physical and chemical processes that keep them alive.

4. Structures within cells that contain DNA and organize genetic information.

6. The molecule that carries genetic information in all living organisms.

7. The basic unit of life in all living organisms.

11. The branch of science that deals with the study of living organisms and their interactions with the environment.

Understanding the Characteristics of Life

Have you ever wondered what makes something alive? It's a fascinating question that scientists have been exploring for centuries. In biology, we study living things, and to do that, we need to understand what characteristics define life. Let's get you introduced to the essential traits that all living organisms share.

Organization and Cells

One of the most fundamental characteristics of life is organization. Living organisms are made up of one or more cells, which are the basic units of life. Cells are like tiny factories, each performing vital functions that keep the organism alive. Some organisms, like bacteria, are made up of a single cell, while others, like humans, are made up of trillions of cells organized into tissues, organs, and systems.

Characteristics of life include organization, metabolism, growth and development, reproduction, response to stimuli, adaptation, and homeostasis.

Metabolism

Metabolism is the set of life-sustaining chemical reactions that occur in living organisms. These reactions allow organisms to grow, reproduce, repair damage, and respond to their environment. Metabolism includes two main processes: anabolism (building up) and catabolism (breaking down). For example, when you eat food, your body breaks it down (catabolism) and uses the nutrients to build and repair tissues (anabolism).

Homeostasis

Have you noticed how your body shivers when it's cold or sweats when it's hot? This is your body's way of maintaining a stable internal environment, a process known as homeostasis. All living organisms have mechanisms to keep their internal conditions within a narrow range, even when external conditions change. This stability is crucial for survival, as it allows organisms to function properly.

Growth and Development

All living things grow and develop. Growth refers to an increase in size and number of cells, while development refers to the process by which organisms change and mature over time. For example, a seed grows into a plant, and a caterpillar develops into a butterfly. Growth and development are guided by the organism's genetic information, which is passed down from generation to generation.

Reproduction

Living organisms have the ability to reproduce, which means they can create new organisms similar to themselves. Reproduction can be sexual, involving the combination of genetic material from two parents, or asexual, involving a single parent. For example, humans reproduce sexually, while bacteria can reproduce asexually by splitting into two identical cells. Reproduction ensures the continuation of a species.

Response to Stimuli

Life is dynamic, and living organisms can respond to changes in their environment. This ability to respond to stimuli helps organisms survive and thrive. For example, plants grow towards light, and animals move away from danger. These responses can be immediate, like pulling your hand away from a hot stove, or they can be more gradual, like a plant growing towards sunlight.

Adaptation Through Evolution

Over time, living organisms adapt to their environments through the process of evolution. Evolution occurs over many generations and involves changes in the genetic makeup of a population. These changes can lead to new traits that help organisms survive and reproduce in their specific environments. For example, the long necks of giraffes evolved to help them reach leaves high in trees.

Energy Use

All living organisms need energy to perform their life functions. They obtain energy in different ways. Plants, for example, use sunlight to make food through photosynthesis, while animals get energy by eating plants or other animals. This energy is then used for growth, reproduction, and other vital activities. Without energy, living organisms cannot sustain life.

Biology is the study of living things and their interactions with the environment.

Understanding the characteristics of life helps us appreciate the complexity and diversity of living organisms. Whether you're looking at a single-celled bacterium or a complex human being, these traits are what make life possible. By studying these characteristics, you gain a deeper understanding of biology and the incredible processes that sustain life on Earth. Remember, life is all around you, and each living thing shares these common traits.

1. Characteristics of Life
GUIDED NOTES

I. Introduction

What is the main question this article explores? _____

_____

II. Eight Characteristics of Life

List the eight main characteristics of life discussed in the article:

1. _____   2. _____

3. _____   4. _____

5. _____   6. _____

7. _____   8. _____

III. Details about Each Characteristic

1. Organization and Cells

Define cells: _____

Single-celled organism example:_____

Multi-celled organism example: _____

2. Metabolism

Definition of metabolism:_____

_____

Two main processes of metabolism:

  a. _____ : building up   b. _____ : breaking down

3. Homeostasis

Definition: _____Example from

the text: _____

4. Growth and Development

Difference between growth and development:

Growth: _____

Development: _____

_____

Example of development from the text: _____

_____

5. Reproduction

Two types of reproduction:

  a. _____   b. _____

Example of each:

  a. _____

  b. _____

6. Response to Stimuli

Why is this ability important?_____Two

examples from the text:

  1. _____

  2. _____

7. Adaptation Through Evolution

Definition of evolution: _____

_____

Example from the text: _____

_____

8. Energy Use

Why do living organisms need energy? _____

How do plants obtain energy? _____

How do animals obtain energy? _____

IV. True or False

Mark each statement as True (T) or False (F):

_____ All living organisms are made up of cells.

_____ Metabolism only involves breaking down substances.

_____ Homeostasis is the ability to maintain a stable internal environment.

_____ Only animals can respond to stimuli.

_____ Evolution occurs within a single organism's lifetime.

#1

How do cells function as the basic units of life in different organisms?

Consider how single-celled organisms like bacteria compare to multi-celled organisms like humans in terms of cell organization and function.

#2

Why is metabolism important for living organisms, and how does it support life processes?

Reflect on the two main processes of metabolism, anabolism and catabolism, and how they enable growth, repair, and response to the environment.

#3

What role does homeostasis play in the survival of living organisms?

Think about examples in your own body, such as sweating or shivering, and why maintaining stable internal conditions is essential for life.

#4

In what ways do organisms grow and develop, and how is this process guided by genetic information?

Consider the journey of a seed growing into a plant or a caterpillar transforming into a butterfly, and how genetic information influences these changes.

#5

How do different organisms reproduce, and why is reproduction vital for the continuation of a species?

Reflect on the differences between sexual and asexual reproduction and the significance of each method for species survival.

#6

How do living organisms respond to stimuli in their environment, and why is this ability important for their survival?

Think about immediate responses, like pulling your hand away from a hot surface, and gradual responses, like a plant growing towards light, and how these responses help organisms adapt.

TERM	DEFINITION
Cell	
Organization	
Metabolism	
Anabolism	
Catabolism	
Homeostasis	
Growth	

TERM	DEFINITION
Development	
Genetic information	
Reproduction	
Sexual reproduction	
Asexual reproduction	
Response to stimuli	
Evolution	

Characteristics of Life

```
D E Q Z S V R V Q Y H L F E U Q H S X X Z J X H
B M A S D Q E X W K I R P M R J D Z W B Y C X W
F E N E G O S L I C W S U E G O N O Q Z H C I W
O T A X I R P J Y J R Z V M Q V I Y G X M A D H
G A O U T Q O M A P H M P Q K E Y M O U H B E O
S B B A G S N L P G Q V W F S Z R T N O L Y V M
A O D L I V S J U F S B K V G G R O W T H I E E
V L H T B R E O K Q R O H L I G F N K R T I L O
A I F M L L T J K J D N C R Q Y I Q K X P O S
Q S F L U J O C E L L X T M P S Q J M W X D P T
B M R X C M S B F R Q C W X Y G T G G C D Q M A
S Q G E N E T I C I N F O R M A T I O N R F E S
Z J N O F M I W N V D F Z A S E X U A L E H N I
D C I R T J M A W E V O L U T I O N B B P X T S
P R W G X H U W U Y N B Q E D K L S O N R E A W
K V O A P B L A N A B O L I S M M O W Z O B F T
G N O N E H I O W B K K J R P R V B Z O D L U I
N C N I L C P X G S A T E R N P H F E Z U V L X
N Z G Z F Z T N K S W V V Q E X W A S M C Y H C
X U J A H I F I A R D L M D K T R M G C T J M A
V N N T Y G N C V H W R S C F O F Z G G I X Q U
O W U I Q B W N C A T A B O L I S M K V O J C T
S H O O O P X R J S X Y G J F N R I J K N W K R
A Q V N Y D F T N D T H C S U Q C A V N E F X N
```

Response to stimuli	Genetic information	Evolution
Asexual	Sexual	Reproduction
Development	Growth	Homeostasis
Catabolism	Anabolism	Metabolism
Organization	Cell	

Characteristics of Life

Across

4. The hereditary material that guides growth, development, and reproduction in organisms. _____ information

9. The production of offspring from a single parent, resulting in identical genetic copies. _____ reproduction

10. The increase in size and number of cells in an organism.

11. The ability of an organism to maintain a stable internal environment despite external changes.

13. The ability of organisms to react to environmental changes for survival and thriving. Response to _____

14. The process by which an organism changes and matures over time.

Down

1. The set of life-sustaining chemical reactions in organisms, including anabolism and catabolism.

2. The structured arrangement of cells into tissues, organs, and systems in multicellular organisms.

3. The biological process of creating new organisms, either sexually or asexually.

5. The process of breaking down complex molecules into simpler ones, releasing energy.

6. The process of adaptation and change in organisms over generations, leading to new traits that enhance survival.

7. The process of building up complex molecules from simpler ones, essential for growth and repair.

8. The basic unit of life, functioning like a tiny factory to perform vital functions.

12. The production of offspring through the combination of genetic material from two parents. _____ reproduction

Water and Macromolecules in Biology

In your biology class, you might have heard that water is essential for life. But have you ever wondered why that is? And what about those big molecules called macromolecules? Let's help you understand the vital roles of water and macromolecules in living organisms.

The Importance of Water

Water is everywhere in living organisms. In fact, about 70% of your body is made up of water! But why is water so crucial? Here are some key reasons:

Solvent Properties: Water is known as the "universal solvent." This means it can dissolve many substances, allowing your cells to use nutrients, minerals, and chemicals efficiently.

Temperature Regulation: Water has a high heat capacity, which means it can absorb and release heat slowly. This helps regulate your body temperature, keeping it stable even when the environment changes.

Chemical Reactions: Many chemical reactions in your body, like digestion and energy production, occur in water. Water molecules help break down and transport substances in these reactions.

Transport: Water is the main component of blood, which carries oxygen and nutrients to cells and removes waste products. Without water, your cells wouldn't get the essentials they need to function.

What are Macromolecules?

Macromolecules are large, complex molecules that are crucial for life. There are four main types of macromolecules: carbohydrates, lipids, proteins, and nucleic acids. Let's take a closer look at each one.

Carbohydrates:
Carbohydrates are your body's main source of energy. They are found in foods like bread, pasta, and fruits. Carbohydrates are made of sugar molecules. Simple carbohydrates have one or two sugar units, while complex carbohydrates have many.

Macromolecules are an important part of the foods we eat.

Lipids: Lipids, or fats, store energy and make up cell membranes. They are also important for insulation and protecting organs. Lipids are made of fatty acids and glycerol. They can be found in foods like oils, butter, and avocados.

Proteins: Proteins are the building blocks of your body. They make up muscles, enzymes, and hormones. Enzymes speed up chemical reactions, and hormones regulate body functions. Proteins are made of amino acids. There are 20 different amino acids that combine in various ways to form proteins.

Nucleic Acids: Nucleic acids store and transmit genetic information. DNA and RNA are the two types of nucleic acids. Nucleic acids are made of nucleotides, which include a sugar, a phosphate group, and a nitrogenous base.

How Water and Macromolecules Work Together

Water and macromolecules have a close relationship. Here's how they interact:

Water has many qualities that are needed for life.

Hydration and Reactions: Water helps dissolve macromolecules so they can participate in chemical reactions. For example, enzymes (proteins) need water to function properly.

Transport and Nutrients: Water carries macromolecules throughout your body. Blood, which is mostly water, transports glucose (a carbohydrate) to cells for energy.

Cell Structure and Function: Water maintains the shape and structure of cells and their components. Proteins and lipids in cell membranes rely on water to keep cells flexible and functional.

Real-Life Applications

Understanding water and macromolecules isn't just for passing your biology class. It has real-life applications:

Nutrition: Knowing which foods provide essential macromolecules can help you make healthier choices. Eating a balanced diet ensures you get enough carbohydrates, lipids, proteins, and nucleic acids.

Medicine: Many medicines are designed to interact with macromolecules like proteins and nucleic acids. Understanding this can help you appreciate how treatments work.

Environmental Science: Water pollution can affect the availability of clean water, impacting all living organisms. Understanding water's role in biology highlights the importance of protecting our water sources.

Water and macromolecules are fundamental to life. Water's unique properties make it an essential part of biological processes, while macromolecules serve as the building blocks and machinery of cells. By understanding their roles, you can better appreciate how your body works and how to take care of it.

2. Water and Macromolecules

I. The Importance of Water

List four key reasons why water is crucial for living organisms:

1. _____

2. _____

3. _____

4. _____

II. Macromolecules

Match each macromolecule with its primary function:

_____ Carbohydrates   A. Store and transmit genetic information

_____ Lipids   B. Main source of energy

_____ Proteins   C. Building blocks of the body

_____ Nucleic Acids   D. Store energy and make up cell membranes

III. Types of Macromolecules

For each macromolecule, provide its basic building block:

1. Carbohydrates: _____

2. Lipids: _____

3. Proteins: _____

4. Nucleic Acids: _____

IV. Water and Macromolecules Interaction

Explain how water interacts with macromolecules in these processes:

1. Hydration and Reactions: _____

_____

2. Transport and Nutrients: _____

_____

3. Cell Structure and Function: _____

_____

V. Real-Life Applications

Write one way understanding water and macromolecules applies to each field:

1. Nutrition: _____

_____

2. Medicine: _____

_____

_____

3. Environmental Science: _____

_____

VI. True or False

_____ Water makes up about 70% of the human body.

_____ There are five main types of macromolecules.

_____ Proteins are made of amino acids.

_____ Nucleic acids include DNA and RNA.

VII. In your own words, explain why learning about water and macromolecules is important for understanding biology:

_____

_____

_____

_____

2. Water and Macromolecules

#1

Why is water called the "universal solvent," and how does this property benefit your cells?

Consider how water dissolves various substances and helps in nutrient absorption and chemical reactions within your body.

#2

How does water help regulate your body temperature, and why is this important for your health?

Reflect on the high heat capacity of water and how it keeps your body temperature stable despite environmental changes.

#3

What roles do carbohydrates play in your body, and how do they provide energy?

Think about the different types of carbohydrates (simple and complex) and their importance as your main energy source.

#4

In what ways do lipids contribute to your body's structure and function?

Consider how lipids store energy, make up cell membranes, and provide insulation and protection for your organs.

#5

How do proteins facilitate various functions in your body, and why are amino acids important?

Reflect on the role of proteins in building muscles, speeding up chemical reactions (enzymes), and regulating body functions (hormones).

#6

How do water and macromolecules interact to maintain cell structure and function?

Think about how water helps dissolve macromolecules for chemical reactions and how it supports the shape and flexibility of cells and their components.

TERM	DEFINITION
Universal solvent	
Heat capacity	
Chemical reactions	
Transport	
Macromolecules	
Carbohydrates	
Lipids	

TERM	DEFINITION
Proteins	
Amino acids	
Nucleic acids	
DNA	
RNA	
Hydration	
Cell membranes	

Water & Macromolecules

```
R U I Y M A C S M I C O K C Y J B P Y B T Y X S
B E H M V V Y K V I A M I N O A C I D S C Z S E
J E A A L F U O N Q Y F F M I L X V X K E W A K
X T D C P J V K U Y Q Q M E U I Q T C W L H O M
V L V R F U Q Z C N G B B U W D F U K U L Y X U
W F F O J T T P L W R F M V B N S R R P M D X W
P S U M U G G R E G S M E Q J A Z H X C E R W D
N W K O E Q M O I V L D Y Q Z T P X H I M A H Y
I Q A L R H Y T C G I S Z M B F Y G A L B T F K
C G H E P W W E A M P M P B Q S L U X G R I A Z
A H P C O N D I C E I J K H F Y P F N G A O G Q
H B J U O P F N I O D J G B V W N G U L N N M I
H H B L J U G S D U S Y K V X R O U I O E H I W
E D X E N V K C S T K Y L O L N B R W S S Q L E
A T G S Q X Y Z B D C L S N M A U M T A P R O R
T F U N I V E R S A L S O L V E N T N W Y F V M
C C A R B O H Y D R A T E S S N J R L L D G H J
A T F U Z U X D B I J H K Q J L X B Y E T B E I
P L E B B J S A B P O K A B F F W S Q J Y R N R
A M C Z Q T J N S M C C X M H D Y G C Y G Y R Q
C M Q A G P Y C E M T R A N S P O R T G W B A A
I C H E M I C A L R E A C T I O N S G U U V Z A
T I N I G L Y Y L K T C X O L E S E C T L Y D X
Y P W Y X R B V L U B N N F O S Y V W C B B C W
```

Universal solvent	Heat capacity	Nucleic acids
Cell membranes	Hydration	RNA
DNA	Amino acids	Proteins
Lipids	Carbohydrates	Macromolecules
Transport	Chemical reactions	

Water & Macromolecules

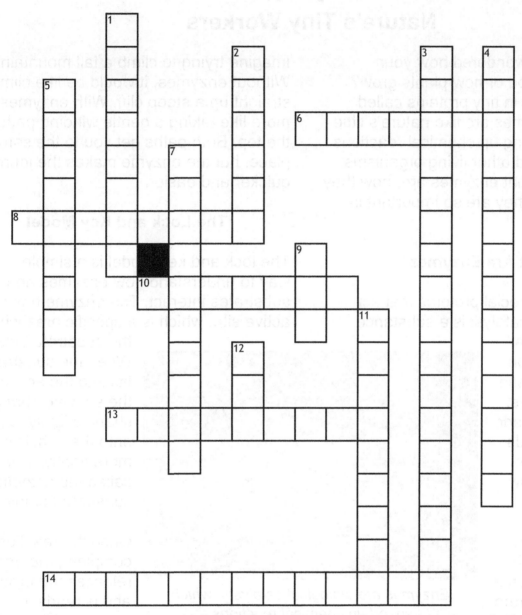

Across

6. Macromolecules that store and transmit genetic information, including DNA and RNA, made of nucleotides. ____ acids

8. Macromolecules that are the building blocks of the body, making up muscles, enzymes, and hormones, and composed of amino acids.

10. A property of water that allows it to dissolve many substances, making it essential for cells to use nutrients, minerals, and chemicals efficiently. Universal ____

13. The process of water helping to dissolve macromolecules so they can participate in chemical reactions, necessary for enzymes to function properly.

14. Macromolecules that serve as the body's main source of energy, found in foods like bread, pasta, and fruits, and made of sugar molecules.

Down

1. The ability of water to absorb and release heat slowly, helping to regulate body temperature and maintain stability. Heat ____

2. Macromolecules, also known as fats, that store energy, make up cell membranes, and provide insulation and protection for organs, made of fatty acids and glycerol.

3. Processes in the body, such as digestion and energy production, that occur in water, where water molecules help break down and transport substances. (Two words)

4. Large, complex molecules essential for life, including carbohydrates, lipids, proteins, and nucleic acids.

5. Structures made of lipids and proteins that rely on water to maintain their shape and flexibility, essential for cell function. Cell ____

7. The building blocks of proteins, with 20 different types that combine in various ways to form proteins. (Two words)

9. A type of nucleic acid involved in protein synthesis and the transmission of genetic information, composed of nucleotides.

11. The role of water in carrying oxygen and nutrients to cells and removing waste products, primarily through the blood.

12. A type of nucleic acid that contains genetic information essential for growth, development, and reproduction, composed of nucleotides.

Enzymes:
Nature's Tiny Workers

Have you ever wondered how your body digests food or how plants grow? The answer lies in tiny proteins called enzymes. Enzymes are like nature's little workers, speeding up chemical reactions in your body and other living organisms. Let's go over what enzymes are, how they work, and why they are so important in biology.

What Are Enzymes?

Enzymes are special proteins that act as catalysts. A catalyst is a substance that speeds up a chemical reaction without being used up in the process. Enzymes are made up of amino acids and have unique shapes that allow them to interact with specific molecules called substrates. Each enzyme works on a particular substrate, much like a key fits into a specific lock.

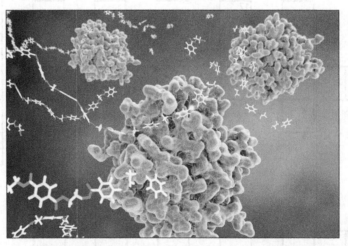

Enzymes are biological catalysts, which speed up chemical reactions.

How Do Enzymes Work?

Enzymes work by lowering the activation energy needed for a chemical reaction to occur. Activation energy is the energy required to start a reaction. By reducing this energy, enzymes make it easier and faster for reactions to happen.

Imagine trying to climb a tall mountain. Without enzymes, it would be like climbing straight up a steep cliff. With enzymes, it's more like taking a gentle winding path to the top. Both paths get you to the same place, but the enzyme makes the journey quicker and easier.

The Lock and Key Model

The lock and key model is a simple way to understand how enzymes and substrates interact. The enzyme has an active site, which is a specific area where the substrate binds. When the substrate fits into the active site, the enzyme changes shape slightly to hold onto the substrate more tightly. This is called the enzyme-substrate complex.

Once the reaction is complete, the enzyme releases the product and is ready to interact with another substrate. This process can happen thousands of times per second, making enzymes incredibly efficient.

Types of Enzymes

There are many types of enzymes, each with a specific function. Here are a few examples:

Amylase: Found in saliva, amylase helps break down carbohydrates into sugars.

Protease: These enzymes break down proteins into amino acids. They are found in your stomach and intestines.

Lipase: Lipase breaks down fats into fatty acids and glycerol. It is produced in your pancreas and works in your small intestine.

DNA Polymerase: This enzyme helps copy DNA during cell division.

Factors Affecting Enzyme Activity
Several factors can affect how well enzymes work.

Temperature: Enzymes work best at specific temperatures. For most human enzymes, this is around 37°C (98.6°F), which is our normal body temperature. Too much heat can denature (damage) enzymes, causing them to lose their shape and function.
pH Levels: Each enzyme has an optimal pH level. For example, pepsin, an enzyme in your stomach, works best in acidic conditions, while amylase works best in neutral conditions.

Substrate Concentration: The more substrate available, the faster the reaction, up to a point. Once all the enzymes are busy, adding more substrate won't speed things up.

Enzymes assist your body with digesting food for energy.

Inhibitors: Some molecules can slow down or stop enzyme activity. These are called inhibitors. Competitive inhibitors compete with the substrate for the active site, while non-competitive inhibitors bind elsewhere on the enzyme, changing its shape.

Real-Life Applications of Enzymes
Enzymes are not just important in your body; they have many practical uses too:

Medicine: Enzymes are used in treatments for diseases like cancer and diabetes. For example, insulin, a hormone that regulates blood sugar, is produced using enzymes.

Food Industry: Enzymes are used to make cheese, bread, and yogurt. They help break down complex molecules, improving texture and flavor.

Laundry Detergents: Enzymes in detergents help break down stains like grease, blood, and grass, making your clothes cleaner.

Enzymes are fascinating and essential molecules that play a crucial role in living organisms. By speeding up chemical reactions, they help your body function smoothly and efficiently.

Understanding enzymes can give you a deeper appreciation of how your body works and how science can harness these tiny workers for various applications.

3. Enzymes

I. What Are Enzymes?

Complete the definition:

Enzymes are special _____ that act as _____. They

speed up chemical reactions without being _____ in the process.

II. How Enzymes Work

Fill in the blanks:

1. Enzymes lower the _____ _____ needed for a

chemical reaction to occur.

2. The "_____ and _____" model explains how

enzymes and substrates interact.

3. The specific area where the substrate binds to the enzyme is called the

_____ _____.

III. Types of Enzymes

Match each enzyme with its function:

_____ Amylase   A. Breaks down proteins

_____ Protease   B. Helps copy DNA

_____ Lipase   C. Breaks down carbohydrates

_____ DNA Polymerase   D. Breaks down fats

IV. Factors Affecting Enzyme Activity

List four factors that can affect enzyme activity:

1. _____   2. _____

3. _____   4. _____

V. Enzyme Applications

Name one application of enzymes in each area:

1. Medicine: _____

2. Food Industry: _____

3. Household Products: _____

VI. True or False

_____ Enzymes are used up in the chemical reactions they catalyze.

_____ Each enzyme works on many different substrates.

_____ The shape of an enzyme is important for its function.

_____ Enzymes can work at any temperature.

VII. Short Answer

1. Explain the "Lock and Key" model of enzyme function in your own words:

_____

_____

_____

2. Why are enzymes important in living organisms?

_____

_____

_____

VIII. Reflection

In your own words, explain why understanding enzymes is important for biology and everyday life:

_____

_____

_____

_____

_____

#1

How do enzymes make chemical reactions happen faster in your body?

Think about the concept of activation energy and how enzymes lower it to speed up reactions.

#2

Why is the lock and key model useful for understanding enzyme function?

Reflect on the analogy between the specific fit of a key into a lock and how an enzyme's active site interacts with its substrate.

#3

What might happen to enzyme activity if your body temperature rises too high?

Consider the effect of temperature on enzyme structure and function, including the concept of denaturation.

#4

How do different pH levels affect enzyme activity?

Think about how enzymes like pepsin and amylase work best at different pH levels and why that might be important for their functions.

#5

Can you think of a real-life example where enzymes are used outside the body?

Reflect on the use of enzymes in everyday products like laundry detergents or in the food industry for making cheese and bread.

#6

Why is enzyme efficiency important for your body's overall function?

Think about how enzymes' ability to speed up reactions thousands of times per second helps maintain bodily functions and processes.

TERM	DEFINITION
Enzyme	
Catalyst	
Amino acids	
Substrate	
Activation energy	
Active site	
Enzyme-substrate complex	

TERM	DEFINITION
Denature	
Amylase	
Protease	
Lipase	
DNA Polymerase	
Inhibitor	
Optimal pH	

Enzymes

```
F C P Y L S S M S S C K W J Z P H W U X J Z I D
H O B T R F V E L A M I N O A C I D S B T I Q E
O H E A C T I V A T I O N E N E R G Y Y S O D N
G H Z V K Z R D Y H M F Q K N V P N L V U F F Z
X U M S F E O N B W U C C D S U Q E O Y B X V Y
O Y Q W P C Z A O I S Q O V W C E U V Y S W I M
P L P I H Y U P C D W W P M I D J U M M T H O E
A U Y H A G D O G K F O R U O V E H E S R F R S
V V J I E F B L B V C J R D I P F N V C A H W U
R T V C Q F T Y M Z A R I Q I J J S R B T R I B
R V F Y C P M M D W T K B L L G P H F P E N B S
K V I N R R M E B K A L I P A S E Y G T G M N T
M L N P O G R R W Z L U F Z A Y F T W R O W Z R
C Y H B U L F A C Z Y M D H A H R Y V D F S X A
D O I M L B Z S D G S G Z V P F Q M X R X M G T
J R B Z Z I Z E Y N T D P S R V U E N Z Y M E E
J X I Z C K P V D S X A X A O Y C S Y C G Z G C
I U T C D F X G C L C Y C N T D E N A T U R E O
J H O Q U R K Y G D E N L V E M N D U H T D I M
K B R O P T I M A L P H O Y A L E D O W N I B P
P A C T I V E S I T E W M C S C L A G V D N A L
J W P P R Q K Q O C Z Z U S E V I K Q U A S A E
C P Q O D I Z L S C J W V W Q K C C H M C X B X
F V V E P G Y Q A M Y L A S E N D E P A H Y J D
```

Optimal pH	DNA polymerase	Enzyme-substrate complex
Activation energy	Inhibitor	Lipase
Protease	Amylase	Denature
Active site	Substrate	Amino acids
Catalyst	Enzyme	

Enzymes

Across

2. The minimum amount of energy required to start a chemical reaction, which enzymes help to lower. _____ energy

5. The building blocks of proteins, including enzymes, which are made up of long chains of these molecules. (Two words)

8. The process by which an enzyme loses its shape and function due to factors like high temperature or extreme pH levels.

10. A special protein that acts as a catalyst to speed up chemical reactions without being consumed in the process.

11. An enzyme found in saliva that helps break down carbohydrates into simpler sugars.

12. The specific pH level at which an enzyme works best, varying from enzyme to enzyme. _____ pH

13. Enzymes that break down proteins into amino acids; found in the stomach and intestines.

14. The specific molecule that an enzyme interacts with during a chemical reaction, fitting into the enzyme's active site like a key into a lock.

Down

1. A molecule that can slow down or stop enzyme activity by blocking the active site or altering the enzyme's shape.

3. An enzyme that breaks down fats into fatty acids and glycerol, produced in the pancreas and active in the small intestine.

4. An enzyme that assists in copying DNA during cell division, ensuring genetic information is passed on accurately. DNA _____

6. The region on an enzyme where the substrate binds and the chemical reaction takes place. (Two words)

7. This forms when an enzyme binds to its substrate, facilitating the chemical reaction. Enzyme-substrate _____

9. A substance that increases the rate of a chemical reaction without being used up or altered in the process.

Cell Theory and Cell Types: Building Blocks of Life

Have you ever wondered what makes up every living thing on Earth? Whether it's a tiny ant or a giant sequoia tree, all living beings are made of cells. Time to get into cell theory and the different types of cells. By the end, you'll have a better understanding of these fundamental building blocks of life.

What is Cell Theory?

Cell theory is one of the most important principles in biology. It helps scientists understand how living organisms are structured and function. Here are the three main ideas of cell theory:

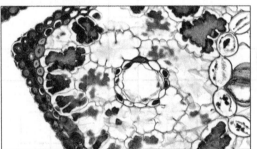
Cells are the basic unit of life for all living things.

1. All living things are made of one or more cells. This means that every plant, animal, and microorganism is composed of cells.

2. The cell is the basic unit of life. Cells are the smallest structures that can be considered alive. They carry out all the functions necessary for an organism to survive.

3. All cells come from pre-existing cells. New cells are created when existing cells divide. This process is essential for growth, repair, and reproduction in living organisms.

Types of Cells

Now that you understand the basics of cell theory, let's dive into the different types of cells. There are two major categories: prokaryotic cells and eukaryotic cells.

Prokaryotic Cells

Prokaryotic cells are the simplest and oldest type of cells. They are usually found in single-celled organisms like bacteria. Here are some key features of prokaryotic cells:

No nucleus: Prokaryotic cells don't have a nucleus. Instead, their genetic material floats freely in the cell.

Simple structure: These cells lack many of the specialized structures, or organelles, found in more complex cells.

Small size: Prokaryotic cells are generally smaller than eukaryotic cells.

Even though they are simple, prokaryotic cells are incredibly important. They can live in extreme environments, like hot springs and deep ocean vents, and play a crucial role in ecosystems.

Eukaryotic Cells

Eukaryotic cells are more complex and are found in plants, animals, fungi, and protists.

Here are some important characteristics of eukaryotic cells:

Nucleus: Eukaryotic cells have a nucleus, which contains the cell's genetic material.

Organelles: These cells have specialized structures called organelles that perform different functions. For example, mitochondria produce energy, while chloroplasts (found in plant cells) carry out photosynthesis.

Larger size: Eukaryotic cells are generally larger than prokaryotic cells.

Eukaryotic cells can form multicellular organisms, which means they can work together to build complex beings like you.

Specialized Cells

In multicellular organisms, cells often become specialized to perform specific tasks. Here are a few examples of specialized cells:

Red blood cells: These cells carry oxygen from your lungs to the rest of your body. They have a unique shape that helps them move through blood vessels easily.

Nerve cells: Also known as neurons, these cells transmit signals throughout your body, allowing you to think, feel, and move.

Muscle cells: Muscle cells contract and relax to enable movement. They are packed with proteins that help them perform this function.

Plant Cells: Plant cells have unique structures like cell walls and chloroplasts. The cell wall provides support, while chloroplasts allow plants to make their own food through photosynthesis.

Importance of Cells

Cells are not just tiny building blocks; they are essential for life. They allow organisms to grow, reproduce, and respond to their environment. By studying cells, scientists can understand diseases, develop new medicines, and improve agricultural practices.

You now know the basics of cell theory and the different types of cells. Remember, all living things are made of cells, which are the basic units of life. Whether simple like prokaryotic cells or complex like eukaryotic cells, each type plays a vital role in the world around us. Keep exploring the amazing world of cells, and you'll discover even more fascinating details about life's building blocks. By understanding cells, you're taking a big step in your science education.

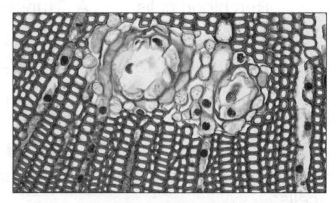

There a variety of cells that are designed to do specific functions.

4. Cell Theory and Types of Cells

I. Cell Theory

List the three main ideas of cell theory:

1. _____

2. _____

3. _____

II. Types of Cells

There are two major categories of cells. Name them:

1. _____   2._____

A. Prokaryotic Cells
List three key features of prokaryotic cells:

1. _____   2._____

3._____

B. Eukaryotic Cells
List three important characteristics of eukaryotic cells:

1. _____   2._____

3._____

III. Specialized Cells

Match each specialized cell type with its function:

_____ Red blood cells   A. Transmit signals in the body

_____ Nerve cells   B. Enable movement

_____ Muscle cells   C. Carry oxygen in the body

_____ Plant cells   D. Make their own food through photosynthesis

IV. Cell Structures

Name two structures found in plant cells that are not typically found in animal cells:

1. _____   2._____

46 | 25x: Biology © 2024 3andB.com

V. True or False

Mark each statement as True (T) or False (F):

_____ All living things are made of one or more cells.

_____ Prokaryotic cells have a nucleus.

_____ Eukaryotic cells can form multicellular organisms.

_____ All cells come from pre-existing cells.

VI. Short Answer

1. Explain why cells are considered the basic unit of life:

_____

_____

_____

2. Describe one way that studying cells can benefit society:

_____

_____

_____

VII. Reflection

In your own words, explain why understanding cell theory and different types of cells is important for your science education:

_____

_____

_____

#1

Why do you think cell theory is considered one of the most important principles in biology?

Think about how cell theory helps scientists understand the structure and function of all living organisms.

#2

What are the main differences between prokaryotic and eukaryotic cells?

Reflect on the presence of a nucleus, the complexity of structures, and the size of these cells.

#3

How do specialized cells, like red blood cells and nerve cells, contribute to the functioning of multicellular organisms?

Consider the specific roles these cells play and how they support the overall health and operation of the body.

#4

Why is it important for new cells to come from pre-existing cells?

Think about the processes of growth, repair, and reproduction in living organisms.

#5

How do prokaryotic cells survive in extreme environments, and why is this important for ecosystems?

Reflect on the adaptability of these cells and their role in maintaining ecological balance.

#6

In what ways can studying cells help scientists develop new medicines and improve agricultural practices?

Consider the importance of understanding cell functions and structures in medical and agricultural advancements.

TERM	DEFINITION
Cell theory	
Cell	
Prokaryotic cell	
Eukaryotic cell	
Nucleus	
Organelle	
Mitochondria	

TERM	DEFINITION
Chloroplast	
Red blood cells	
Nerve cells	
Muscle cells	
Cell wall	
Photosynthesis	
Growth	

Cell Theory & Types Of Cells

```
Q Y C E X A B S P T W I E Y Q F R A N A O Q R S
W E H H P K W F M I I L L G J O H B F D G O T F
U G L P E Q K S Z C P K Z L F P U R A Q R A Y Y
P A O Z Z Q R S I N K N M I T O C H O N D R I A
H R R J S C P B A P A A Z G P I K L E B Q M X V
U Q O Z F N O W S O X C T V O R G A N E L L E W
Y B P L W X N Y V I G R G K E Q P L Z Z V D Y P
M U L I P J Y T I R P E G W L G E O V S T V I N
N G A Z I H W Q U U C D J P F H G B V P I C C B
T T S R Y C N R V N R B B B V M T H E O R Y L F
A P T I G Y G J A Z N L P B R L A C T I Y U A P
B Y W A J D R Y W O E O M U S C L E C E L L S H
Y U X H P D O D T F R O M H R U F L M R I A Z O
P C I R A R W R R O V D R O P A W K V C G M T T
N E B L Y J T C R F E C M X R Q H J Y V M H T O
W L N L B H H R J I C E P M O J X Z H P I B S S
O L U C W T W U T C E L V O K S Y B V V Y A X P Y
M W C S T C O C D O L L M B A D J M O H P A H N
C A L M O J B H M B L S V J R W O C C K M S V T
H L E X D B A C J A S P T W Y Q D F W S L D C H
B L U N P H R T Z V Q O I S O D A Q N F R T D E
M O S E U K A R Y O T I C B T Y D Y M I H O M S
L X M C O M L Z K Q Z O I D I S D Z W V A I D I
M C E L L T H E O R Y A Z S C M Z S H G I L Z S
```

Muscle cells	Nerve cells	Red blood cells
Cell theory	Growth	Photosynthesis
Cell wall	Chloroplast	Mitochondria
Organelle	Nucleus	Eukaryotic
Prokaryotic	theory	

Cell Theory & Types Of Cells

Across

6. A rigid structure found in plant cells that provides support and protection. (Two words)

7. Cells that transmit signals throughout the body, allowing for communication between the brain and other parts of the body. ____ cells

10. The control center of a eukaryotic cell that contains the cell's genetic material (DNA).

11. Organelles in eukaryotic cells that produce energy through cellular respiration.

13. An organelle found in plant cells that carries out photosynthesis, converting light energy into chemical energy.

14. The process by which chloroplasts in plant cells convert sunlight, carbon dioxide, and water into glucose and oxygen.

Down

1. Cells that contract and relax to enable movement and support body functions. ____ cells

2. A complex cell with a nucleus and organelles, found in plants, animals, fungi, and protists. ____ cell

3. The principle that all living things are made of cells, cells are the basic unit of life, and new cells come from pre-existing cells. Cell ____

4. The smallest unit of life that can perform all life processes; cells can be unicellular or multicellular.

5. Specialized cells that carry oxygen from the lungs to the rest of the body and return carbon dioxide to the lungs. __ ___ cells

8. A simple, small cell without a nucleus, typically found in bacteria and archaea. ____ cell

9. Specialized structures within a cell that perform specific functions, such as mitochondria and chloroplasts.

12. The process by which organisms increase in size and number of cells, largely driven by cell division and replication.

Understanding Cell Organelles:
Organs of Cells

Have you ever wondered what makes up the cells in your body? Cells are the basic units of life, and they contain many smaller structures called organelles. Each organelle has a specific job that helps the cell function properly. You will learn about the different types of cell organelles and their functions. By understanding these tiny but powerful components, you will gain a deeper appreciation for the complexity and wonder of life at the microscopic level.

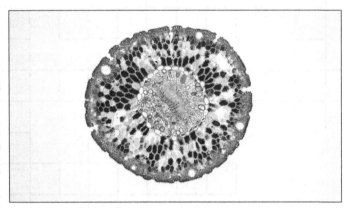

Organelles are like tiny organs within cells that help them live and function.

The Nucleus: The Control Center

Imagine a cell as a factory. The nucleus is like the manager's office, where important decisions are made. The nucleus contains the cell's genetic material, or DNA, which holds the instructions for making proteins and other vital substances. This organelle controls the cell's growth, reproduction, and many other functions. Think of the nucleus as the brain of the cell, sending out orders to ensure everything runs smoothly.

Mitochondria: The Powerhouses

Next, let's talk about mitochondria. These organelles are often called the powerhouses of the cell because they generate energy. Mitochondria take in nutrients and convert them into energy that the cell can use. This energy is essential for all the cell's activities, from moving to dividing. Without mitochondria, cells wouldn't have the power they need to function. It's like having a generator that keeps the lights on in your house.

Ribosomes: The Protein Factories

Ribosomes might be small, but they play a huge role in the cell. These tiny structures are the sites where proteins are made. Proteins are crucial for many cell functions, including building cell structures and carrying out chemical reactions. Ribosomes can be found floating freely in the cytoplasm or attached to another organelle called the endoplasmic reticulum. Think of ribosomes as little factories that produce the proteins your body needs to stay healthy.

Endoplasmic Reticulum: The Production Line

The endoplasmic reticulum (ER) is like a production line in a factory, where products are assembled and processed. There are two types of ER: rough and smooth. The rough ER is covered with ribosomes, giving it a bumpy appearance. It helps in the production and packaging of proteins. The smooth ER, on the other hand, is involved in making lipids (fats) and breaking down toxic substances. Both types of ER play vital roles in keeping the cell running efficiently.

Golgi Apparatus: The Shipping Department

Once proteins and lipids are made, they need to be sorted and sent to their proper destinations. This is where the Golgi apparatus comes in. Think of it as the cell's shipping department. The Golgi apparatus modifies, sorts, and packages molecules for transport to different parts of the cell or outside the cell. It ensures that everything gets to where it needs to go, just like a postal service.

The mitochondria is known as the powerhouse of the cell.

Lysosomes: The Cleanup Crew

Cells need to stay clean and organized to function well. Lysosomes are the organelles responsible for breaking down waste materials and cellular debris. They contain enzymes that digest unwanted substances, preventing them from accumulating and harming the cell. Lysosomes are like the cell's janitors, keeping everything tidy and in working order.

Vacuoles: The Storage Units

Vacuoles are storage organelles that hold various substances the cell might need later. In plant cells, vacuoles are large and central, storing water, nutrients, and waste products. In animal cells, they are smaller but still important. Vacuoles help maintain the cell's shape and provide storage space for essential materials, similar to how you might use a closet to store items you don't need every day.

Cytoplasm: The Cellular Jelly

The cytoplasm is the jelly-like substance that fills the inside of the cell. It surrounds all the organelles and provides a medium where they can move and interact. The cytoplasm is mostly made of water but also contains salts, nutrients, and other molecules. It helps maintain the cell's shape and allows for the movement of materials within the cell. Think of the cytoplasm as the space in a room where all the furniture and people can move around.

You should have a better understanding of the different cell organelles and their functions. Each organelle plays a unique and vital role in ensuring that the cell operates smoothly. Remember, cells are the building blocks of life, and their organelles are the key players that keep everything running. Now you can appreciate the incredible work happening inside every single cell.

5. Cell Organelles and Functions
GUIDED NOTES

I. Introduction

Cells are the basic units of life and contain smaller structures called

_____.

II. Cell Organelles and Their Functions

Match each organelle with its primary function:

_____ Nucleus   A. Generates energy for the cell

_____ Mitochondria   B. Breaks down waste and cellular debris

_____ Ribosomes   C. Controls cell activities and contains DNA

_____ Endoplasmic   D. Modifies, sorts, and packages molecules

                            Reticulum

_____ Golgi Apparatus E. Produces proteins

_____ Lysosomes   F. Assembles and processes cell products

_____ Vacuoles   G. Stores water, nutrients, and waste products

III. Organelle Details

Fill in the blanks with key information about each organelle:

1. Nucleus: Often called the _____ of the cell, it contains

_____ which holds instructions for making proteins.

2. Mitochondria: Known as the _____ of the cell because

they _____.

3. Ribosomes: These can be found _____

or _____.

4. Endoplasmic Reticulum (ER):

Rough ER: Covered with _____ and helps in _____

_____.

Smooth ER: Involved in making _____ and _____

_____.

5. **Golgi Apparatus:** Ensures that cellular products get to where they need

to go, similar to a _____.

6. **Lysosomes:** Contain _____ that digest unwanted substances,

acting like the cell's _____.

7. **Vacuoles:** In plant cells, they are _____ and _____,

while in animal cells, they are _____.

8. **Cytoplasm:** The _____-like substance that fills the inside

of the cell, mostly made of _____.

IV. True or False

Mark each statement as True (T) or False (F):

_____ The nucleus is responsible for generating energy in the cell.

_____ Ribosomes are the sites where proteins are made.

_____ The Golgi apparatus is responsible for breaking down cellular debris.

_____ Vacuoles help maintain the cell's shape and provide storage space.

_____ The cytoplasm is a solid substance that fills the cell.

V. Short Answer

Explain in your own words why understanding cell organelles is important for comprehending life at the microscopic level:

_____

_____

_____

_____

#1

How does the nucleus control the cell's activities?

Think about the role of DNA and why having a control center (nucleus) is crucial for coordinating the cell's functions.

#2

Why are mitochondria referred to as the powerhouses of the cell?

Reflect on how energy is important for cell activities and what might happen if the cell didn't have a reliable source of energy.

#3

What role do ribosomes play in the cell, and why are proteins so important?

Consider how proteins contribute to various cell functions and why having "factories" for protein production is essential.

#4

How do the rough and smooth endoplasmic reticulum differ in their functions?

Think about the specific tasks each type of endoplasmic reticulum handles and why a cell might need both types.

#5

In what ways does the Golgi apparatus function like a shipping department?

Reflect on the process of modifying, sorting, and packaging molecules, and how this ensures that the cell operates efficiently.

#6

Why are lysosomes important for maintaining cellular health?

Consider the consequences of waste buildup in the cell and how lysosomes help to prevent these issues by breaking down unwanted materials.

TERM	DEFINITION
Cell	
Organelle	
Nucleus	
DNA	
Mitochondria	
Ribosome	
Endoplasmic reticulum	

TERM	DEFINITION
Rough endoplasmic reticulum	
Smooth endoplasmic reticulum	
Golgi apparatus	
Lysosome	
Vacuole	
Cytoplasm	
Protein	

Cell Organelles & Functions

```
Q  L  D  H  H  A  O  N  J  U  S  D  X  V  K  V  O  G  J  D  M  H  C  E
O  P  P  H  R  R  N  U  R  M  G  Z  N  T  N  J  Q  P  P  I  P  G  W  U
E  L  J  C  B  W  B  C  I  I  D  L  M  W  O  E  U  K  O  S  G  O  H  W
L  G  H  K  P  E  D  L  B  R  S  D  C  O  B  D  C  W  R  T  C  L  U  U
Y  J  R  Z  U  Z  M  E  O  X  M  G  S  O  O  E  J  N  G  P  F  G  R  F
V  A  C  U  O  L  E  U  S  W  O  V  X  O  M  T  W  T  A  N  W  I  Q  R
K  L  J  L  C  Q  N  S  O  R  O  U  G  H  E  R  F  P  N  A  S  A  M  D
Q  P  F  I  Y  E  U  R  M  U  T  Q  X  C  L  E  T  T  E  P  M  P  J  C
L  R  D  Y  T  N  Z  L  E  S  H  J  Y  K  A  H  V  B  L  L  J  P  E  V
S  O  A  H  O  B  B  J  X  A  E  A  O  P  A  J  C  M  L  Y  T  A  L  A
L  T  J  T  P  P  F  M  B  A  R  V  H  J  U  G  Z  A  E  S  P  R  H  F
T  E  C  I  L  H  Q  I  A  B  O  T  Z  Y  S  U  D  N  A  O  E  A  Y  F
Q  I  R  B  A  F  U  T  V  T  D  Y  X  D  E  I  M  K  S  S  E  T  Z  Q
D  N  A  V  S  U  G  O  R  B  T  X  U  U  K  H  F  D  G  O  Q  U  J  G
V  P  U  P  M  F  L  C  C  W  Z  Z  S  W  M  A  F  X  J  M  K  S  A  O
O  D  L  L  U  R  D  H  E  Q  L  E  B  O  C  K  R  L  Q  E  D  C  Z  H
Q  Y  Q  U  E  N  D  O  P  L  A  S  M  I  C  R  E  T  I  C  U  L  U  M
Y  D  Q  T  X  O  H  N  N  E  B  K  B  F  M  D  A  K  N  K  J  E  T  L
N  E  W  B  G  R  Q  D  G  G  B  A  K  B  Q  T  B  X  J  T  F  M  P  Y
T  S  P  E  Q  M  L  R  V  Z  I  Y  L  S  R  G  G  B  R  R  F  K  M  W
U  D  C  T  O  E  B  I  L  E  C  O  O  Y  M  F  Q  L  P  G  Q  F  B
H  E  I  Q  J  B  T  A  H  N  A  C  R  F  D  L  E  S  E  Z  Q  V  I  P
Z  S  E  N  U  W  L  R  C  E  L  L  B  A  I  A  Y  E  P  N  N  I  R  R
D  Z  H  W  I  H  O  R  L  B  I  Y  E  E  M  C  I  N  M  M  K  S  H  A
```

Golgi apparatus	Smooth ER	Rough ER
Endoplasmic reticulum	Protein	Cytoplasm
Vacuole	Lysosome	Ribosome
Mitochondria	DNA	Nucleus
Organelle	Cell	

Cell Organelles & Functions

Across

4. Deoxyribonucleic acid, the molecule that carries the genetic instructions for life, found within the nucleus of a cell.

8. The cleanup crew of the cell, containing enzymes that break down waste materials and cellular debris.

9. The part of the ER studded with ribosomes, involved in protein production and packaging. ____ endoplasmic reticulum

10. The basic unit of life, containing various organelles that each have specific functions necessary for its survival and operation.

12. The cell's shipping department, which modifies, sorts, and packages proteins and lipids for distribution within or outside the cell. ____ apparatus

13. A tiny structure where proteins are synthesized; these can be free in the cytoplasm or attached to the endoplasmic reticulum.

14. The part of the ER that lacks ribosomes and is involved in lipid production and detoxification processes. ____ endoplasmic reticulum

Down

1. A storage organelle that holds water, nutrients, and waste products; large and central in plant cells, smaller in animal cells.

2. Known as the powerhouses of the cell, these organelles generate energy by converting nutrients into usable cellular energy.

3. A network of membranous tubules within the cell, involved in the production, folding, and transport of proteins (rough ER) and lipids (smooth ER). ____ reticulum

5. A specialized structure within a cell that performs a distinct function, much like different departments in a factory.

6. A molecule produced by ribosomes that is essential for building cell structures and carrying out various cellular functions.

7. The control center of the cell, containing DNA, which holds the genetic instructions for making proteins and managing cell activities.

11. The jelly-like substance inside the cell that surrounds organelles and provides a medium for their movement and interaction.

Understanding the Cell Cycle: Cellular Growth and Division

Have you ever wondered how your body grows, repairs itself, and maintains all its functions? The answer lies in a process called the cell cycle. This cycle is crucial for all living organisms, including you! It ensures that cells divide correctly to produce new cells, replacing old or damaged ones. Let's get into the the cell cycle to explore its stages and significance.

What is the Cell Cycle?

The cell cycle is a series of events that cells go through as they grow and divide. Think of it like a life cycle for cells, complete with its own stages and checkpoints. The main purpose of the cell cycle is to create two identical daughter cells from one parent cell. This cycle is essential for growth, development, and tissue repair in your body.

The Stages of the Cell Cycle
The cell cycle has four main stages: G1, S, G2, and M.

Mitosis creates two identical daughter cells.

G1 Phase (Gap 1)

During the G1 phase, the cell grows and carries out its normal functions. It's like the cell is preparing for the big task ahead. Here, the cell checks if it has enough energy and materials to duplicate its DNA. If everything is in order, the cell moves to the next stage.

S Phase (Synthesis)

In the S phase, the cell duplicates its DNA. DNA is the genetic material that carries all the instructions for the cell's functions. Imagine making a copy of a book; the cell ensures that the new copy is identical to the original. This step is crucial because each daughter cell needs a complete set of DNA.

G2 Phase (Gap 2)

After DNA replication, the cell enters the G2 phase. During this stage, the cell continues to grow and produces proteins necessary for cell division. It's like double-checking everything before a big event, ensuring that the cell is ready for the final stage.

M Phase (Mitosis)

The M phase is where the magic happens – cell division! Mitosis is the process where the cell's nucleus divides, followed by the division of the entire cell. Mitosis has its own stages: prophase, metaphase, anaphase, and telophase, followed by cytokinesis. By the end of mitosis, you have two identical daughter cells, each with a complete set of DNA.

Checkpoints in the Cell Cycle

The cell cycle has built-in checkpoints to ensure everything goes smoothly. These checkpoints act like quality control inspectors, checking for errors and making sure the cell is ready to move on to the next stage. If something is wrong, the cell cycle can pause to fix the issue or, in some cases, trigger cell death to prevent damaged cells from dividing.

The main checkpoints are at the end of G1, during the S phase, and at the end of G2. These checkpoints are crucial for preventing diseases like cancer, where cells divide uncontrollably.

Why is the Cell Cycle Important?

Understanding the cell cycle can help you appreciate how your body functions and grows. Here are some reasons why the cell cycle is important:

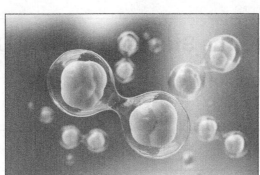

The cell cycle is need for growth, development, and repair.

Growth and Development: The cell cycle allows organisms to grow from a single cell into a complex, multicellular organism. All the cells in your body originated from a single fertilized egg cell that underwent countless cycles of division.

Tissue Repair and Regeneration: When you get a cut or injury, the cell cycle kicks in to produce new cells that replace the damaged ones, helping you heal.

Maintenance of Tissues: Your body constantly replaces old and worn-out cells with new ones through the cell cycle. For example, your skin cells are continuously renewed to keep your skin healthy.

The cell cycle is a fundamental process that keeps living organisms, including you, functioning correctly. By understanding its stages and importance, you gain insight into how your body grows, repairs itself, and maintains balance. Any time you grow a little taller or heal a wound, it's all thanks to the incredible work of the cell cycle.

6. Cell Cycle
GUIDED NOTES

I. What is the Cell Cycle?

Define the cell cycle in your own words: _____

_____

Main purpose of the cell cycle: _____

_____

II. The Stages of the Cell Cycle

List the four main stages of the cell cycle:

1. _____   2. _____

3. _____   4. _____

III. Matching

Match each phase with its description:

_____ G1 Phase   A. DNA duplication occurs

_____ S Phase   B. Cell division takes place

_____ G2 Phase   C. Cell grows and prepares for DNA replication

_____ M Phase   D. Cell produces proteins necessary for cell
                            division

IV. Fill in the Blanks

1. During the _____ phase, the cell duplicates its DNA.

2. The M phase is also known as _____.

3. Mitosis has its own stages: _____, _____,

_____, and _____.

4. The process where the entire cell divides is called _____.

V. Short Answer

Explain the role of checkpoints in the cell cycle: _____

_____

_____

VI. True or False

_____ The cell cycle is only important for growth and development.

_____ Checkpoints in the cell cycle help prevent diseases like cancer.

_____ All the cells in your body originated from a single fertilized egg cell.

_____ The G1 phase occurs after DNA replication.

VII. Importance of the Cell Cycle

List three reasons why the cell cycle is important:

1. _____   2. _____

3. _____

VIII. In your own words, explain how the cell cycle relates to tissue repair and regeneration:

_____

_____

IX. Reflection

How does understanding the cell cycle help you appreciate your body's functions? (2-3 sentences)

_____

_____

_____

#1

How does the cell cycle contribute to your body's growth and development?

Consider how a single fertilized egg cell multiplies and differentiates into the various types of cells that make up your body.

#2

Why is it important for the cell cycle to have checkpoints?

Reflect on the role of these checkpoints in ensuring cells divide correctly and the potential consequences if errors go unchecked.

#3

What might happen if the cell cycle's checkpoints fail and cells divide uncontrollably?

Think about diseases like cancer and how unchecked cell division can lead to health problems.

#4

How does the G1 phase prepare a cell for DNA replication in the S phase?

Consider the activities that take place in the G1 phase, such as cell growth and the gathering of necessary materials.

#5

In what way does the S phase ensure that each daughter cell receives a complete set of DNA?

Reflect on the process of DNA replication and why it is crucial for genetic consistency in new cells.

#6

Why is the cell cycle essential for tissue repair and regeneration?

Think about how your body responds to injuries and the role of new cell production in healing damaged tissues.

TERM	DEFINITION
Cell cycle	
G1 phase (Gap 1)	
S phase (Synthesis)	
G2 phase (Gap 2)	
M phase (Mitosis)	
Prophase	
Metaphase	

TERM	DEFINITION
Anaphase	
Telophase	
Cytokinesis	
Checkpoints	
DNA replication	
Cell division	
Tissue Repair	

Cell Cycle

```
D R A S V E V Y 1 2 S G C H U U P S A H T E 1 R
E K G 2 P H A S E V M K H V C K K Y G A D T L S
E N T V Y Y C L D N A R E P L I C A T I O N M Y
A P I 2 M P H P U H R C C K K O M G C L 2 C M V
I H V 2 L Y K R D D L P K H A U Y P C N M S A D
P N G H R S U O R R U R P E U N N A Y 2 A G C C
U N M E N 1 T P Y A O C O E C N P P T S G T G D
Y C I 1 V A M H P G S P I N E E S 2 O A M L E L
R E E 1 V L E A Y D C A N N I P A M K N E V O R
L L V D N L T S G M P A T O L S C K I A T A N O
U L L E V N A E H T A V S L A Y S I N P C P T D
A C P V E O P L H I E C O V R V A U E H V L T V
K Y I K D M H S G S U S U T 1 H L A S A S 2 E 2
L C H M I K A I G S C U A A I O E T I S I I H G
I L K P V D S T U U S O O R Y Y S S E R A U M
K E H C G O E 2 G E C E L L D I V I S I O N T D
L U M I N U T U L R E I P E V 1 S N U S D N U H
U L R C M I R H Y E D R G R H M S O R I G U O U
M K 2 D S K 1 I R P 2 I A A 1 M C S 1 T U A V I
M I T O S I S A U A C U O V 1 K E N P V V E A A
P L S K K A 1 G 1 I T T R G 1 P H A S E L K 2 S
V O I Y T M H S E R O T U K R 1 C S P H A S E I
S C Y I N A 1 V V K V U E D G T E L O P H A S E
I 2 S U I 1 A I A A M P P K C G K R H P A T D I
```

Tissue repair

Checkpoints

Anaphase

Mitosis

G1 Phase

Cell division

Cytokinesis

Metaphase

G2 Phase

Cell cycle

DNA replication

Telophase

Prophase

S Phase

Cell Cycle

Across

2. Built-in mechanisms in the cell cycle that ensure each stage is completed correctly before the cell moves to the next stage.

8. The process of copying the cell's DNA during the S phase, ensuring each daughter cell gets an identical set of genetic material. DNA ____

11. The overall process where a single cell divides to form two new, identical daughter cells. Cell ____

12. The stage of mitosis where nuclear membranes start to form around each set of chromosomes, and the cell begins to split.

13. A series of events that cells go through as they grow and divide, ensuring the production of two identical daughter cells from one parent cell. (Two words)

14. The stage of the cell cycle where the cell duplicates its DNA, ensuring each daughter cell receives a complete set of genetic instructions. _ ____

Down

1. The final part of cell division where the cytoplasm divides, resulting in two separate daughter cells.

3. The process where the cell cycle produces new cells to replace damaged or old cells, aiding in the healing of injuries. Tissue ____

4. The stage after DNA replication, where the cell continues to grow and produces proteins necessary for cell division. __ ____

5. The first stage of mitosis where the chromosomes condense, and the nuclear envelope begins to break down.

6. The stage of mitosis where sister chromatids are pulled apart to opposite ends of the cell.

7. The first stage of the cell cycle, where the cell grows and carries out normal functions while preparing for DNA replication. __ ____

9. The stage of mitosis where chromosomes align in the center of the cell, ensuring equal separation to each daughter cell.

10. The stage where the cell's nucleus and then the entire cell divide, resulting in two identical daughter cells.

Photosynthesis:
How Plants Make Their Own Food

Have you ever wondered how plants grow and survive? You might think they need someone to feed them, like we need food. But plants are unique. They have a special ability to make their own food using sunlight. This amazing process is called photosynthesis. Let's get into the details of photosynthesis and discover how it works.

What is Photosynthesis?

Photosynthesis is a process used by plants, algae, and some bacteria to convert light energy from the sun into chemical energy. This chemical energy is stored in the form of glucose, a type of sugar. Plants use glucose as their food to grow, reproduce, and carry out their life functions. The word "photosynthesis" comes from the Greek words "photo," which means light, and "synthesis," which means putting together. So, photosynthesis means "putting together with light."

The Ingredients for Photosynthesis

Just like you need ingredients to bake a cake, plants need ingredients for photosynthesis. These ingredients are:

1. Sunlight: The energy source for photosynthesis.

2. Water (H_2O): Absorbed by the plant roots from the soil.

3. Carbon Dioxide (CO_2): Taken from the air through tiny openings on the leaves called stomata.

4. Chlorophyll: The green pigment in leaves that captures sunlight.

Photosynthesis converts sunlight into usable energy for plants.

The Photosynthesis Equation

The process of photosynthesis can be summed up by a simple chemical equation:

$$6CO_2 + 6H_2O \rightarrow C_6H_{12}O6 + 6O_2$$

This equation represents the process of photosynthesis, where six molecules of carbon dioxide (CO_2) and six molecules of water (H_2O) react in the presence of sunlight and chlorophyll to produce glucose ($C_6H_{12}O_6$) and six molecules of oxygen (O_2).

The Two Stages of Photosynthesis

Photosynthesis happens in two main stages: the light-dependent reactions and the Calvin cycle.

1. Light-Dependent Reactions: These reactions occur in the thylakoid membranes of the chloroplasts. When sunlight hits the chlorophyll, it excites the electrons, giving them energy. This energy is used to split water molecules into oxygen, protons, and electrons. The oxygen is released into the atmosphere, and the energy is stored in molecules called ATP and NADPH.

2. The Calvin Cycle: This stage occurs in the stroma of the chloroplasts. It does not require light, which is why it is sometimes called the light-independent reactions. The ATP and NADPH produced in the light-dependent reactions provide the energy to convert carbon dioxide into glucose.

Why is Photosynthesis Important?

Photosynthesis is crucial for life on Earth for several reasons:

Provides Food: It is the primary source of food for plants. Without photosynthesis, plants would not have the energy to grow and produce fruits, vegetables, and grains that you eat.

Produces Oxygen: Photosynthesis releases oxygen into the atmosphere, which is essential for you and all other living organisms to breathe.

Supports Ecosystems: Plants form the base of the food chain. Herbivores eat plants, and carnivores eat herbivores. Without photosynthesis, the entire food chain would collapse.

Regulates the Atmosphere: By absorbing carbon dioxide and releasing oxygen, photosynthesis helps regulate the

levels of these gases in the atmosphere, contributing to a balanced environment.

Photosynthesis and You

You might not realize it, but photosynthesis affects your daily life in many ways. The food you eat, the air you breathe, and even the fuel you use are all connected to photosynthesis. For example, fossil fuels like coal and oil are formed from the remains of ancient plants that stored energy from photosynthesis millions of years ago.

Fun Facts about Photosynthesis

• Some plants can perform photosynthesis underwater, using dissolved carbon dioxide.

The glucose from photosynthesis is the base of food chains in ecosystems.

• The Amazon rainforest produces about 20% of the world's oxygen through photosynthesis.

• Algae in the oceans perform more photosynthesis than all the land plants combined!

Photosynthesis is a fascinating process that allows plants to harness the power of the sun to make their own food. It plays a vital role in sustaining life on Earth by producing oxygen and forming the base of the food chain. Next time you see a plant, think about the incredible process happening inside its leaves, turning sunlight into the energy that fuels the world.

7. Photosynthesis

I. What is Photosynthesis?

Define photosynthesis in your own words:

_____

_____

Break down the word "photosynthesis":

1. "Photo" means: _____

2. "Synthesis" means: _____

II. Ingredients for Photosynthesis

List the four main ingredients needed for photosynthesis:

1. _____ 2. _____

3. _____ 4. _____

III. The Photosynthesis Equation

Fill in the blanks in the photosynthesis equation:

$$\_\_\ CO_2 + \_\_\ H_2O \rightarrow _____ + \_\_\ O_2$$

IV. Two Stages of Photosynthesis

Match each stage with its description:

____ Light-Dependent Reactions   A. Converts carbon dioxide into glucose

____ Calvin Cycle   B. Splits water molecules and stores energy in ATP and NADPH

V. Importance of Photosynthesis

List four reasons why photosynthesis is important:

1. _____

2. _____

3. _____

4. _____

VI. Photosynthesis in Daily Life

Explain how photosynthesis affects your daily life:

_____

_____

_____

VII. True or False

_____ Photosynthesis only occurs in plants.

_____ The Amazon rainforest produces about 20% of the world's oxygen.

_____ Fossil fuels are unrelated to photosynthesis.

VIII. Fun Facts

Write two interesting facts about photosynthesis that you learned:

1. _____

_____

2. _____

_____

IX. In your own words, explain why learning about photosynthesis is important:

_____

_____

_____

_____

#1

How do plants obtain the ingredients necessary for photosynthesis?

Think about the role of roots, leaves, and sunlight in providing water, carbon dioxide, and energy to the plant.

#2

Why is chlorophyll important in the process of photosynthesis?

Reflect on how chlorophyll captures sunlight and why it is essential for converting light energy into chemical energy.

#3

What would happen to life on Earth if photosynthesis stopped?

Consider the impact on food production, oxygen levels, and the balance of ecosystems.

#4

How do the light-dependent reactions and the Calvin cycle work together to produce glucose?

Think about what each stage accomplishes and how they depend on each other to complete the process of photosynthesis.

#5

In what ways does photosynthesis affect your everyday life?

Reflect on the connection between photosynthesis and the food you eat, the air you breathe, and the environment around you.

#6

How does the photosynthesis equation summarize the entire process?

Break down the equation into its components and think about how each part represents a step in the photosynthesis process.

TERM	DEFINITION
Photosynthesis	
Glucose	
Sunlight	
Water (H_2O)	
Carbon dioxide (CO_2)	
Chlorophyll	
Thylakoid membranes	

TERM	DEFINITION
ATP (Adenosine Triphosphate)	
NADPH	
Light-dependent reactions	
Calvin cycle	
Stomata	
Ecosystem	
Fossil fuels	

Photosynthesis

```
S P G R X T C A B H R I N G I Y Y E T W A T E R
G N A Y N P J E C O S Y S T E M Q B B L E G E W
N G Y Z B L K Z U J B D I U Y D H U I M R N P Z
T N N C Q Y X O B G G R W E A T P U Q F M J S L
J C Z Q T W H J M H R I W V U G D W L T X W Z Q
L I G H T D E P E N D E N T R E A C T I O N S K
S Y L E B T A J C K W R B G W E Z P S D G M T C
T E G J F X F J H E F S L D Y Y U K A R X V H T
Y Y L G U K M F L M S Y N P I E I P V E L P Y V
E S U W U V F K O R Z Y F I R U Y H W H Q Y L E
Z T C K E X U C R N J U Q C H Q H O Z C A G A Y
B O O J E J Y A O A L H E L V T N T B A R U K Z
F M S Z Q Z W D P V I X T V U C O Z R T I O H
O A E M V J Y B H F R R Q F P U Q S V B D O I R
O T D S G T U D Y O F I X Q L R Z Y T O M U D Y
T A T I N T A Y L S S W C L R O U N B N Q U M T
D R O Y S J M H L S E O J W E B U T G D Y X E O
F R H A T C A L V I N C Y C L E J H U I Z X M E
X Z N R W P G V K L T T S B X G R E J O R U B U
S U N L I G H T X F F Q Z V N O V S U X W V R S
A J O Q H Y N A X U H T H X A S B I Q I P G A A
U O W S J T A F H E E W G G D W I S B D B P N S
O H M D P P Q K N L B W T Z P M C L E E J U E D
F D T K F U R H U S Y F Q K H L L Y Z D I Z S J
```

Fossil fuels	Ecosystem	Stomata
Calvin cycle	Light-dependent reactions	NADPH
ATP	Thylakoid membranes	Chlorophyll
Carbon dioxide	Water	Sunlight
Glucose	Photosynthesis	

Photosynthesis

Across
3. An essential ingredient for photosynthesis, absorbed by plant roots from the soil.

7. Tiny openings on the surface of leaves that allow for the exchange of gases, including the intake of carbon dioxide and release of oxygen.

10. Structures within the chloroplasts where the light-dependent reactions of photosynthesis occur. _____ membranes

11. The primary energy source for photosynthesis, providing the light energy needed to drive the process.

13. The process by which plants, algae, and some bacteria convert light energy from the sun into chemical energy stored in glucose.

14. The first stage of photosynthesis, occurring in the thylakoid membranes, where sunlight excites electrons to split water molecules, releasing oxygen and storing energy in ATP and NADPH. _____ _____ reactions

Down
1. A gas taken from the air by plants through tiny openings on the leaves called stomata, used in the photosynthesis process. (Two words)

2. The green pigment in plant leaves that captures sunlight and is crucial for converting light energy into chemical energy.

4. Energy sources like coal and oil, formed from the remains of ancient plants that stored energy from photosynthesis millions of years ago. (Two words)

5. The second stage of photosynthesis, occurring in the stroma of the chloroplasts, where ATP and NADPH are used to convert carbon dioxide into glucose; also known as the light-independent reactions. _____ cycle

6. A community of living organisms and their physical environment, where photosynthesis supports the food chain by providing energy and oxygen.

8. An energy-carrying molecule produced during the light-dependent reactions, used in the Calvin cycle to help convert carbon dioxide into glucose.

9. An energy-rich molecule produced during the light-dependent reactions, used alongside ATP in the Calvin cycle to synthesize glucose.

12. A type of sugar produced during photosynthesis that plants use as food to grow, reproduce, and carry out life functions.

Cellular Respiration:
How Your Cells Turn Food into Energy

Have you ever wondered how your body gets the energy it needs to run, jump, and even think? The answer lies in a process called cellular respiration. This is a vital function that happens in every cell of your body, turning the food you eat into usable energy. Let's get into some details about cellular respiration and discover how it keeps you alive and active.

What is Cellular Respiration?

Cellular respiration is the process by which your cells convert glucose, a type of sugar, into adenosine triphosphate (ATP), the energy currency of the cell. Think of ATP as the fuel that powers all of your body's activities, from simple movements like blinking your eyes to complex ones like playing sports or solving math problems.

ATP from cellular respiration powers all of your biological processes, including muscle contractions.

The Three Stages of Cellular Respiration

Cellular respiration occurs in three main stages: Glycolysis, the Krebs cycle, and the Electron Transport Chain (ETC). Each stage plays a crucial role in breaking down glucose and producing ATP.

1. Glycolysis: The Sugar Breaker

The first stage of cellular respiration is glycolysis, which takes place in the cytoplasm of the cell. During glycolysis, one molecule of glucose is split into two molecules of a compound called pyruvate. This process produces a small amount of ATP and also releases high-energy electrons that are captured by molecules called NADH.

The word "glycolysis" means "sugar splitting," and it's an apt description of what happens here. You might be surprised to learn that glycolysis doesn't require oxygen, which is why it's sometimes called anaerobic respiration.

2. The Krebs Cycle: The Energy Extractor

Once glycolysis is complete, the pyruvate molecules move into the mitochondria, the powerhouse of the cell, where the second stage of cellular respiration occurs: the Krebs cycle.

Also known as the citric acid cycle, this stage is all about extracting energy.

In the Krebs cycle, each pyruvate molecule is broken down further, releasing carbon dioxide as a waste product. More NADH and another molecule called FADH2 are produced, which carry high-energy electrons to the next stage. While the Krebs cycle only produces a small amount of ATP directly, its main job is to prepare for the big energy payoff in the final stage.

3. Electron Transport Chain: The ATP Factory

The final stage of cellular respiration takes place in the inner membrane of the mitochondria. The Electron Transport Chain (ETC) is where most of the ATP is produced. High-energy electrons from NADH and FADH2 are passed along a series of proteins in the inner mitochondrial membrane. As these electrons move along the chain, they release energy, which is used to pump hydrogen ions across the membrane, creating a gradient.

This gradient acts like a dam holding back water. When the hydrogen ions flow back across the membrane through a protein called ATP synthase, it's like releasing the water through a

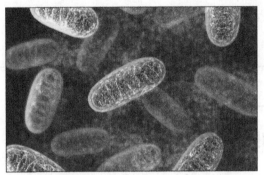

The Krebs cycle and Electron Transport Chain take place in the mitochondria of cells.

turbine. The flow of hydrogen ions spins the ATP synthase, generating ATP from ADP (adenosine diphosphate). Finally, oxygen combines with the electrons and hydrogen ions to form water, which is why you need to breathe in oxygen and exhale carbon dioxide.

Why is Cellular Respiration Important?

Cellular respiration is essential for life because it provides the energy your cells need to function. Without it, your muscles wouldn't have the power to contract, your brain wouldn't have the energy to think, and your heart wouldn't have the strength to pump blood. Essentially, cellular respiration is the engine that drives all of your biological processes.

Now that you have a better understanding of cellular respiration, you can appreciate just how amazing your body is. Every single one of your cells is a mini power plant, working tirelessly to convert the food you eat into the energy you need to live and thrive. Whenever you enjoy a meal or take a deep breath, remember that your cells are hard at work, keeping you energized and healthy.

8. Cellular Respiration
GUIDED NOTES

I. What is Cellular Respiration?

Define cellular respiration in your own words: _____

_____

What does ATP stand for, and what is its role in the cell?

_____

_____

II. The Three Stages of Cellular Respiration

List the three main stages of cellular respiration:

1. _____   2. _____

3. _____

III. Stage 1: Glycolysis

1. Where does glycolysis occur in the cell? _____

2. What does the word "glycolysis" mean? _____

3. True or False: Glycolysis requires oxygen. _____

IV. Stage 2: The Krebs Cycle

1. Where does the Krebs cycle take place? _____

2. What is another name for the Krebs cycle? _____

3. Name two important molecules produced during the Krebs cycle:

   a) _____   b) _____

V. Stage 3: Electron Transport Chain (ETC)

1. Where does the ETC occur in the cell?

_____

2. What is the main function of the ETC?

_____

3. How is ATP produced in this stage?

_____

VI. Importance of Cellular Respiration

List three reasons why cellular respiration is important for living organisms:

1. _____

2. _____

3. _____

VII. Key Terms

Match each term with its correct definition:

_____ Glucose   A. The energy currency of the cell

_____ Mitochondria   B. The first stage of cellular respiration

_____ ATP   C. Where the Krebs cycle and ETC occur

_____ Glycolysis   D. The type of sugar broken down in cellular respiration

VIII. Reflection

In your own words, explain how understanding cellular respiration helps you appreciate the complexity of living organisms:

_____

_____

_____

#1

How does cellular respiration contribute to your daily activities, like playing sports or doing homework?

Consider how ATP, the energy currency produced by cellular respiration, powers both your physical movements and mental tasks.

#2

Why is glycolysis referred to as "sugar splitting," and why doesn't it require oxygen?

Reflect on the process of breaking down glucose into pyruvate and the fact that glycolysis can occur without oxygen, making it an anaerobic process.

#3

What role does the Krebs cycle play in cellular respiration, and why is it important for energy extraction?

Think about how the Krebs cycle processes pyruvate to produce molecules like NADH and FADH2, which are essential for the next stage of energy production.

#4

How does the Electron Transport Chain (ETC) function like an "ATP factory," and why is oxygen crucial in this process?

Consider the role of high-energy electrons, the creation of a hydrogen ion gradient, and the importance of oxygen in forming water at the end of the ETC.

#5

What would happen to your body's energy levels if cellular respiration suddenly stopped?

Reflect on the impacts on muscle movement, brain function, and overall bodily processes without the continuous production of ATP.

#6

In what ways do the three stages of cellular respiration work together to ensure efficient energy production?

Think about how glycolysis, the Krebs cycle, and the Electron Transport Chain are interconnected and how they collectively contribute to the production of ATP.

TERM	DEFINITION
Cellular respiration	
Glucose	
Adenosine triphosphate (ATP)	
Glycolysis	
Pyruvate	
NADH	
Anaerobic respiration	

TERM	DEFINITION
Mitochondria	
Krebs cycle	
FADH2	
Electron transport chain (ETC)	
ATP synthase	
Aerobic respiration	
Carbon dioxide (CO_2)	

Cellular Respiration

```
I B C M U A C C N F B C X T S A U I G K S F R 2
N K D H L K T A T A U O O 2 O M F U G 2 D X N D
E B B G Y T E R M E E R F G F N 2 V I V P E K D
R T G R G U L B A R Y R X T O T H S R N D E S P
K C D I L Y E O H O I F M I T O C H O N D R I A
G E D P 2 L C N X B F A R M H H F T Y S K E D D
F L O K L I T D S I P N O R I P M N H S H S H B
A L K P A P R I L C A G 2 C V E E H F G B G G L
D U L O L V O O G R I N H P S Y T T U M G N T V
H L V H L R N X V E A T P S Y N T H A S E S X A
2 A B Y G B T I G S M C X D V K O R P R M X G U
I R N R A R R D L P K R U E T 2 A E G V U K D K
A R A E E F A E Y I Y P R R 2 X L P G P 2 Y A R
P E P C K C N L C R H M B E E 2 M S N M V I T E
D S X Y U K S K O A G Y M U D M X B Y G C H N B
G P V O T L P M L T P 2 P E M G L U C O S E A S
L I K B C P O O Y I D C E Y H G F G B R M X 2 C
X R M I T 2 R 2 S O B K M B E X T K L M Y 2 C Y
R A N N R R T I I N U K Y T G P Y R U V A T E C
M T C Y A T C E S N L M F V G T I U P G P G T L
S I T C 2 H H D S V N A D H R N L B U A A K E
X O S B A N A E R O B I C R E S P I R A T I O N
P N A U G T I K G 2 B M H A G A G C H L V B K V
S L U M E M N B C D G F P T K F S Y A T P E P I
```

Aerobic respiration

ATP synthase

Electron transport chain

Anaerobic respiration

Cellular respiration

Carbon dioxide

FADH2

Krebs cycle

Mitochondria

NADH

Pyruvate

Glycolysis

ATP

Glucose

Cellular Respiration

Across

3. A type of sugar that is a primary energy source for cells, broken down during cellular respiration to produce ATP.

6. A compound formed from the splitting of glucose during glycolysis, which then enters the Krebs cycle.

7. A waste product released during the Krebs cycle, exhaled by the lungs during breathing. (Two words)

8. The first stage of cellular respiration, occurring in the cytoplasm, where glucose is split into two molecules of pyruvate, producing a small amount of ATP and NADH.

9. A molecule that carries high-energy electrons produced during glycolysis and the Krebs cycle to the Electron Transport Chain.

12. The process by which cells convert glucose into adenosine triphosphate (ATP), providing energy for all cellular activities. Cellular ____

13. The organelles in the cell known as the "powerhouses," where the Krebs cycle and Electron Transport Chain occur.

14. A protein in the inner mitochondrial membrane that uses the flow of hydrogen ions to generate ATP from ADP. ATP ____

Down

1. A type of respiration that does not require oxygen, such as glycolysis. ____ respiration

2. The final stage of cellular respiration, taking place in the inner mitochondrial membrane, where most ATP is produced through the movement of high-energy electrons and hydrogen ions. ____ ____ chain

4. The second stage of cellular respiration, occurring in the mitochondria, where pyruvate is broken down to produce carbon dioxide, NADH, FADH2, and a small amount of ATP.

5. A type of respiration that requires oxygen, involving the Krebs cycle and Electron Transport Chain. ____ respiration

10. The energy currency of the cell, used to power various functions within the body.

11. A molecule similar to NADH that carries high-energy electrons to the Electron Transport Chain.

How Your Cells Generate Energy

Have you ever wondered how your body gets the energy it needs to keep you moving, thinking, and even sleeping? The answer lies in two essential processes: aerobic and anaerobic respiration. These processes help your cells produce the energy required for everything you do. Time to get into cellular respiration and explore how your body generates energy.

What is Cellular Respiration?

Cellular respiration is how your cells convert the food you eat into energy. This energy is stored in a molecule called ATP (adenosine triphosphate), which powers various cellular activities.

There are two main types of cellular respiration: aerobic and anaerobic.

The build of lactic acid can be the cause of the burning sensation during exercise.

Aerobic Respiration

Aerobic respiration requires oxygen to produce energy. When you breathe in, oxygen enters your lungs and is transported to your cells. This oxygen is crucial for aerobic respiration, which takes place in the mitochondria (the powerhouse of the cell).

Here's a simple breakdown of the aerobic respiration process:

1. Glycolysis: This is the first step, occurring in the cytoplasm of the cell. One molecule of glucose (a type of sugar) is broken down into two molecules of pyruvate, producing a small amount of ATP and NADH (another energy-carrying molecule).

2. Krebs Cycle: The pyruvate molecules enter the mitochondria and go through the Krebs cycle. This cycle produces more NADH and FADH2 (yet another energy-carrying molecule) and releases carbon dioxide as a waste product.

3. Electron Transport Chain: The NADH and FADH2 molecules created in the earlier steps donate electrons to the electron transport chain, located in the inner mitochondrial membrane. As electrons move through the chain, they help produce a significant amount of ATP. Oxygen is the final electron acceptor in this chain, combining with electrons and hydrogen ions to form water.

In total, aerobic respiration can produce up to 38 molecules of ATP from a single molecule of glucose. This makes it a very efficient way for your cells to generate energy.

Anaerobic Respiration

Anaerobic respiration, on the other hand, does not require oxygen. This type of respiration occurs in the cytoplasm of the cell and is used when oxygen levels are low, such as during intense exercise or in certain microorganisms that live in oxygen-free environments.

There are two main types of anaerobic respiration:

1. Lactic Acid Fermentation: This process occurs in your muscle cells when they are working hard and can't get enough oxygen. During lactic acid fermentation, glucose is broken down into pyruvate, just like in glycolysis. However, instead of entering the Krebs cycle, pyruvate is converted into lactic acid. This conversion regenerates NAD+, allowing glycolysis to continue and produce a small amount of ATP. The buildup of lactic acid in your muscles can cause the burning sensation you feel during intense exercise.

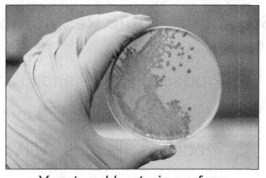

Yeast and bacteria perform alcohol fermentation, a type of anaerobic respiration

2. Alcoholic Fermentation: This type of anaerobic respiration is used by yeast and some bacteria. Like lactic acid fermentation, glucose is broken down into pyruvate during glycolysis. However, in alcoholic fermentation, pyruvate is converted into ethanol (a type of alcohol) and carbon dioxide.

This process also regenerates NAD+, allowing glycolysis to continue and produce ATP.

Anaerobic respiration is much less efficient than aerobic respiration, producing only 2 molecules of ATP per glucose molecule. However, it provides a quick burst of energy when oxygen is scarce.

Why Are Both Types Important?

Both aerobic and anaerobic respiration are vital for your body. Aerobic respiration is the preferred method for producing energy because it generates a lot of ATP. However, during activities like sprinting or heavy lifting, your muscles might not get enough oxygen. In these situations, anaerobic respiration kicks in to provide the energy you need to keep going.

Understanding how your cells generate energy through aerobic and anaerobic respiration can help you appreciate the incredible processes happening in your body every day. Whether you're running a marathon or simply breathing, your cells are hard at work, converting food into the energy you need to live, learn, and play.

9. Aerobic and Anaerobic Respiration
GUIDED NOTES

I. Types of Cellular Respiration

List the two main types of cellular respiration:

1. _____ 2._____

II. Aerobic Respiration

Fill in the blanks:

1. Aerobic respiration requires _____ to produce energy.

2. It takes place in the _____, also known as the

   powerhouse of the cell.

3. The three main steps of aerobic respiration are:

   a. _____ b. _____ c. _____

III. Steps of Aerobic Respiration

Match each step with its description:

_____ Glycolysis   A. Produces NADH and FADH2, releases CO_2

_____ Krebs Cycle   B. Breaks down glucose into pyruvate

_____ Electron Transport   C. Produces the most ATP, uses oxygen as final

                                         electron acceptor Chain

IV. Anaerobic Respiration

Name the two main types of anaerobic respiration:

1. _____ 2._____

V. Compare and Contrast

Fill in the table comparing aerobic and anaerobic respiration:

Feature	Aerobic Respiration	Anaerobic Respiration
Oxygen requirement		
Location in the cell		
ATP yield per glucose		

VI. True or False

_____ Anaerobic respiration is more efficient than aerobic respiration.

_____ Lactic acid fermentation occurs in muscle cells during intense exercise.

_____ The Krebs cycle takes place in the cytoplasm of the cell.

_____ Alcoholic fermentation is used by yeast and some bacteria.

VII. Fill in the Blanks

1. ATP stands for _____.

2. The burning sensation in muscles during intense exercise is caused by

_____.

3. The final electron acceptor in the electron transport chain is

_____.

VIII. Short Answer

Explain why both aerobic and anaerobic respiration are important for the human body:

_____

_____

_____

IX. In your own words, describe why learning about cellular respiration is important for understanding how our bodies function:

_____

_____

_____

_____

#1

How does aerobic respiration differ from anaerobic respiration in terms of oxygen use and energy production?

Think about the role of oxygen in aerobic respiration and how it affects the amount of ATP produced compared to anaerobic respiration.

#2

Why might your muscles use anaerobic respiration during intense exercise, and what are the consequences?

Reflect on the conditions under which your muscles can't get enough oxygen and what happens to the byproducts of anaerobic respiration.

#3

What are the main steps of aerobic respiration, and why is each step important?

Consider how glycolysis, the Krebs cycle, and the electron transport chain each contribute to the production of ATP.

#4

How do the byproducts of anaerobic respiration differ between lactic acid fermentation and alcoholic fermentation?

Think about what happens to pyruvate in each type of fermentation and the substances that are produced.

#5

In what ways are aerobic and anaerobic respiration both essential for your body's energy needs?

Reflect on the situations in which your body relies on each type of respiration and how they complement each other.

#6

How does the efficiency of ATP production compare between aerobic and anaerobic respiration?

Consider the number of ATP molecules produced by each type of respiration and how this affects your energy levels during different activities.

TERM	DEFINITION
Cellular respiration	
ATP (Adenosine Triphosphate)	
Aerobic respiration	
Anaerobic respiration	
Mitochondria	
Glycolysis	
Krebs Cycle (Citric Acid Cycle)	

TERM	DEFINITION
Electron Transport Chain	
NADH	
FADH2	
Lactic acid fermentation	
Alcoholic fermentation	
Pyruvate	
Carbon dioxide (CO_2)	

Aerobic & Anaerobic Respiration

```
U C U 2 D K M O O O V G I X O P E T L V B U G H
R E T E T 2 U N B P B A P X F F U N P M I T O R
O L T P M F D C A R B O N D I O X I D E X Y M N
H L O R 2 A H 2 C G P L M C I V H 2 V N S M N U
E U I K P E E U 2 2 P A K H B X H T U 2 O O U 2
A L B L Y I R U B A A C B B C B D N X P Y M V R
A A V E L E C T R O N T R A N S P O R T E A T P
E R A N A E R O B I C I B R B O C X M B K C D C
R R D V F A D H 2 K H C S O T U T H K G S M F U
O E A F G U L G X D E A V Y F X C B F K M V E 2
B S I A C S S G N T 2 C D N A N D L Y U H A U 2
I P X V B D M L V B G I M T E R F C A R B O N L
C I H R T N N Y R 2 V D X E P H L N R B D E 2 E
M R X L D E K C O E N 2 U C Y H A A X P K 2 G M
N A P O U L V O F T R K B K Y S A D P M I V V B
U T M L B A Y L X O L A X N X C Y H G X S U D D
C I V E V V L Y T U G R B M N F 2 G C N 2 Y D K
E O U K R E B S C Y C L E D U V L T H S G R 2 K
O N K P Y E D I M F T K B T 2 A C G L U C B E I
A I U G S H 2 S F E D 2 2 S G D H R R S K Y K L
T K T C D C K R M I T O C H O N D R I A I I I F
T L 2 K K G D B F G P P P T G E G B N K S P N Y
V U V S C G K A K O N X M P Y R U V A T E R T S
X K A L C O H O L I C F E R M E N T A T I O N S
```

Carbon dioxide	Alcoholic fermentation	Krebs Cycle
Cellular respiration	Pyruvate	Lactic acid
FADH2	NADH	Electron transport
Glycolysis	Mitochondria	Anaerobic
Aerobic	ATP	

Aerobic & Anaerobic Respiration

Across

2. A three-carbon molecule produced during glycolysis from the breakdown of glucose, which can be further processed in respiration.

4. The process by which cells convert food into energy, stored in the form of ATP, to power various cellular activities. Cellular ____

5. The first step in cellular respiration where one molecule of glucose is broken down into two molecules of pyruvate, producing a small amount of ATP and NADH.

7. A type of anaerobic respiration in muscle cells where pyruvate is converted into lactic acid, regenerating NAD+ and allowing glycolysis to continue. ___ ___ fermentation

9. A type of cellular respiration that does not require oxygen, occurring in the cytoplasm, and used during low oxygen conditions. ____ respiration

11. A type of cellular respiration that requires oxygen to produce energy, mainly occurring in the mitochondria. ____ respiration

14. Organelles in cells known as the powerhouse, where aerobic respiration and most ATP production occur.

Down

1. A sequence of proteins in the inner mitochondrial membrane that uses electrons from NADH and FADH2 to produce a significant amount of ATP. ____ ____ chain

3. A series of chemical reactions in the mitochondria that further break down pyruvate, producing NADH, FADH2, and carbon dioxide. ____ Cycle

6. A type of anaerobic respiration in yeast and some bacteria where pyruvate is converted into ethanol and carbon dioxide, regenerating NAD+. ____ fermentation

8. The primary energy-carrying molecule in cells, used to fuel a wide range of cellular functions.

10. A waste product released during the Krebs cycle and alcoholic fermentation, expelled from the body during exhalation. ____ dioxide

12. An energy-carrying molecule produced during glycolysis and the Krebs cycle, used in the electron transport chain to generate ATP.

13. Another energy-carrying molecule produced during the Krebs cycle, also used in the electron transport chain to generate ATP.

How Microorganisms Transform Our Food and Bodies

Imagine life without bread, cheese, yogurt, or even chocolate! These delicious foods wouldn't exist without a process called fermentation. But fermentation isn't just about creating tasty treats; it's also a crucial biological process that happens inside your body. Let's get into fermentation and uncover how it works, its types, and why it's essential for both food production and human health.

What is Fermentation?

Fermentation is a natural process where microorganisms like bacteria and yeast convert sugars into other substances, such as acids, gases, or alcohol. This process usually occurs in the absence of oxygen, making it an anaerobic process. Fermentation has been used for thousands of years to produce foods and beverages, and it also takes place in your body, helping you digest food and generate energy.

Fermentation has been used for thousands of years to make foods and beverages.

Types of Fermentation

There are two main types of fermentation: alcoholic fermentation and lactic acid fermentation.

1. Alcoholic Fermentation: This type is carried out by yeast, a type of fungus. When yeast consumes sugars in foods like grapes or grains, it produces alcohol and carbon dioxide. This process is what makes wine, beer, and other alcoholic beverages possible. The carbon dioxide produced also helps bread rise, giving it that fluffy texture.

2. Lactic Acid Fermentation: This type is performed by certain bacteria, such as Lactobacillus. These bacteria convert sugars into lactic acid, which gives foods like yogurt, sauerkraut, and kimchi their tangy taste. Lactic acid fermentation is also vital for your muscles, especially during intense exercise. When your muscles run out of oxygen, they switch to lactic acid fermentation to produce energy, resulting in the familiar "burn" you feel during strenuous activity.

The Science Behind Fermentation

At its core, fermentation is a way for microorganisms to generate energy. When they break down sugars, they release energy that they use to grow and reproduce. Here's a simplified version of the chemical reaction for alcoholic fermentation:

$$C_6H_{12}O_6 \rightarrow 2C_2H_5OH + 2CO_2$$

In this equation, glucose (a type of sugar) is broken down into ethanol (alcohol) and carbon dioxide. For lactic acid fermentation, the equation looks like this:

$$C_6H_{12}O_6 \rightarrow 2C_3H_6O_3$$

Here, glucose is converted into lactic acid.

Why Fermentation Matters

Fermentation plays a crucial role in various aspects of life:

Food Preservation: Before refrigeration, fermentation was one of the main methods to preserve food. The acids and alcohols produced during fermentation inhibit the growth of harmful bacteria, keeping the food safe to eat for longer periods.

Fermentation is used to help preserve food.

Nutritional Benefits: Fermented foods are loaded with beneficial bacteria known as probiotics. These probiotics are good for your gut health, aiding digestion and boosting your immune system.

Energy Production: As mentioned earlier, fermentation helps your muscles produce energy during intense exercise. It's a backup system your body uses when oxygen levels are low.

Fermentation in Everyday Life

You might be surprised at just how many common foods and beverages rely on fermentation.

Here are a few examples:

Bread: Yeast fermentation produces the carbon dioxide that makes bread rise.

Yogurt: Bacteria ferment the sugars in milk, creating lactic acid and giving yogurt its texture and flavor.

Pickles: Cucumbers are fermented in a salty brine, which preserves them and adds a tangy taste.

Cheese: Bacteria and sometimes molds are used to ferment milk, resulting in a wide variety of cheeses.

Experimenting with Fermentation

You can even try simple fermentation experiments at home to see the process in action. For example, you can make your own yogurt or ferment some vegetables. Just make sure to follow proper guidelines to ensure safety and success.

Fermentation is a fascinating process that has been part of human life for centuries. From the foods you enjoy to the energy your muscles need, fermentation is all around you. By understanding how it works and its importance, you gain a deeper appreciation for both biology and the everyday wonders of science. When you bite into a slice of bread or savor a spoonful of yogurt, you'll know that tiny microorganisms have been hard at work, transforming simple sugars into something truly amazing.

10. Fermentation

I. What is Fermentation?

Define fermentation in your own words:

_____

_____

II. Types of Fermentation

List and briefly describe the two main types of fermentation:

1. _____ : _____

_____

2. _____ : _____

_____

III. The Science of Fermentation

Match each equation to the correct type of fermentation:

____ $C_6H_{12}O_6 \rightarrow 2C_2H_5OH + 2CO_2$ A. Lactic Acid Fermentation

____ $C_6H_{12}O_6 \rightarrow 2C_3H_6O_3$ B. Alcoholic Fermentation

IV. Importance of Fermentation

Explain three reasons why fermentation is important:

1. _____

_____

2. _____

_____

3. _____

_____

V. Fermented Foods

Name four common foods or beverages that rely on fermentation:

1. _____   2. _____

3. _____   4. _____

VI. True or False

_____ Fermentation only occurs in the presence of oxygen.

_____ Yeast is responsible for alcoholic fermentation.

_____ Lactic acid fermentation gives yogurt its tangy taste.

_____ Fermentation cannot occur in the human body.

VII. Fill in the Blanks

1. Fermentation is carried out by _____ like bacteria and yeast.

2. During intense exercise, muscles may switch to _____ fermentation when oxygen is low.

3. The carbon dioxide produced during fermentation helps _____ rise.

4. Fermented foods are loaded with beneficial bacteria known as _____.

VIII. Short Answer

Explain how fermentation was used for food preservation before refrigeration:

_____

_____

IX. In your own words, explain why learning about fermentation is important for high school students:

_____

_____

_____

#1

How does fermentation impact the foods you eat daily?

Think about common foods like bread, yogurt, and cheese. How would their taste and texture be different without fermentation?

#2

What are the main differences between alcoholic fermentation and lactic acid fermentation?

Consider the microorganisms involved and the end products they produce. How do these differences affect the foods and drinks created?

#3

Why is fermentation considered an anaerobic process, and why is this important?

Reflect on what it means for a process to occur without oxygen. How does this affect where and how fermentation can take place?

#4

How does fermentation benefit your body during intense exercise?

Think about the role of lactic acid fermentation in your muscles. How does this help you continue exercising when oxygen levels are low?

#5

In what ways has fermentation been used historically to preserve food?

Consider how acids and alcohols produced during fermentation can prevent the growth of harmful bacteria. How did people use this before modern refrigeration?

#6

What are some simple fermentation experiments you can try at home, and what do they teach you about the process?

Think about making yogurt or pickles. What steps are involved, and what do you observe about the transformation of sugars into other substances?

TERM	DEFINITION
Fermentation	
Microorganisms	
Anaerobic process	
Yeast	
Alcoholic fermentation	
Lactic acid fermentation	
Lactobacillus	

TERM	DEFINITION
Ethanol	
Carbon dioxide (CO_2)	
Probiotics	
Food preservation	
Glucose	
Energy production	
Muscle fatigue	

Fermentation

```
J Y U I J F B P S T W J V O P K F A A P Q O Q Y
R C N E D Z W O F H T N A Y E A S T L A N J H C
L H Z Q H L Z N J H H S R I L Y C Q C N Q Q E V
B Y E B L A C T O B A C I L L U S A O A A S O Y
K G N X H W X J B E Y Z Y I I K P K H E X G M B
T F E M I C R O O R G A N I S M S O O R J T L D
I Y R G G T F E T P K D S U J A P G L O T H M C
F W G E F Q C M Z T H M T X R W U C I B Z Y M K
O V Y M R F I U X N N D U N R Y I W C I F H X T
O M P G A V T S R Z P Y W B K B F S F C E R V V
D S R G S Z H C L W U V P L X V Y B E P R Q S R
P H O X A M F L L A C T I C A C I D R R M I F F
R P D U M R U E V H R I L B K L P W M O E P E M
E Q U R Y D P F D P Y B F Z K I S B E C N R R Y
S S C X K U W A Y I W F O Q I B K P N E T O Z H
E D T R N E T T V F H Y O N P O L K T S A B M K
R S I X C T G I A R Q D G H X U G U G A S T I H P
V S O Y I H I G A M S Q Y V G G Z Z T G I O K I
A L N Y W A Y U O U N D K V F P H Y I S O T G G
T I B L L N E O L J W T R N P L F O L N I N V
I M B N W O J H B G D E O C Q I Z T B N C M C Z U
O D M M C L E Z G L U C O S E E F Z T U B S I Y
N T U U Y K J I Y M U K I B W C W J L A Z Y W S
R R C A C A R B O N D I O X I D E I Z N Q F K K
```

Lactic acid	Muscle fatigue	Energy production
Food preservation	Alcoholic fermentation	Anaerobic process
Glucose	Probiotics	Carbon dioxide
Ethanol	Lactobacillus	Yeast
Microorganisms	Fermentation	

Fermentation

Across
2. The "burn" felt in muscles during intense exercise, caused by lactic acid fermentation when muscles run out of oxygen. Muscle ____

3. A type of alcohol produced during alcoholic fermentation.

8. A type of fermentation where bacteria convert sugars into lactic acid, found in foods like yogurt and sauerkraut and also occurs in muscles during intense exercise. ____ ____ fermentation

10. A type of sugar that is broken down during fermentation to produce energy.

12. The process of keeping food safe to eat for longer periods, often achieved through fermentation by producing acids and alcohols that inhibit harmful bacteria. Food ____

13. A type of bacteria involved in lactic acid fermentation, producing lactic acid from sugars.

14. Beneficial bacteria found in fermented foods that aid digestion and boost the immune system.

Down
1. A gas produced during fermentation that helps bread rise and gives beverages their fizz. (Two words)

4. The process by which cells generate energy, including through fermentation when oxygen levels are low. Energy ____

5. A type of fermentation where yeast converts sugars into alcohol and carbon dioxide, used in making beverages like wine and beer. ____ fermentation

6. Tiny living organisms like bacteria and yeast that are involved in processes like fermentation.

7. A natural process where microorganisms like bacteria and yeast convert sugars into substances such as acids, gases, or alcohol, often in the absence of oxygen.

9. A process that occurs in the absence of oxygen, such as fermentation. ____ process

11. A type of fungus used in alcoholic fermentation to convert sugars into alcohol and carbon dioxide.

Unraveling the Secrets of Nature's Code

Imagine holding the instructions for building every living thing on Earth, from the tiniest bacteria to the largest whale. These instructions are written in a special code called DNA. DNA, or deoxyribonucleic acid, is the molecule that carries all the information needed for an organism to grow, develop, and reproduce. Let's get into the structure and function of DNA, helping you understand why it is often called the blueprint of life.

What is DNA?

DNA stands for deoxyribonucleic acid. It is a molecule found in the cells of all living organisms. If you could look inside your cells with a powerful microscope, you would see long, twisted strands of DNA. These strands are coiled up tightly to fit inside the cell's nucleus.

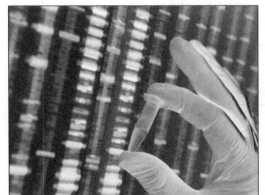

DNA is considered the blueprint of life.

The Structure of DNA

DNA has a unique and fascinating structure. It looks like a twisted ladder, known as a double helix. This double helix is made up of two long strands that run in opposite directions. The sides of the ladder are made of sugar and phosphate molecules. The rungs of the ladder are made of smaller molecules called nitrogenous bases.

There are four types of nitrogenous bases in DNA: adenine (A), thymine (T), cytosine (C), and guanine (G). These bases pair up in a very specific way: adenine always pairs with thymine, and cytosine always pairs with guanine. This pairing is crucial because it ensures that DNA can copy itself accurately.

How DNA Copies Itself

One of the most important functions of DNA is its ability to replicate, or make copies of itself. This process is essential for growth and repair in living organisms. When a cell divides, it needs to pass on an exact copy of its DNA to the new cells. Here's how DNA replication works:

1. Unwinding the Helix: The double helix unwinds, and the two strands separate.

2. Pairing Up: Free-floating nitrogenous bases in the cell pair up with the exposed bases on each strand. Adenine pairs with thymine, and cytosine pairs with guanine.

3. Forming New Strands: Enzymes help form new sugar-phosphate backbones, creating two new DNA molecules. Each new molecule has one old strand and one new strand.

This semi-conservative method of replication ensures that each new cell has an exact copy of the DNA.
The Role of DNA in Protein Synthesis

DNA doesn't just sit in the nucleus. It has a very active role in making proteins, which are the building blocks of your body. Proteins are responsible for almost everything your body does, from building muscles to fighting off infections.

The process of making proteins from DNA involves two main steps: transcription and translation.

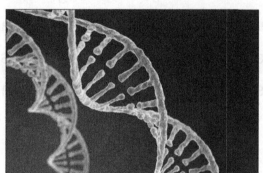
DNA is famously known for its unique double helix structure.

1. Transcription: In this step, a section of DNA is copied into a molecule called messenger RNA (mRNA). This happens in the nucleus. The mRNA carries the genetic code from the DNA out of the nucleus and into the cytoplasm.

2. Translation: In the cytoplasm, the mRNA attaches to a ribosome. This is where the genetic code is read, and amino acids are assembled into a protein. Each set of three bases on the mRNA (called a codon) corresponds to a specific amino acid. Transfer RNA (tRNA) molecules bring the correct amino acids to the ribosome, and the protein chain is built.

Why DNA is Important

DNA is essential for life. It contains all the instructions needed to make you who you are. Your unique combination of DNA determines everything from your eye color to your risk of certain diseases. Understanding DNA also helps scientists in many fields, including medicine, forensics, and agriculture.

In medicine, for example, scientists study DNA to understand genetic diseases and develop new treatments. In forensics, DNA fingerprinting helps solve crimes by matching DNA samples from crime scenes with suspects. In agriculture, scientists use DNA to create crops that are more resistant to pests and diseases.

DNA is truly the blueprint of life. Its unique structure allows it to store and transmit genetic information accurately. By understanding DNA, you unlock the secrets to how living organisms grow, develop, and function. As you continue your studies in biology, remember that DNA is at the heart of it all, guiding the processes that keep life thriving. By grasping the basics of DNA, you are taking the first step in exploring the intricate and fascinating world of genetics.

11. Structure and Function of DNA and RNA
GUIDED NOTES

I. What is DNA?

1. DNA stands for: _____

2. DNA is found in: _____

3. Describe what DNA looks like inside a cell: _____

_____

II. The Structure of DNA

Match each part of DNA with its description:

_____ Double helix   A. Made of sugar and phosphate molecules

_____ Sides of the ladder   B. Twisted ladder shape

_____ Rungs of the ladder   C. Nitrogenous bases

_____ Nitrogenous bases   D. Adenine (A), Thymine (T), Cytosine (C),

                               Guanine (G)

III. Base Pairing

Fill in the correct base pair:

1. Adenine (A) pairs with: _____

2. Cytosine (C) pairs with: _____

IV. DNA Replication

List the three steps of DNA replication in order:

1. _____   2. _____

3. _____

V. Protein Synthesis

Name and briefly describe the two main steps in protein synthesis:

1. _____

_____

2. _____

_____

VI. Importance of DNA

List three fields where understanding DNA is important and give one example for each:

1. Field: _____ Example: _____

_____

2. Field: _____ Example: _____

_____

3. Field: _____ Example: _____

_____

VII. True or False

_____ DNA is the same in all living organisms.

_____ The structure of DNA is a single straight line.

_____ DNA contains instructions for making proteins.

_____ DNA replication creates two identical copies, each with one old and one new strand.

VIII. In your own words, explain why DNA is called the "blueprint of life":

_____

_____

_____

_____

#1

How does the structure of DNA resemble a twisted ladder, and why is this structure important for its function?

Think about the components of the double helix, such as the sugar-phosphate backbone and the nitrogenous base pairs.

#2

Why is the specific pairing of nitrogenous bases (A with T and C with G) crucial for DNA replication?

Reflect on how accurate copying of DNA ensures that new cells receive the correct genetic information.

#3

Describe the process of DNA replication and its significance in growth and repair of living organisms.

Focus on the steps of unwinding the helix, base pairing, and forming new strands.

#4

Explain the roles of transcription and translation in protein synthesis and how they contribute to the functions of your body.

Think about how mRNA carries the genetic code from the DNA to the ribosome and how proteins are assembled.

#5

In what ways does understanding DNA help in fields like medicine, forensics, and agriculture?

Consider how genetic information is used to treat diseases, solve crimes, and improve crop resistance.

#6

Why is DNA often called the blueprint of life, and what does this mean for our understanding of living organisms?

Reflect on how DNA contains all the instructions for an organism's growth, development, and function.

TERM	DEFINITION
DNA **(Deoxyribonucleic Acid)**	
Nucleus	
Double helix	
Sugar-phosphate backbone	
Nitrogenous bases	
Base pairing	
Replication	

TERM	DEFINITION
Semi-conservative replication	
Transcription	
Translation	
mRNA (Messenger RNA)	
Codon	
tRNA (Transfer RNA)	
Protein synthesis	

Structure & Function of DNA and RNA

```
L E N D S A P Y F L U E R K H I E U R W N N N L T P W P K P M
H W L C F P U X W W V G Y W V D U S E D I P X O W P N T Q O J
I W Y G J I V U B Y M R K O R K M Y W B B I E N P U N Y G R A
S Q P K A I T T H C Y O B I C A O S R M N V A M S T U B C T M
G E V C I J R F S I B Q F J O P Z L G W G B P L G K C Y P C S
C B Z C X L D O Q P W T O K M I Z H Q U C Z V Y M H L Z O C U
M J D X J H D U U L I R N T H D O U B L E H E L I X E X I F H
L W M M Z J B D J L K A H J J P U M M R Z F O Z H X U K R Z Z
H D Z L K C K E Z Q D N U U D J Y D Z S R B P R E U S P P C S
Y N Y X L C O D O N A S G K R F L Z B G T B Q R A N O H Q W L
M M A X Y L B W A D C L M P V G M W N H H L S L R U F M R N G
S E M I C O N S E R V A T I V E R E P L I C A T I O N R G G A
S W Z D H L I X B L G T O T P R O T E I N S Y N T H E S I S R
W J C S E P F M T G P I A Q D T Y G Y P B H W U V Z R K M W P
S L T F X Q C Z M S K O R I H T O I R L F U R D A W K J Y I H
E F R B A A Z K F C F N B B R U X S E M C K O S F O Z C K X O
M O A R E V E Y Q F L Y G C U A K Q P T Z H L B X V U D W M S
I G N D N A K I S R Q D B P A A P Z L U W O M L P Q X N G Y P
C F S A J D R R O D E M A W O B C Z I F X B B M R M I X X E H
O W C A P R R U N S P S S Y L B H F C C X Y V B J D Y C D W A
N S R K V R X I R T R G E A C A I N A G G Q H L O P P N I R T
S C I L X G L J U B N S P D D Z Q S T L I G K D J U X T U U E
E P P D L V D W I B J I A P U O Q Q I N Z N H K P Z Q H V J B
R F T S N I D G K U N N I W T Z V Y O L U L O N N M J F U M A
V D I G F I Q F L W O X R J X G G F N S H Q A Z T Q O E U X C
A D O N E A C K X J O D I C U F E H K T K I F K R C K K G T K
T Z N O W K V N N L V A N A U T R G A Q Q G D R N N W T B X B
I F J Q E G P F R G C P G A E X F H Y O R R N M A B P J N K O
V J Z R E W T F X U E O K M T N W G V L U Z G R J V U E N D N
E L H U D F L L A M J S R V R O T C X M T E P N P X R N F D E
E N I T R O G E N O U S B A S E S P T D H X G A Z N B O F V W
```

Semi-conservative replication	Base pairing	Nitrogenous bases
Sugar-phosphate backbone	Protein synthesis	tRNA
Codon	mRNA	Translation
Transcription	Replication	Double helix
Nucleus	DNA	

Structure & Function of DNA and RNA

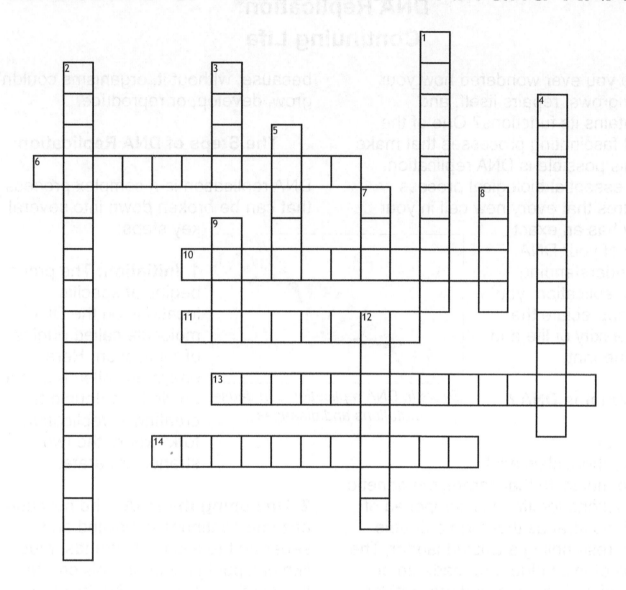

Across

6. The molecules that form the rungs of the DNA ladder; includes adenine (A), thymine (T), cytosine (C), and guanine (G). _____ bases

10. The process by which the genetic code carried by mRNA is read by a ribosome to assemble amino acids into a protein.

11. The sides of the DNA ladder, made up of alternating sugar and phosphate molecules. Sugar-phosphate _____

13. The process of copying a section of DNA into messenger RNA (mRNA), which carries the genetic code out of the nucleus.

14. The twisted ladder-like structure of DNA, consisting of two long strands that run in opposite directions. (Two words)

Down

1. The process of making proteins from the genetic code in DNA, involving transcription and translation. Protein _____

2. A method of DNA replication where each new DNA molecule consists of one old strand and one new strand. _____-_____ replication

3. The specific pairing of nitrogenous bases in DNA; adenine pairs with thymine, and cytosine pairs with guanine. _____ pairing

4. The process by which DNA makes a copy of itself during cell division, ensuring that each new cell receives an exact copy of the DNA.

5. A set of three bases on the mRNA that corresponds to a specific amino acid.

7. The molecule that contains the genetic instructions for the development, functioning, growth, and reproduction of all living organisms.

8. The molecule that carries the genetic instructions from DNA in the nucleus to the ribosome in the cytoplasm.

9. The molecule that brings the correct amino acids to the ribosome during protein synthesis.

12. The membrane-bound structure within a cell that contains the DNA.

DNA Replication:
Continuing Life

Have you ever wondered how your body grows, repairs itself, and maintains its functions? One of the most fascinating processes that make all this possible is DNA replication. This essential biological process ensures that every new cell in your body has an exact copy of your DNA. By understanding DNA replication, you can appreciate the complexity of life and its blueprint.

What is DNA?

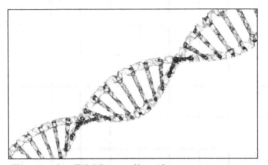

Errors in DNA replication can cause mutations and diseases.

DNA, or deoxyribonucleic acid, is the molecule that carries the genetic instructions for life. It is composed of two long strands that form a double helix, resembling a twisted ladder. The rungs of this ladder are made up of pairs of molecules called nucleotides. There are four types of nucleotides in DNA: adenine (A), thymine (T), cytosine (C), and guanine (G). These nucleotides pair up in a specific way: A with T and C with G.

Why is DNA Replication Important?

DNA replication is crucial because it ensures that each new cell produced during growth or repair has the same genetic information as the original cell. This process is fundamental to life because, without it, organisms couldn't grow, develop, or reproduce.

The Steps of DNA Replication

DNA replication is a complex process that can be broken down into several key steps:

1. Initiation: The process begins at specific locations on the DNA molecule called origins of replication. Here, enzymes called helicases unwind the double helix, creating a "replication fork" where the two strands separate.

2. Unzipping the DNA: The helicase enzyme continues to unwind and separate the two DNA strands, much like unzipping a zipper. This creates two single strands of DNA that will serve as templates for the new strands.

3. Building the New Strands: Another enzyme called DNA polymerase adds new nucleotides to each template strand. It follows the base-pairing rules (A with T and C with G) to ensure that the new strand is a perfect complement to the template strand. This process occurs in opposite directions for each template strand, forming what is known as the leading strand and the lagging strand.

4. Leading and Lagging Strands:
The leading strand is synthesized continuously in the direction of the replication fork. In contrast, the lagging strand is synthesized in short segments called Okazaki fragments, which are later joined together by an enzyme called DNA ligase.

5. Proofreading and Error
Correction: DNA polymerase also has a proofreading function, which helps correct any mistakes made during replication. This ensures that the new DNA molecules are as accurate as possible.

6. Termination: Once the
entire DNA molecule has been replicated, the two new double helices rewind into their classic shape. Each new DNA molecule consists of one original strand and one newly synthesized strand, a process known as semi-conservative replication.

Enzymes Involved in DNA Replication

Several key enzymes play vital roles in DNA replication:

Helicase: Unwinds the double helix and separates the two DNA strands.

DNA Polymerase: Adds new nucleotides to the growing DNA strand and performs proofreading.

Primase: Synthesizes a short RNA primer to provide a starting point for DNA polymerase.

DNA Ligase: Joins the Okazaki fragments on the lagging strand to create a continuous DNA strand.

Topoisomerase: Prevents the DNA from becoming too tightly coiled during replication.

The Importance of Accuracy

Accurate DNA replication is critical for maintaining the integrity of an

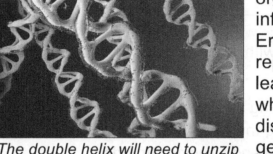
The double helix will need to unzip so the DNA strands can be copied.

organism's genetic information. Errors during replication can lead to mutations, which can cause diseases or other genetic disorders. Fortunately, the proofreading ability of DNA polymerase and other repair mechanisms help keep these errors to a minimum.

DNA replication is a remarkable process that ensures the continuity of life. By understanding how it works, you can gain a deeper appreciation for the complexity and precision of cellular functions. The next time you think about how your body grows or heals, remember that it all starts with the incredible process of DNA replication. This intricate dance of molecules is what keeps life going, one cell at a time.

12. DNA Replication
GUIDED NOTES

I. DNA Basics

1. What does DNA stand for? _____

2. DNA is composed of two long strands that form a _____

List the four types of nucleotides in DNA:

1. _____ (A)   3. _____ (C)

2. _____ (T)   4. _____ (G)

II. Importance of DNA Replication

Explain in your own words why DNA replication is important:

_____

_____

III. Steps of DNA Replication

Match each step with its description:

___ Initiation
___ Unzipping the DNA
___ Building the New Strands
___ Leading and Lagging Strands
___ Proofreading and Error Correction
___ Termination

A. Helicase continues to separate DNA strands
B. DNA polymerase adds new nucleotides to template strands
C. Process begins at origins of replication
D. New double helices rewind into classic shape
E. DNA polymerase corrects mistakes during replication
F. Leading strand synthesized continuously, lagging strand in fragments

IV. Enzymes Involved in DNA Replication

Name the enzyme responsible for each function:

1. Unwinds the double helix: _____

2. Adds new nucleotides and performs proofreading: _____

3. Synthesizes short RNA primer: _____

4. Joins Okazaki fragments: _____

5. Prevents DNA from becoming too tightly coiled: _____

V. True or False

_____ DNA replication ensures that each new cell has different genetic information from the original cell.

_____ The leading strand is synthesized in short segments called Okazaki fragments.

_____ DNA polymerase follows base-pairing rules: A with T and C with G.

_____ Errors during replication can lead to mutations and genetic disorders.

VI. Short Answer

1. Describe the structure of DNA: _____

_____

_____

2. Explain what is meant by "semi-conservative replication": _____

_____

_____

3. Why is accurate DNA replication critical? _____

_____

_____

VII. In your own words, explain why understanding DNA replication is important for high school students:

_____

_____

_____

_____

#1

Why is DNA replication important for the growth and repair of your body?

Think about how your body needs to create new cells to heal cuts or grow taller.

#2

How do the base-pairing rules (A with T and C with G) ensure accurate DNA replication?

Imagine what would happen if the pairs didn't match correctly.

#3

What roles do enzymes like helicase and DNA polymerase play in DNA replication?

Reflect on how these enzymes help in the process of unzipping and building new DNA strands.

#4

What is the difference between the leading strand and the lagging strand during DNA replication?

Think about why one strand can be synthesized continuously while the other is made in short segments.

#5

Why is the proofreading function of DNA polymerase crucial for DNA replication?

Consider what might happen if errors in DNA replication were not corrected.

#6

How does understanding DNA replication help you appreciate the complexity of life?

Think about the precision and coordination required for your cells to function properly.

TERM	DEFINITION
DNA (Deoxyribonucleic Acid)	
Nucleotides	
Double helix	
DNA replication	
Replication fork	
Helicase	
DNA polymerase	

TERM	DEFINITION
Primase	
Leading strand	
Lagging strand	
Okazaki fragments	
DNA ligase	
Topoisomerase	
Semi-conservative replication	

DNA Replication

```
P R E J G T E E P I T T U S L Y E C X B F U N M M D L H U S X
L E P U X U O R D N A R E P L I C A T I O N M Y U B B P T E R
R P Q W Q T D E U A E U R T B O K F G Q T T R I W J O I O B Y
P L F U C E F G U L V O Q K L K H T Q U F Z V J L V F K P M M
K I T S J J D C L S V F Q X U S H H O W Z J E I I S F O O H S
L C W Z M J V O I B Y Z O N I F Z B N I F T Q S E I R G I G H
M A W S Z X O S D P J H Q L V P Z B A E M J M I W V F D S T D
X T D W Y Q Y J G Y X S B N D Y U Q R X D W X Y A X R F O B C
A I V H B V V R Y R H K G C C R Q P S Z H D T W E O W K M B K
P O O H B S B J U H B O Z W Q L A G G I N G S T R A N D E L Y
Q N E W Y Q S W J M E J T H Z K Q H I P Y J Q S S T O E R K Z
A F F M Q H Q A G S E W D O X Q X U B U D D S J R K Q J A W T
A O A S A R O K A Z A K I F R A G M E N T S Q W F U I Y S C J
T R K I Q N A Y L E A D I N G S T R A N D K E E F E J Z E E O
Y K X I X R U S P S U U Z S X W M M A A Y T E P Q B B D E K I
X V R W X W M U P A F W F H R O Y Y Q W E P I F L K X J B Z L
J V Y P W L J D Z F L D A I Z V Z Y M J L K Q R O U R Z T S E
P B M R W F J N G L I X T O A C C C Z W S P Y Z H A X H X M D
D H N I N D T A K I N C C R L K I N R P G D W Y E L Z W G C M
V D U M N H P L D P D A O B B N I E Z A A J M B L R H Z D C F
W J C A S E M I C O N S E R V A T I V E R E P L I C A T I O N
Q D L S S C C G R I W E X R L K G S S B X C Y V C J W L S N V
N N E E R G A A Q J W B L E X O C C H K R D G A A H Q E T G W
R A O O L J Y S D O U B L E H E L I X J Q F D K S Z C O Y T I
B E T A W Z Q E Y S X R M Q C L U Y G R G I H Z E E K C L N B
H I I G M B Y U T J L F F J Z A K X C D Y J S A Y G K V L T O
A Q D J F N A S S S K S U S L P A C P V B E H Y G W V Q P B S
T F E Z M T B Z C G X K J S D N A P O L Y M E R A S E J C W N
D L S U R Q J U Y Y O N Y D E D Q V J R C J L F A C B C T E S
V R T Y K D S R W L K R S A H G B N K V W A K K L P G O E J
P K W Y B D N K Q I P J J R X S Y G H F W J S G B X L E M U M
```

Semi-conservative replication	DNA ligase	Okazaki fragments
Lagging strand	Leading strand	DNA polymerase
Replication fork	DNA replication	Topoisomerase
Primase	Helicase	Double helix
Nucleotides	DNA	

DNA Replication

Across
2. The building blocks of DNA, consisting of adenine (A), thymine (T), cytosine (C), and guanine (G), which pair up in specific ways (A with T and C with G).

5. The enzyme that synthesizes a short RNA primer to provide a starting point for DNA polymerase.

8. Short segments of DNA synthesized on the lagging strand during replication. ____ fragments

11. The enzyme that unwinds the double helix and separates the DNA strands during replication.

12. The process by which DNA makes an exact copy of itself before cell division. DNA ____

14. The twisted ladder-like structure of DNA formed by two strands of nucleotides. (Two words)

Down
1. The method of DNA replication where each new DNA molecule consists of one original strand and one newly synthesized strand. ___-___ replication

3. The enzyme that prevents the DNA from becoming too tightly coiled during replication.

4. The enzyme that adds new nucleotides to the template strand and proofreads the new DNA strand for errors. DNA ____

6. The DNA strand that is synthesized in short segments, called Okazaki fragments, opposite to the direction of the replication fork. ____ strand

7. The enzyme that joins Okazaki fragments together to create a continuous DNA strand. DNA ___

9. The molecule that carries the genetic instructions for life, composed of two long strands forming a double helix.

10. The DNA strand that is synthesized continuously in the direction of the replication fork. ____ strand

13. The point where the two DNA strands separate to allow replication. Replication ____

Protein Synthesis:
Making Important Macromolecules

Have you ever wondered how your body grows, repairs itself, and stays healthy? The secret lies in tiny machines inside your cells called proteins. Proteins are essential for almost everything your body does. But how does your body make these important molecules? The process is called protein synthesis, and it's an amazing journey that happens inside your cells.

What is Protein Synthesis?

Protein synthesis is the process by which your cells create proteins. Think of it like a factory assembly line where raw materials are turned into a finished product. In this case, the raw materials are amino acids, and the finished product is a protein. This process happens in two main stages: transcription and translation.

Proteins are essential for growth, repair, and maintaining your health.

Stage 1: Transcription

Transcription is the first step in protein synthesis. It takes place in the nucleus of your cells, which is like the control center. Inside the nucleus, you have DNA, which contains the instructions for making proteins.

1. DNA Unzips: The DNA double helix unwinds and unzips into two separate strands.

2. RNA Polymerase: An enzyme called RNA polymerase attaches to one of the DNA strands. It reads the DNA sequence and makes a copy of it called messenger RNA (mRNA).

3. mRNA Formation: The mRNA is a single-stranded copy of the DNA's instructions. It carries the genetic code from the DNA to the ribosomes, where proteins are made.

Stage 2: Translation

Translation is the second step in protein synthesis. It occurs in the cytoplasm of your cells, specifically at the ribosomes. Ribosomes are like tiny factories where proteins are assembled.

1. mRNA Travels: The mRNA leaves the nucleus and travels to a ribosome in the cytoplasm.

2. tRNA Brings Amino Acids: Transfer RNA (tRNA) molecules carry amino acids to the ribosome. Each tRNA has a specific amino acid and a three-letter code called an anticodon.

3. Reading the Code: The ribosome reads the mRNA sequence three letters at a time, known as codons.

4. Building the Protein: For each codon on the mRNA, a tRNA with a matching anticodon brings the correct amino acid.

These amino acids are linked together to form a protein chain.

5. Completion: Once the ribosome reaches the end of the mRNA, the protein chain is complete. The protein then folds into its final shape and is ready to do its job in the cell.

Why is Protein Synthesis Important?

Protein synthesis is crucial because proteins are involved in nearly every function of your body. Here are a few examples of what proteins do:

Enzymes: Proteins called enzymes speed up chemical reactions in your body, like digesting food.

Hormones: Some proteins are hormones, which send signals between different parts of your body.

Antibodies: Proteins in your immune system help fight off infections.

Structural Proteins: Proteins like collagen give structure to your skin, bones, and muscles.

Without protein synthesis, your body wouldn't be able to perform these essential tasks.

Fun Facts About Protein Synthesis

Speedy Process: A single ribosome can add up to 20 amino acids to a protein chain every second!

Accuracy Matters: Your cells have proofreading mechanisms to ensure that proteins are made accurately. Mistakes can lead to faulty proteins, which can cause diseases.

Universal Code: The genetic code used in protein synthesis is nearly universal, meaning it's the same in almost all living organisms. This is why scientists can use bacteria to produce human insulin for diabetes treatment.

Protein synthesis is a fascinating and vital process that keeps your body functioning smoothly. By understanding how your cells make proteins, you gain insight into the incredible complexity and efficiency of life itself. Whether you're growing, healing, or just going about your daily activities, protein synthesis is always at work behind the scenes. When you eat a meal or exercise, remember the amazing process of protein synthesis that's helping your body stay strong and healthy.

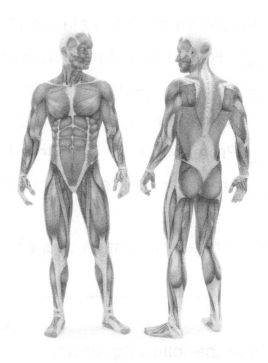

Proteins give structure to your muscles, skin, and bones.

13. Protein Synthesis
GUIDED NOTES

I. What is Protein Synthesis?

Define protein synthesis in your own words:_____

_____

List the two main stages of protein synthesis:

1. _____   2._____

II. Stage 1: Transcription

Match each step with its description:

_____ DNA Unzips   A. Forms a single-stranded copy of DNA
                         instructions

_____ RNA Polymerase   B. The DNA double helix separates

_____ mRNA Formation   C. Reads DNA sequence and makes a copy

Where does transcription take place? _____

III. Stage 2: Translation

Order the steps of translation (1-5):

___ mRNA travels to the ribosome

___ tRNA brings amino acids

___ Ribosome reads mRNA codons

___ Protein chain is completed

___ Amino acids are linked to form a protein chain

Where does translation occur? _____

_____

IV. Key Terms

Define the following terms:

1. Amino acids: _____

2. Codons: _____

3. Anticodons: _____

4. Ribosomes:_____

V. Importance of Protein Synthesis

List four types of proteins and their functions:

1. _____

2. _____

3. _____

4._____

VI. True or False

_____ Protein synthesis occurs only in the nucleus.

_____ mRNA carries genetic information from DNA to ribosomes.

_____ tRNA molecules carry amino acids to the ribosome.

_____ The genetic code is different for every living organism.

VII. Fun Facts

Write down two interesting facts about protein synthesis:

1. _____

2._____

VIII. In your own words, explain why understanding protein synthesis is important for your body's health:

_____

_____

_____

_____

#1

Why do you think protein synthesis is often compared to a factory assembly line?

Think about how raw materials are turned into a finished product in a factory and how this is similar to the way amino acids are turned into proteins.

#2

How does the role of mRNA in transcription help ensure that proteins are made correctly?

Think about the process of copying instructions and delivering them accurately.

#3

What might happen if there were errors in the transcription or translation stages of protein synthesis?

Consider how mistakes in making a product can affect its function and quality.

#4

Why is it important for your body to have different types of proteins like enzymes, hormones, and antibodies?

Reflect on the various tasks these proteins perform and how they keep your body functioning well.

#5

How do tRNA molecules know which amino acids to bring to the ribosome during translation?

Think about the role of the anticodon and how it matches with the codon on the mRNA.

#6

Why do you think the genetic code used in protein synthesis is nearly universal across all living organisms?

Reflect on the idea of a common blueprint for life and how it might benefit scientific research and medicine.

TERM	DEFINITION
Protein synthesis	
Amino acids	
Transcription	
Translation	
Nucleus	
DNA (deoxyribonucleic acid)	
RNA polymerase	

TERM	DEFINITION
mRNA (messenger RNA)	
Ribosome	
tRNA (transfer RNA)	
Codon	
Anticodon	
Enzymes	
Hormones	

Protein Synthesis

```
S T R A N S L A T I O N R K T J O P M C O D O N
V J L U E U F L N C L B B K A R O J P A W I A K
F T R N A J M I U W O T E B E X Z G L B Z K M X
M O Z K W N W Q Z W I Q I V P R S L J I N G I S
T Z K W L O K A W P N D P S P L Y I P M U Z N X
V K Q F M B R T J F N M H X E I N B Z R C M O B
X B G V A B Q G F G T R V O D F T X C V L E A X
P O L Y M E R A S E P N A E Y V H G T M E W C X
A N Z A C T Y D G N B A D F N Q E O S M U V I D
J J M U X X P N C S O M O J E I S X X G S E D F
R E G X Q J W D N A U W O R U W I R Q H E K S J
I A O T S Y H J Z E I J G I Y T S T C K Z P D A
D R V N W H O V Y W Q J Y B L C D Z N Q U Z M M
J Q R O J T R P U T V T Y O V V W W Z E T Y H G
U D V O M G M C Y T R A N S C R I P T I O N H A
N B L B Y V O M B C K N P O W X M Y C Q Q O X N
Y V V I F E N Z C K E L D M O L P N Z X T B A N
P X J O Y M E T D K D A P E V W D X K L R C T J
I R Y P Y L S X O X D N C V F X P Z W O Q C Y O
T R P P R O T E I N S Y N T H E S I S P Z K V G
L W Y E Z C M W N F L F T G B E N Z Y M E S V C
U G A J C J N X M O C I F A B Y I P J Z I X A I
U Z J B X S S G X K U N V M G W X I I V J U V T
T E N I E R J C B W K J B D C A N T I C O D O N
```

Protein synthesis	Hormones	Enzymes
Anticodon	Codon	tRNA
Ribosome	mRNA	polymerase
DNA	Nucleus	Translation
Transcription	Amino acids	

Protein Synthesis

Across

6. The process by which cells create proteins, essential for almost every function in the body. Protein ____

7. The control center of the cell where transcription takes place, containing the cell's DNA.

9. A single-stranded copy of DNA's instructions that carries the genetic code to the ribosomes.

12. The cell's protein-making factory where translation occurs and proteins are assembled.

13. The molecule that carries genetic instructions for making proteins.

14. The first stage of protein synthesis, where DNA instructions are copied into messenger RNA (mRNA).

Down

1. Proteins that speed up chemical reactions in the body, such as digesting food.

2. Proteins that send signals between different parts of the body to regulate various functions.

3. The second stage of protein synthesis, where mRNA is used to assemble amino acids into a protein.

4. The enzyme that reads the DNA sequence and makes a copy of it called mRNA during transcription. RNA ____

5. The building blocks of proteins that are linked together during protein synthesis. (Two words)

8. A three-letter code on tRNA that matches a codon on mRNA, ensuring the correct amino acid is added to the protein chain.

10. The molecule that carries amino acids to the ribosome during translation, matching them to the mRNA codons.

11. A sequence of three nucleotides on mRNA that corresponds to a specific amino acid.

How Meiosis Creates Genetic Diversity

Have you ever wondered how organisms, including humans, pass on their traits from one generation to the next? Or why siblings can look so different from each other? The answer lies in a special type of cell division called meiosis. This fascinating process is essential for sexual reproduction and genetic diversity.

What is Meiosis?

Meiosis is a type of cell division that reduces the number of chromosomes by half, creating four unique daughter cells. These cells are called gametes—sperm in males and eggs in females. Unlike mitosis, which produces identical cells for growth and repair, meiosis ensures that each gamete has a unique combination of genes. This is why you share some traits with your parents and siblings but are still one-of-a-kind.

The genetic variation from meiosis has led to many unique adaptions.

The Two Stages of Meiosis

Meiosis occurs in two main stages: Meiosis I and Meiosis II. Each stage has several phases, and we'll explore these step-by-step.

Meiosis I: Reducing Chromosome Number

1. Prophase I: Chromosomes condense and become visible under a microscope. Each chromosome pairs up with its homologous chromosome (the same type of chromosome from the other parent), forming a tetrad. Here, a process called crossing over occurs, where sections of DNA are exchanged between homologous chromosomes. This exchange creates new combinations of genes.

2. Metaphase I: The tetrads align in the middle of the cell. Spindle fibers attach to the chromosomes, preparing them for separation.

3. Anaphase I: The spindle fibers pull the homologous chromosomes apart to opposite ends of the cell. Unlike mitosis, the sister chromatids (the identical copies of each chromosome) stay together.

4. Telophase I and Cytokinesis: The cell splits into two new cells, each with half the original number of chromosomes. These cells are now haploid, meaning they contain one set of chromosomes.

Meiosis II: Creating Four Unique Cells

1. Prophase II: Chromosomes condense again in the two new cells. This stage is similar to prophase in mitosis.

2. Metaphase II: Chromosomes line up in the middle of each cell, and spindle fibers attach to the centromeres of the sister chromatids.

3. Anaphase II: The spindle fibers pull the sister chromatids apart, moving them to opposite ends of the cell.

4. Telophase II and Cytokinesis: Each of the two cells divides again, resulting in four haploid daughter cells, each with a unique combination of genes.

The process of meiosis is how traits are passed from parents to their child.

Importance of Meiosis

Genetic Diversity: Meiosis introduces genetic variation through crossing over and the random assortment of chromosomes. This variation is crucial for evolution and adaptation. It explains why you might inherit your mom's eye color but your dad's hair type.

Reproduction: Meiosis is essential for sexual reproduction. Without it, organisms couldn't produce gametes with the correct number of chromosomes. This balance ensures that offspring have the right amount of genetic material.

Evolution and Adaptation: Genetic diversity helps populations adapt to changing environments. It provides a pool of different traits that can be beneficial for survival. For example, in a population of animals, some might have a gene that makes them more resistant to disease. If that disease spreads, those animals are more likely to survive and pass on their genes.

Key Terms to Remember

Chromosome: A structure made of DNA and proteins that contains genetic information.

Gametes: Reproductive cells (sperm and eggs) that are produced by meiosis.

Haploid: A cell with one set of chromosomes (half the usual number).

Homologous Chromosomes: Pairs of chromosomes, one from each parent, that are similar in shape, size, and genetic content.

Crossing Over: The exchange of genetic material between homologous chromosomes during meiosis.

Meiosis might seem complex, but it's a vital process that allows for genetic diversity and successful reproduction. By understanding meiosis, you can appreciate the intricate dance of chromosomes that makes each living organism unique. Next time you look in the mirror, remember that the process of meiosis played a big role in making you who you are.

14. Meiosis
GUIDED NOTES

I. What is Meiosis?

Define meiosis in your own words:_____

_____

_____

List two key differences between meiosis and mitosis:

1. _____

2. _____

II. The Two Stages of Meiosis

Fill in the blanks:

Meiosis occurs in two main stages: _____ and _____.

III. Meiosis I: Reducing Chromosome Number

Match each phase with its description:

___ Prophase I   A. Chromosomes align in the middle of the cell

___ Metaphase I   B. Homologous chromosomes are pulled apart

___ Anaphase I   C. Cell splits into two haploid cells

___ Telophase I   D. Chromosomes condense and crossing over occurs

IV. Meiosis II: Creating Four Unique Cells

List the four phases of Meiosis II in order:

1. _____   2._____

3. _____   4._____

V. Importance of Meiosis

Explain three reasons why meiosis is important:

1. _____

   _____

2. _____

   _____

3. _____

   _____

VI. Key Terms

Match each term with its definition:

____ Chromosome   A. Cells with half the usual number of chromosomes

____ Gametes   B. Exchange of genetic material between chromosomes

____ Haploid   C. Structure made of DNA containing genetic information

____ Homologous   D. Reproductive cells (sperm and eggs) Chromosomes

____ Crossing   E. Pairs of chromosomes, one from each parent Over

VII. True or False

_____ Meiosis produces four identical daughter cells.

_____ Crossing over occurs during Prophase I.

_____ Meiosis is necessary for asexual reproduction.

_____ Genetic diversity is a result of meiosis.

VIII. In your own words, explain why understanding meiosis is important for students:

_____

_____

_____

#1

How does meiosis contribute to the genetic uniqueness of siblings?

Think about the processes of crossing over and the random assortment of chromosomes during meiosis.

#2

Why is it important for gametes to have half the number of chromosomes compared to other cells?

Reflect on what would happen if gametes had the same number of chromosomes as regular cells during fertilization.

#3

What are the main differences between meiosis and mitosis?

Compare the purposes of these two types of cell division and the outcomes they produce.

#4

Why is genetic diversity important for a population's survival?

Think about how genetic variation can help populations adapt to changing environments and withstand diseases.

#5

What role does crossing over play in meiosis?

Reflect on how the exchange of genetic material between homologous chromosomes during Prophase I affects genetic diversity.

#6

How do the stages of Meiosis I differ from those of Meiosis II?

Pay attention to how the processes and outcomes of each stage contribute to reducing chromosome number and creating genetic diversity.

TERM	DEFINITION
Meiosis	
Chromosome	
Gametes	
Haploid	
Homologous chromosomes	
Crossing over	
Prophase I	

TERM	DEFINITION
Metaphase I	
Anaphase I	
Telophase I and cytokinesis	
Prophase II	
Metaphase II	
Anaphase II	
Telophase II and cytokinesis	

Meiosis

```
U C F M A B V Y R P F T P M G O D K S Z M G U V L B U N Q Z U
F E I P T K L H T P Z T I O F K M E M X Q R F E Y Q Z T M C E
H U K S O G Z A E T K B H G G C H R O M O S O M E C I A R K Z
Y Y T W L D K J L B J A B W A Z I T S J M Y O R H G Y G K U W
D N C Q K Z D V O O V S R E N U U B W C B I U A W P E H B I V
A N B E H Q H U P C U T F I B U M H C F A O R K M Y O O P O X
D H N J Y C F K H W K A S F M P B Z O O N B N B Z A V Q C U L
N S N B B P F U A W X D E B E Q T E X H A W E E K K C R M N C
O A P R O P H A S E I I I Q I C E T A H P D W N W H K B Q U N
I E R H N T F N E Y I N Z Z O U A S R G H Z C S K D K G V P U
T F R H G L U O I V C D M Z S U C Y R X A G X T K L G I W S P
U X G N A O N L I K P O V X I T I X F G S J Q M J J Q V H T L
I U X C M X T X A E X S P L S F Z Q Q C E F N A D E O T A C I
P M W H E G B U N O M E T A P H A S E I I R O E X L B K P V P
E E C V T C X S D C Y F P C I V Q U A C I T E G H P H U L R A
H T O E E E H R C D B G E C R O S S I N G O V E R M B C O B B
P A B A S C C V Y D P P H O D O B N E V V K Y A W K Z Q I F X
K P A I K N H X T O N D O B O T K J G X E S D F U J O O D V B
X H Y J J K K O X Q Z U O R S Y G Y E I K E R Z O U U E L Z
A A H G V U O M K B N O D B F F C Z V X Y G B O I G I C I V U
L S U L W L Q G I I S X J D S I E R X A J G X C S V N U R D M
S E R T Z W F L N U M F G P G B Q B X B W Q K T O Z C Q D E K
J I B I W A Q L E I P G T J K F C K K N J K V M U T P Z J H B
U I I F E I L F S N H O M O L O G O U S C H R O M O S O M E S
H U L C B U R J I M Q W Y X M Z V L R G O H N F N D D D L A D
P E D E D Y J W S K H S V K S N A C K R S M W U W B A O O U H
U V D W B E I C Z A P R O P H A S E I V U Y J C K D D R A J D
C P B M O K O F Q B D O E W Y R R X W W T T O F H F E F P K P
P Y J B I G P G D H S S E W Z S A Q E I H P D U I P M J J M A
J N P A N A P H A S E I Q U Z E G O X W X C E Y O D M X G L A
T E L O P H A S E I A N D C Y T O K I N E S I S J H S J T K N
```

Telophase II and cytokinesis	Anaphase II	Metaphase II
Prophase II	Telophase I and cytokinesis	Anaphase I
Metaphase I	Prophase I	Crossing over
Homologous chromosomes	Haploid	Gametes
Chromosome	Meiosis	

Meiosis

Across

2. The final phase of Meiosis II, where each of the two haploid cells divides again, resulting in four unique haploid daughter cells. ___ II and cytokinesis

3. The first phase of Meiosis I, where chromosomes condense, homologous chromosomes pair up to form tetrads, and crossing over occurs. _____ I

8. The phase of Meiosis I where tetrads align in the middle of the cell, and spindle fibers attach to the chromosomes. ____ I

10. Pairs of chromosomes, one from each parent, that are similar in shape, size, and genetic content. ____ chromosomes

12. The final phase of Meiosis I, where the cell splits into two haploid cells, each with half the original number of chromosomes. Telophase I and ____

13. Reproductive cells (sperm in males and eggs in females) produced by meiosis, each containing half the usual number of chromosomes.

14. A structure made of DNA and proteins that contains genetic information necessary for the development and function of an organism.

Down

1. The phase of Meiosis II where chromosomes line up in the middle of each haploid cell, and spindle fibers attach to the centromeres of the sister chromatids. ____ II

4. The phase of Meiosis II where spindle fibers pull sister chromatids apart, moving them to opposite ends of the cell. ____ II

5. The exchange of genetic material between homologous chromosomes during Prophase I of meiosis, resulting in new combinations of genes. ____ over

6. A type of cell division that reduces the number of chromosomes by half, creating four unique daughter cells called gametes.

7. A cell that has one set of chromosomes, which is half the number of chromosomes found in a typical body cell.

9. The first phase of Meiosis II, where chromosomes condense again in the two new haploid cells. ____ II

11. The phase of Meiosis I where spindle fibers pull homologous chromosomes to opposite ends of the cell, while sister chromatids remain together. ____ I

Inheritance:
How Traits Are Passed Down

Have you ever wondered why you have your mom's curly hair or your dad's blue eyes? Or why some traits, like freckles or dimples, seem to run in families? The answer can be found in the process called inheritance. Inheritance is all about how traits and characteristics are passed from parents to their children.

What is Inheritance?

Inheritance is the process through which genetic information is passed from parents to their offspring. This genetic information is stored in structures called genes, which are found on chromosomes inside the cells of every living organism. You have 46 chromosomes in each of your cells, 23 from your mom and 23 from your dad.

Some traits are dominant while others are recessive.

The Role of DNA

DNA, or deoxyribonucleic acid, is the molecule that carries the genetic instructions for life. Think of DNA like a recipe book that contains all the instructions needed to build and maintain your body. Each gene is like a specific recipe or set of instructions within that book. These instructions determine everything from your eye color to your blood type.

Dominant and Recessive Traits

Genes come in different versions called alleles. When it comes to traits, you can have dominant alleles and recessive alleles. Dominant alleles are like the bossy ones; they tend to show up more often. Recessive alleles are quieter and only show up when you have two copies of them (one from each parent).

For example, if you inherit a dominant allele for brown eyes from one parent and a recessive allele for blue eyes from the other, you will have brown eyes. However, if you inherit two recessive alleles for blue eyes, then you'll have blue eyes.

Punnett Squares

One way scientists predict how traits are inherited is by using Punnett squares. These are simple charts that help you see how different combinations of alleles can result in different traits. By filling out a Punnett square, you can predict the likelihood of inheriting particular traits.

Mendel's Peas

The study of inheritance began with a scientist named Gregor Mendel. Mendel was a monk who loved gardening. He conducted experiments with pea plants and discovered the basic principles of inheritance. By crossbreeding pea plants with different traits, like flower color and seed shape, Mendel figured out how traits are passed down through generations. His work laid the foundation for modern genetics.

Genetic Disorders

Sometimes, the inheritance of genes can lead to genetic disorders. These are conditions caused by mutations or changes in the DNA. Some genetic disorders are inherited in a dominant manner, while others are recessive. For example, cystic fibrosis is a recessive disorder, meaning a person needs to inherit two copies of the faulty gene to have the condition. On the other hand, Huntington's disease is a dominant disorder, so only one copy of the faulty gene is needed to cause the disease.

Environmental Influence

While your genes provide the blueprint for who you are, the environment also plays a crucial role. Factors like diet, lifestyle, and exposure to different environments can influence how genes are expressed. For instance, you might have a genetic predisposition to be tall, but if you don't get enough nutrition while growing up, you might not reach your full height potential.

Modern Genetics

Today, scientists have advanced tools to study genetics. Techniques like DNA sequencing allow us to read the genetic code and understand more about how genes work. This knowledge has led to breakthroughs in medicine, agriculture, and many other fields. Genetic testing can now help detect the risk of certain diseases, and gene therapy holds the promise of treating genetic disorders by correcting faulty genes.

Traits are passed from parents to offspring.

Understanding inheritance is crucial not only for biology but for understanding who you are and how you became that way. Whether it's through the color of your eyes, the shape of your nose, or the presence of a genetic condition, the genes you inherit from your parents play a significant role in your life. By learning about inheritance, you're getting a glimpse into the fascinating science that connects all living things.

15. Inheritance
GUIDED NOTES

I. Key Concepts

Define the following terms:

1. Inheritance:_____

_____

2. Genes: _____

_____

3. Chromosomes: _____

4. DNA: _____

II. DNA and Genes

1. What does DNA stand for? _____

2. How many chromosomes do humans have in each cell?_____

3. Explain the analogy used to describe DNA in the text:_____

_____

_____

III. Alleles and Traits

1. What are alleles? _____

2. Complete the table: _____

Type of Allele	Description
Dominant	
Recessive	

3. Give an example of how dominant and recessive alleles work:

_____

_____

_____

IV. Punnett Squares

1. What is a Punnett square? _____

2. What is the purpose of using Punnett squares? _____

_____

V. Gregor Mendel

1. Who was Gregor Mendel? _____

_____

2. What did Mendel study? _____

_____

3. Why is Mendel's work important? _____

_____

VI. Genetic Disorders

1. What causes genetic disorders? _____

2. Complete the table with examples from the text:

Type of Disorder	Example	How it's Inherited
Recessive		
Dominant		

VII. Nature vs. Nurture

1. Explain how the environment can influence genetic traits: _____

_____

2. Give an example from the text: _____

_____

VIII. Modern Genetics

List two advancements in modern genetics mentioned in the article:

1. _____   2. _____

_____

#1

Why do you think it's important to understand the process of inheritance?

Think about how knowing your genetic background can help you understand your health and traits better.

#2

How do dominant and recessive alleles influence the traits you inherit from your parents?

Reflect on the examples of dominant and recessive traits, like eye color, and how they appear in your family.

#3

What role does DNA play in determining your physical characteristics?

Consider how DNA acts like a recipe book for building and maintaining your body.

#4

How can using Punnett squares help in predicting the traits of offspring?

Think about how these charts show possible combinations of alleles and help predict traits.

#5

How did Gregor Mendel's experiments with pea plants contribute to our understanding of genetics?

Reflect on Mendel's method of crossbreeding plants and what he discovered about trait inheritance.

#6

How do environmental factors influence the expression of genetic traits?

Think about how diet, lifestyle, and other environmental factors might affect how your genes are expressed.

TERM	DEFINITION
Inheritance	
Genes	
Chromosomes	
DNA (Deoxyribonucleic Acid)	
Alleles	
Dominant alleles	
Recessive alleles	

TERM	DEFINITION
Punnett squares	
Gregor Mendel	
Genetic disorders	
Cystic fibrosis	
Huntington's disease	
Environmental influence	
DNA sequencing	

Inheritance

```
I N H E R I T A N C E Y U K C A F M Q J X B Z B
H G K D O M I N A N T A L L E L E S W T W A R I
P J S E Q U E N C I N G O J D Q X R C H I S K Q
E H E N V I R O N M E N T A L I N F L U E N C E
N P Y H L F H Z L S M K K G D Q K T A N R M C G
K U H Q S S N D L C E Z A E E C B H U T R V W S
G N O Y T J W C Y Y V R B N X V E V O I N I A H
E N G D Q J S V M F K G R E G O R M E N D E L L
N E L N U Z L P U C L V H T Z T R B X G M W R V
E T J A K N W J O B J G B I U Q B E D T H G E G
S T H S J O I D P K R I K C I E I N G O R E C B
V S D E L X U J Q J T M H U D J J Z J M N K J E R
B Q P Q H U E L P O Q S L I H L W S I S R Q S W
J U Z U C K L W C W H D G S I D G E L D D E S Z
K A W E M R Q T N D J S P O N O C S V I C H I D
L R J N W Q J U Y Q H H N R M C I Q G S U T V N
I E C C G Q D Q B B H I C D W Y H G Z E O F E O
Y S S I H Q S Y G P O W C E N W J M F A K Z A C
O O D N P H A L L E L E S R R A T U Y S F P L F
W R W G Y V U R J S R C Y S D D P F V E G F L L
D N A P Q O X B Y U D W L E Y W H E U N W J E I
R C Y S T I C F I B R O S I S Y V V X N K K L Y
B R C J C H R O M O S O M E S R F P P H O O E K
M T R S K K N H O X X W K V P I E M U R B G S C
```

DNA sequencing	Environmental influence	Huntington's disease
Cystic fibrosis	Genetic disorders	Gregor Mendel
Punnett squares	Recessive alleles	Dominant alleles
Alleles	DNA	Chromosomes
Genes	Inheritance	

Inheritance

Across

2. The process through which genetic information is passed from parents to their offspring.

7. Advanced techniques used by scientists to read the genetic code and understand more about how genes work, leading to breakthroughs in various fields. DNA ____

8. Conditions caused by mutations or changes in DNA, which can be inherited in a dominant or recessive manner. Genetics ____

11. Different versions of a gene that can lead to variations in traits.

12. Structures found on chromosomes that contain the instructions for the development and functioning of living organisms.

13. A dominant genetic disorder that requires only one copy of the faulty gene to be present for the condition to develop. ____ disease

14. Simple charts used by scientists to predict the likelihood of inheriting particular traits based on different combinations of alleles. ___ squares

Down

1. Alleles that tend to show up more often and mask the presence of recessive alleles. ____ alleles

3. Thread-like structures located inside cells that carry genetic information in the form of genes.

4. Alleles that are only expressed when two copies are present, one from each parent. ____ alleles

5. A scientist and monk who conducted experiments with pea plants and discovered the basic principles of inheritance, laying the foundation for modern genetics. Gregor ____

6. A recessive genetic disorder that requires two copies of the faulty gene to be present for the condition to develop. Cystic ____

9. The role that factors like diet, lifestyle, and exposure to different environments play in influencing how genes are expressed. Environmental ____

10. The molecule that carries the genetic instructions for life, acting like a recipe book for building and maintaining an organism's body.

The Basics of Heredity

Have you ever wondered why you have your mother's eyes or your father's hair color? Or why some traits seem to be passed down from generation to generation, while others do not? This is because of genetics, specifically Mendelian genetics. Named after Gregor Mendel, a monk and scientist, Mendelian genetics is the study of how traits are inherited from one generation to the next. Let's learn the basic principles of Mendelian genetics and how they explain the inheritance of traits.

Who Was Gregor Mendel?

Gregor Mendel was an Austrian monk who lived in the 19th century. He is often called the "father of modern genetics" because of his groundbreaking work with pea plants. Mendel conducted experiments in his monastery's garden, where he studied how traits like flower color and seed shape were passed from one generation of pea plants to the next. His work laid the foundation for what we now know as Mendelian genetics.

Mendel was able to observe and describe several principles of inheritance through pea plants.

Mendel's Experiments

Mendel chose pea plants for his experiments because they have easily observable traits and can be quickly and easily bred. He focused on seven different traits, including flower color (purple or white) and seed shape (round or wrinkled). By cross-pollinating plants with different traits and carefully recording the results, Mendel was able to develop several key principles of inheritance.

The Principles of Mendelian Genetics

1. Law of Segregation: This principle states that every individual has two alleles (versions of a gene) for each trait, one inherited from each parent. These alleles separate, or segregate, during the formation of gametes (sperm and egg cells), so each gamete carries only one allele for each trait. When gametes combine during fertilization, the offspring inherits one allele from each parent.

2. Law of Independent Assortment: According to this principle, alleles for different traits are distributed to gametes independently of one another. This means the inheritance of one trait does not affect the inheritance of another. For example, the gene for flower color does not influence the gene for seed shape.

3. Dominant and Recessive Alleles:

Mendel discovered that some alleles are dominant, meaning they will express (show) their trait even if only one copy is present. Other alleles are recessive, meaning their traits are only expressed if two copies are present. For example, in pea plants, the allele for purple flowers is dominant over the allele for white flowers. A plant with one purple-flower allele and one white-flower allele will have purple flowers.

Punnett Squares: Predicting Inheritance

To help predict the inheritance of traits, scientists often use a tool called a Punnett square. A Punnett square is a simple grid that allows you to visualize the possible combinations of alleles that offspring can inherit from their parents. By filling in the squares with the alleles from each parent, you can determine the likelihood of different traits appearing in the offspring.

Mendel would cross pollinate pea plants with different traits and see how often those traits would occur in the offspring plants.

Real-World Applications of Mendelian Genetics

Mendelian genetics is not just about pea plants. The principles Mendel discovered apply to many organisms, including humans. Understanding these principles can help us with many real-world applications, such as:

Medicine: Geneticists can identify and understand the inheritance patterns of certain genetic diseases. This knowledge can help in diagnosing, treating, and even preventing these diseases.

Agriculture: Farmers use Mendelian genetics to breed plants and animals with desirable traits, such as higher crop yields or disease resistance.

Forensics: DNA analysis in forensic science is based on genetic principles, helping to solve crimes and identify individuals.

Mendelian genetics provides a clear and simple explanation for how traits are passed from one generation to the next. By understanding the basic principles discovered by Gregor Mendel, you can gain insight into the fascinating world of heredity and genetics. Whether you're studying biology, interested in medicine, or just curious about why you look the way you do, Mendelian genetics offers valuable knowledge that can help you understand the natural world.

16. Mendelian Genetics
GUIDED NOTES

I. Key Figures in Genetics

1. Who is considered the "father of modern genetics"? _____

2. What was his occupation? _____

II. Mendel's Experiments

1. What plant did Mendel use for his experiments? _____

2. List two traits Mendel studied in these plants:

   a. _____   b. _____

III. Principles of Mendelian Genetics

Match each principle with its correct description:

_____ Law of Segregation

_____ Law of Independent

_____ Dominant and

A. Alleles for different traits are distributed to gametes independently

B. Every individual has two alleles for each trait, one from each parent Assortment

C. Some alleles express their trait even if only one copy is present Recessive Alleles

IV. Key Terms

Define the following terms:

1. Allele: _____

_____

2. Gamete: _____

_____

3. Punnett square: _____

_____

V. Real-World Applications

Name one real-world application of Mendelian genetics for each field:

1. Medicine: _____

_____

2. Agriculture: _____

_____

3. Forensics: _____

_____

VI. True or False

_____ Mendel conducted his experiments with sunflowers.

_____ The inheritance of one trait affects the inheritance of another trait.

_____ A Punnett square helps predict the likelihood of traits in offspring.

VII. Short Answer

Explain why Mendel chose pea plants for his experiments:

_____

_____

VIII. In your own words, explain why learning about Mendelian genetics is important:

_____

_____

_____

#1

Why do you think Mendel chose pea plants for his experiments?

Consider the traits of pea plants that make them suitable for studying inheritance.

#2

How do the concepts of dominant and recessive alleles impact the traits you may have inherited?

Reflect on traits you have from your parents and whether they are dominant or recessive.

#3

In what ways do you think understanding Mendelian genetics can be beneficial in medicine?

Think about how genetic information could help in diagnosing or treating diseases.

#4

How does the Law of Segregation relate to your own family traits?

Consider how traits from both parents can appear in you or your siblings.

#5

Why do you think the Law of Independent Assortment is important when predicting traits?

Reflect on how different traits can be inherited independently from one another.

#6

How can Punnett squares help us understand our own genetics?

Think about how this tool could be used to predict traits in a family scenario.

TERM	DEFINITION
Genetics	
Mendelian genetics	
Gregor Mendel	
Alleles	
Law of Segregation	
Law of Independent Assortment	
Dominant allele	

TERM	DEFINITION
Recessive allele	
Punnett square	
Cross-pollination	
Trait	
Gametes	
Heredity	
Genetic variation	

Mendelian Genetics

```
B L T X G L K K C D U J E Y K O Y F W O P I H U W N F X E L E
S A E Y D B I N D W T Q B O A C R O S S P O L L I N A T I O N
C W X F C S Q L R M O N X F Y Q T Q W K U D Q H S J P S D V L
T O R C O V O B N K M O A J L P G V T S B O B K D U N A V A E
T F X Y R M B Q P O C G T O D M T J M O F M U A M K W S Z T R
E S H K S F J T U C Y T C N X X E G V L Q I D L K C U R Y J E
T E C N Z C P K A B V U E A N Y C I S F Q N X L D T Q Y L P C
Y G I B T X F Y I L O G U T X I Z D K U T A T E X Q P D Z B E
C R R C I R B P V N C J C W V B S P H E D N I L O B M E I O S
S E V H T I X Q U A B I P M Y B Z W S L L T M E O T V X J U S
Q G S K R O W S I B E D A W D D B X K Y E A A S K J Y N D N I
T A Q R Y M Q B L S S I N Z Y J N F J M E L V C G E M N Q V V
S T H R K W J F U U K M O H E R E D I T Y L Q F U P Y U Q Q E
Q I M G U M R W W D R D W I A D R G J U P E L W V W S T A T A
Q O M D D V B B T G G Z Z W H G V L Y C J L V U D N W G U M L
E N P K X M C H B Q W F R R E L T I I A Z E R M U C U B R G L
N G E N E T I C S L F H K M A Z A T V Y C S V H N H O V F H E
N A G H D L K T T I R G X C A X O F S H Q B U X O Y Y T S D L
H A I Q S X W F R N K Y Y J N J M X L O B K O M V I Q M D G E
T V G T M T D Y A E P L W N L J R Y D G R E G O R M E N D E L
Z A T C O A G B I O U H H G R Z Y U P U N N E T T S Q U A R E
Q R W U G U I W T T L W U X F I G O V E R F C C H R I O J F A
I I B Z Y G J N F R R C N Q H F Z N U J G C D W Z S Q K C L Q
L A W O F I N D E P E N D E N T A S S O R T M E N T L X H Q Z
M T B H L W W A P R W F D E Z W M P O P W M Q Y J I V L S A G
T I B P T F I E E X K E Y P T J Y P S S T C D P Z C I V H S A
V O Y C E F F C F B D N U U E T S E W U O V F G B N G O J B M
P N D Z A W J K U B D E H U Z A L G D S M D Z Q B H S G P E E
F G E F O T G C X H K T T L Z Z X F X D U J B C C J D J B A T
C P F S K L I I A J A K M E N D E L I A N G E N E T I C S I E
T Q F A G P R E D Q F T S E R M X B Z Y V W S B H Y E Z F P S
```

Punnett square	Recessive allele	Dominant allele
Law of Independent Assortment	Law of Segregation	Mendelian genetics
variation	Heredity	Gametes
Trait	Cross-pollination	Alleles
Gregor Mendel	Genetics	

Mendelian Genetics

Across

7. A diagram used to predict the genetic outcome of a cross between two individuals, showing all possible allele combinations in their offspring. ____ square

9. An allele that expresses its trait even if only one copy is present; it masks the effect of a recessive allele. ____ allele

10. Different versions of a gene that determine specific traits, with each individual inheriting two alleles for each trait, one from each parent.

11. An allele that only expresses its trait when two copies are present; its effect is masked by a dominant allele. ____ allele

12. The diversity in gene frequencies among individuals in a population, which contributes to differences in traits. Genetic ____

13. A specific characteristic of an organism that can be inherited, such as flower color or seed shape.

14. A principle that describes how alleles for different traits are distributed to gametes independently, meaning the inheritance of one trait does not affect another. Law of ___ ____

Down

1. The study of how traits are inherited through generations, based on the principles established by Gregor Mendel. ___ genetics

2. An Austrian monk known as the "father of modern genetics" for his research on pea plants and the inheritance of traits. (Two words)

3. The process of transferring pollen from one plant to the stigma of another plant to produce seeds with varying traits.

4. A principle stating that alleles for a trait separate during the formation of gametes, so each gamete carries only one allele for each trait. Law of ___

5. Reproductive cells (sperm and egg) that carry alleles from each parent and combine during fertilization.

6. The branch of biology that studies heredity and the variation of inherited characteristics.

8. The passing of traits from parents to offspring through genes.

Tiny Changes
with Big Effects

Have you ever wondered why some people have different eye colors or why certain diseases run in families? These differences often come down to something called mutations. Time to get into what mutations are, how they happen, and why they are so important to our lives and the world around us.

What Is a Mutation?

A mutation is a change in the DNA sequence of an organism. DNA is like a set of instructions for building and running every living thing. These instructions are made up of tiny chemical units called nucleotides. Think of DNA as a very long book written in a special code. A mutation is like a typo in this book. Sometimes the typo is so small you might not even notice it, but other times it can change the meaning of a whole sentence or even a chapter.

Types of Mutations

There are several types of mutations, and each can have different effects on an organism. Here are some of the most common types:

Point Mutations: This is when a single nucleotide in the DNA sequence is changed. Imagine changing one letter in a word; sometimes it makes no difference, but other times it completely changes the meaning.

Insertions and Deletions: These mutations involve adding or removing nucleotides in the DNA sequence. Think of inserting or deleting a letter in a word; it can make the word unreadable or create a completely new word.

Frameshift Mutations: These occur when insertions or deletions change the way the DNA sequence is read. It's like changing the spaces between words in a sentence, making it hard to understand.

Mutations can be beneficial, harmful, or have no impact on an organism.

How Do Mutations Happen?

Mutations can happen in several ways. Some occur naturally when DNA is copied during cell division. Our cells are pretty good at copying DNA accurately, but mistakes can happen. Environmental factors like UV radiation from the sun, chemicals, and even some viruses can also cause mutations.

Are All Mutations Bad?

You might think that mutations are always harmful, but that's not true. Some mutations have little to no effect. Others can be beneficial, giving an organism an advantage in its environment. For example, a mutation might make a plant more resistant to drought or an animal better at finding food.

On the other hand, some mutations can be harmful and lead to diseases. For instance, a mutation in a specific gene might cause a genetic disorder like cystic fibrosis or sickle cell anemia. Scientists study these mutations to understand how they cause diseases and to develop treatments.

Mutations and Evolution

Mutations play a crucial role in evolution. They create genetic diversity, which is the variation in DNA among individuals. This diversity is important because it allows populations to adapt to changing environments. Over time, beneficial mutations can spread through a population, helping a species survive and thrive.

Real-Life Examples of Mutations

Mutations occur when there are changes to the DNA sequence.

Let's look at some real-life examples to see how mutations affect living things:

Blue Eyes: The blue eye color in humans is caused by a mutation in a gene that affects the pigmentation in the iris. This mutation likely occurred thousands of years ago and spread through populations in Europe.

Antibiotic Resistance: Some bacteria have mutations that make them resistant to antibiotics. These bacteria can survive even when treated with antibiotics, making infections harder to cure.

Peppered Moths: During the Industrial Revolution in England, pollution darkened tree bark. A mutation in peppered moths made some of them dark-colored, which helped them blend in and avoid predators. This mutation increased in the population because it provided a survival advantage.

Studying Mutations

Scientists use various tools and techniques to study mutations. One common method is DNA sequencing, which allows scientists to read the DNA code and identify changes. By comparing DNA sequences from different individuals, scientists can find mutations associated with diseases or traits.

Mutations are fascinating and complex changes in our DNA that can have a wide range of effects. They are a natural part of life and play a key role in evolution and diversity. Understanding mutations helps scientists learn more about genetics, develop medical treatments, and explore the incredible variety of life on Earth.

17. Mutations
GUIDED NOTES

I. What is a Mutation?

Define mutation in your own words:

_____

Compare DNA to a: _____

II. Types of Mutations

List and briefly describe the three main types of mutations:

1. _____

   Description: _____

2. _____

   Description: _____

3. _____

   Description: _____

III. Causes of Mutations

List three ways mutations can occur:

1. _____

2. _____

3. _____

IV. Effects of Mutations

Fill in the blanks:

1. Some mutations have _____ or _____ effect.

2. _____ mutations can give an organism an advantage in its environment.

3. _____ mutations can lead to diseases.

V. Mutations and Evolution

Explain how mutations contribute to evolution:

_____

_____

_____

VI. Real-Life Examples of Mutations

Match each mutation example with its description:

_____ Blue Eyes

_____ Antibiotic Resistance

_____ Peppered Moths

A. Helped moths blend in during Industrial Revolution

B. Caused by a mutation affecting iris pigmentation

C. Makes bacteria survive antibiotic treatment

VII. Studying Mutations

Name one method scientists use to study mutations:

_____

VIII. True or False

_____ All mutations are harmful to organisms.

_____ Mutations play a crucial role in evolution.

_____ DNA sequencing can help identify mutations.

IX. In your own words, explain why understanding mutations is important:

_____

_____

_____

#1

What is a mutation, and how can it be like a typo in a book?

Consider how a small change in a DNA sequence can alter the instructions for building an organism.

#2

How do point mutations differ from insertions and deletions, and what are the effects of each?

Reflect on how changing one letter in a word differs from adding or removing letters, and how this might affect the meaning.

#3

What are some natural and environmental causes of mutations?

Think about the different ways mutations can occur during cell division or due to external factors like UV radiation.

#4

Can mutations be beneficial, and if so, how?

Consider examples where mutations might help an organism survive better in its environment.

#5

How do mutations contribute to genetic diversity and evolution?

Reflect on how variations in DNA can help populations adapt and evolve over time.

#6

What are some real-life examples of mutations, and what effects do they have?

Think about how mutations like blue eyes or antibiotic resistance impact individuals and populations.

TERM	DEFINITION
Mutation	
DNA (deoxyribonucleic acid)	
Nucleotide	
Point mutation	
Insertion	
Deletion	
Frameshift mutation	

TERM / DEFINITION

TERM	DEFINITION
Cell division	
Genetic disorder	
Genetic diversity	
DNA sequencing	
Antibiotic resistance	
Evolution	
Pigmentation	

Mutations

```
Y R G C M E M L O O E V O L U T I O N B O A I X
Y W R S T H L B D G P O I N T M U T A T I O N E
F W E N P Z A Q A N E N Z N P X U S I E L F H J
D D C A G U A N N G E N E T I C D I S O R D E R
N Q Y T G K I P T K D P H U L S B O E V W G U Y
R D U O F Y G V I Y C E B E U H U P L I J O M I
P H Y C R R J W B N R T O E I N S E R T I O N W
S X Y U A J D P I G M E N T A T I O N C J U N K
L W S T M O I A O L L Y X I G D S I H D Z X D Y
I G T F E Z V L T Y D Q S C Q A Y A S I O Q T X
Z W Q A S H E N I O N U S W B D E L E T I O N I
R A U F H P R K C A A H A A E L Y E P P Q B J F
N G U Z I E S B R I H G X B C L M I X C P M I W
B Z M E F O I K E P J V Y Z M V W S S E B A U T
N I T G T G T P S J V F N M P A O S H L E B U Z
O Z K V M A Y F I F H Q H X C K W A X L A C U O
Q P C S U T P S S Y M U T A T I O N P D G A X B
E B P E T C P N T R I D Q Y Z V L O F I Q C N D
O Y F S A S Q P A V D S E U A B V A H V P M T P
I K J X T R S V N B K H Q L Z D F Q A I T U Y Z
G A L C I L T K C S S A A W X V D Z B S F X S S
D G O Q O I K S E P S D Q G V J F A N I N H A U
K C S C N K D N A S E Q U E N C I N G O N K Y D
D E R L L G L Q W N U C L E O T I D E N W S D S
```

Antibiotic resistance	DNA sequencing	Genetic disorder
Cell division	Frameshift mutation	Point mutation
Pigmentation	Evolution	Deletion
diversity	Insertion	Nucleotide
DNA	Mutation	

Mutations

Across
3. A technique used by scientists to read the DNA code and identify mutations. DNA ____

6. The process by which a cell replicates its DNA and divides into two new cells. Cell ____

8. A disease caused by a mutation in one or more genes, such as cystic fibrosis or sickle cell anemia. Genetic ____

10. A type of mutation where one or more nucleotides are added to the DNA sequence.

12. The molecule that carries the genetic instructions for living organisms, composed of nucleotides.

13. The building blocks of DNA, consisting of a sugar, a phosphate group, and a nitrogenous base.

14. A mutation caused by insertions or deletions that change the way the DNA sequence is read, often leading to significant changes in the protein produced. ____ mutation

Down
1. A change in the DNA sequence of an organism, which can affect how the organism develops and functions.

2. A type of mutation where one or more nucleotides are removed from the DNA sequence.

4. The coloring of an organism's tissues, such as the iris of the eye, which can be affected by genetic mutations.

5. A type of mutation where a single nucleotide in the DNA sequence is changed. ____ mutation

7. A phenomenon where bacteria develop mutations that allow them to survive treatment with antibiotics. Antibiotic ____

9. The process by which populations change over time through variations in their genetic material, often influenced by mutations.

11. The variation in DNA sequences among individuals in a population, which is important for evolution and adaptation. Genetic ___

18. Evolution and Natural Selection
by 3andB Staff Writer | October 1, 2024

How Life Changes Over Time

Have you ever wondered why some animals can blend perfectly into their surroundings, or why certain plants thrive in particular environments? This is the work of evolution and natural selection, fundamental ideas in biology that explain how life on Earth changes and adapts over time. Let's learn more and uncover the secrets of life's incredible diversity.

What is Evolution?

Evolution is the process by which different kinds of living organisms develop and diversify from earlier forms during

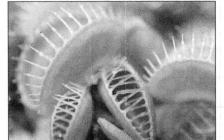

Evolution and natural selection have created a diverse collection of life on our planet.

the history of the Earth. It explains how simple early life forms have transformed into the vast array of species we see today. Evolution occurs over long periods, sometimes taking millions of years.

Think of evolution as a giant, ever-changing tree. Each branch represents a different species, and as time goes on, new branches grow, representing new species, while others might shrink or disappear entirely.

The Role of Genetics

At the heart of evolution is genetics, the study of heredity and the variation of inherited traits. Every living organism has DNA, which carries the genetic information that makes you unique. When organisms reproduce, they pass on their DNA to their offspring, but sometimes, small changes, or mutations, occur in the DNA.

These mutations can introduce new traits. For example, a mutation might result in a butterfly having a slightly different wing color. If this new color helps the butterfly survive better in its environment, it will be more likely to reproduce and pass on this trait to its offspring.

Natural Selection: The Driving Force

Natural selection is the process by which organisms better adapted to their environment tend to survive and produce more offspring. It was first proposed by Charles Darwin, who is often called the father of evolution.

Imagine a group of rabbits living in a snowy area. Some rabbits have white fur, while others have brown fur. The white-furred rabbits are better camouflaged against the snow, making it harder for predators to spot them. These white rabbits are more likely to survive and reproduce, passing the white fur trait to their offspring. Over time, the population will have more white-furred rabbits because they are better suited to the snowy environment.

Adaptations: Nature's Toolkit

Adaptations are the traits that help an organism survive and reproduce in its environment. These can be physical, like the shape of a bird's beak, or behavioral, like the way certain animals hunt in packs.

For example, the long neck of a giraffe is an adaptation that allows it to reach leaves high up in trees, giving it access to food that other animals can't reach. This adaptation helps giraffes survive in their environment.

Speciation: The Creation of New Species

Sometimes, a group of organisms becomes isolated from the rest of their species. This can happen due to geographic barriers like mountains or rivers. Over time, the isolated group may evolve differently from the original population, leading to the creation of a new species. This process is called speciation.

Consider a population of birds separated by a mountain range. On one side, the birds might develop longer beaks to eat certain types of insects, while on the other side, they might develop shorter beaks to eat seeds. Eventually, these differences can become so significant that the two groups can no longer interbreed, resulting in two distinct species.

Natural selection selects for traits that are useful and will be passed down between generations.

Examples of Evolution in Action

One of the most famous examples of evolution in action is the peppered moth in England. Before the Industrial Revolution, most peppered moths were light-colored, which helped them blend in with the lichen-covered trees. However, as pollution increased, the trees became covered in soot, and the dark-colored moths, which were once rare, became more common because they were better camouflaged against the darkened trees.

Another example is the development of antibiotic resistance in bacteria. When antibiotics are used to kill bacteria, some may have mutations that make them resistant to the drug. These resistant bacteria survive and reproduce, leading to a population that can no longer be killed by the antibiotic.

Understanding evolution and natural selection helps us appreciate the incredible diversity of life on Earth. These processes explain how organisms change over time and adapt to their environments. By studying evolution, we gain insights into the history of life and the ongoing changes that shape the natural world. The next time you observe a bird with a unique beak or a plant thriving in a harsh environment, you'll know that these traits are the result of millions of years of evolution and natural selection.

18. Evolution and Natural Selection
GUIDED NOTES

I. Key Concepts

Define the following terms:

1. Evolution: _____

_____

2. Natural Selection: _____

_____

3. Genetics: _____

_____

4. Adaptation: _____

_____

5. Speciation: _____

_____

II. The Process of Evolution

Match each concept with its description:

_____ DNA   A. Small changes in genetic material

_____ Mutations   B. Carries genetic information

_____ Offspring   C. Better suited organisms survive and
                               reproduce

_____ Natural Selection   D. The next generation of organisms

III. Natural Selection Example

Fill in the blanks to complete the rabbit example:

In a snowy area, rabbits with _____ fur are better _____ against the snow. These rabbits are more likely to _____ and _____, passing on their traits to their _____. Over time, the population will have more _____-furred rabbits.

IV. Adaptations

List one physical and one behavioral adaptation mentioned in the text:

1. Physical:_____

2. Behavioral: _____

V. Speciation

Explain the bird example of speciation in your own words:

_____

_____

_____

VI. Examples of Evolution in Action

Describe the two examples given in the text:

1. Peppered moth: _____

_____

_____

2. Antibiotic resistance in bacteria: _____

_____

_____

VII. True or False

_____ Evolution occurs rapidly, usually within a few years.

_____ All mutations are beneficial to an organism.

_____ Natural selection was first proposed by Charles Darwin.

_____ Adaptations always involve physical changes to an organism.

VIII. Reflection

In your own words, explain why understanding evolution and natural selection is important:

_____

_____

#1

How do you think mutations contribute to the process of evolution?

Consider how small changes in DNA can introduce new traits and affect an organism's survival and reproduction.

#2

Why is natural selection important for the survival of a species?

Reflect on how certain traits can give organisms an advantage in their environment, helping them survive and reproduce more successfully.

#3

Can you think of an example of an adaptation in an animal or plant that helps it survive in its environment?

Think about specific traits, like the long neck of a giraffe or the camouflage of a chameleon, and how these traits help the organisms live and thrive.

#4

How might geographic isolation lead to the creation of a new species?

Consider how being separated by barriers like mountains or rivers can cause groups of the same species to evolve differently over time.

#5

What is an example of evolution you can observe in everyday life?

Reflect on examples like antibiotic resistance in bacteria or changes in peppered moth populations, and how these demonstrate evolutionary principles.

#6

Why is understanding evolution and natural selection important for studying biology?

Think about how these concepts help explain the diversity of life on Earth and how organisms adapt to their environments over time.

TERM	DEFINITION
Evolution	
Natural selection	
Genetics	
Mutation	
Adaptation	
Speciation	
DNA (deoxyribonucleic acid)	

TERM	DEFINITION
Trait	
Camouflage	
Reproduction	
Population	
Environment	
Industrial revolution	
Antibiotic resistance	

Evolution & Natural Selection

```
F J B W G D N O N S O O T S P E C I A T I O N T
H T Y K T U J Q G V X T D W Z D H D W T X L C F
I D V S R P Q S T I Y G Q A N V C B A B X J Z J
N R W Y A F P W V D X T D N A Y L N Z D I B G U
D E M G I M L P W J J B O G D I L Q I Z K E G T
U P F P T G S C U G B X N M U T A T I O N T V F
S R W E N V I R O N M E N T V Y M F H U X U D S
T O D P E V O L U T I O N V Q H K W L E B W L I
R D D G I V S V Y R B X H G X C O F W U W P P O
I U L E K M A E P L N G A O P J L U C V L H O N
A C T N X L Y E J S Z T D O F X C L Y F E O P Y
L T N E H R F Y E N F H A S P G R U D U C X U B
R I C T J K H B M M X E P O F D U D U G A X L G
E O Q I F S Y J W S D Y T N X I D E I U M L A F
V N Q C D J K F L T U I A Q H R A G Y V O B T J
O P Y S W R H D X B W A T U D U Q L R X U W I M
L Y H A J Y B X X X N Q I S I A W M P G F U O T
U B Z M I R W L F D Q W O N A I Z A A P L K N S
T S Y F V I B X J H X B N N K A M R Z A A E O R
I N A T U R A L S E L E C T I O N N M X G I Q N
O K H Q K V N O O Y R N B Z P R V O Y M E C V J
N W Z L G I B J S E I T I J R N V N M S X U I G
J O J G O A D K Q E E N E G S D Y N H N F U S N
M O A N T I B I O T I C R E S I S T A N C E W N
```

Antibiotic resistance	Industrial revolution	Environment
Population	Reproduction	Camouflage
Trait	DNA	Speciation
Adaptation	Mutation	Genetics
Natural selection	Evolution	

Evolution & Natural Selection

Across

5. A group of individuals of the same species living in a particular area.

9. The ability of bacteria to survive and reproduce despite being exposed to antibiotics, often due to mutations. Antibiotic ____

10. The molecule that carries genetic information in living organisms.

11. A characteristic or feature of an organism, such as eye color or leaf shape, that can be passed from one generation to the next.

12. The process by which organisms better adapted to their environment tend to survive and produce more offspring. (Two words)

13. The formation of new and distinct species through evolutionary processes, often due to geographic isolation.

14. An adaptation that allows an organism to blend into its surroundings to avoid predators.

Down

1. The surrounding conditions in which an organism lives, including natural elements and other living things.

2. A period of major industrialization and pollution that significantly impacted the environment and species like the peppered moth. Industrial ____

3. The process by which different kinds of living organisms develop and diversify from earlier forms over long periods of time.

4. A change in the DNA sequence that can introduce new traits to an organism.

6. A trait that helps an organism survive and reproduce in its environment.

7. The biological process by which new individual organisms are produced.

8. The study of heredity and the variation of inherited traits in living organisms.

How Genes Shape Populations

Have you ever wondered why some people have blue eyes while others have brown? Or why animals in one part of the world look different from the same species in another region? We can learn the answers by exploring population genetics. This area of science helps us understand how genes, the tiny instructions inside our cells, change and spread within groups of living things over time.

What is Population Genetics?

Population genetics is the study of how genes vary within groups of organisms. A population is a group of individuals of the same species that live in the same area and can interbreed. Scientists look at the frequencies of different genes in a population and how these frequencies change due to various factors.

Populations are groups of species living in the same area that can interbreed.

Genes and Alleles

To understand population genetics, you need to know about genes and alleles. Genes are segments of DNA that determine specific traits, like eye color or blood type. Each gene can have different versions, called alleles. For example, the gene for eye color has alleles for blue, brown, and green eyes.

Gene Pool

The gene pool is the total collection of alleles in a population. It's like a big pot of genetic ingredients from which individuals get their traits. The more diverse the gene pool, the healthier and more adaptable the population can be. Genetic diversity helps populations survive changes in the environment, like new diseases or climate changes.

Factors Affecting Gene Frequencies

Several factors influence gene frequencies in a population:

Mutations: These are changes in the DNA sequence. They can introduce new alleles into a population. While most mutations are neutral or harmful, some can be beneficial and increase an organism's chances of survival.

Natural Selection: This is the process where individuals with traits that are better suited to their environment are more likely to survive and reproduce. Over time, these beneficial traits become more common in the population.

Genetic Drift: This is a random change in allele frequencies, especially in small populations. Sometimes, by pure chance, certain alleles become more or less common.

Gene Flow: This happens when individuals from different populations interbreed, mixing their genes. It can introduce new alleles to a population and increase genetic diversity.

Understanding genetic diversity can help conservationists protect different endangered species.

The Hardy-Weinberg Principle

Scientists use the Hardy-Weinberg principle to predict how gene frequencies will behave in a population that is not evolving. According to this principle, if no mutations, natural selection, genetic drift, or gene flow occurs, and if the population is large with random mating, the gene frequencies will remain constant. This creates a baseline to compare real populations against to see if and how they are evolving.

Applications of Population Genetics

Population genetics isn't just theoretical; it has real-world applications. For instance, it helps conservationists understand how to protect endangered species by maintaining genetic diversity. It's also used in medicine to track the spread of genetic diseases and develop treatments. Population genetics is also important in agriculture for breeding plants and animals with desirable traits.

Population genetics gives us a window into the invisible world of genes and how they shape the living world around us. By studying how gene frequencies change in populations, scientists can make predictions, understand past events, and even plan for the future. Whether it's conserving wildlife, improving healthcare, or enhancing crops, the principles of population genetics are at work, making our world a better and more diverse place.

19. Population Genetics
GUIDED NOTES

I. Key Concepts
Define the following terms:

1. Population Genetics: _____

_____

2. Population: _____

_____

3. Gene: _____

4. Allele: _____

5. Gene Pool:_____

II. Factors Affecting Gene Frequencies
Match each factor with its description:

_____ Mutations   A. Random changes in allele frequencies

_____ Natural Selection   B. Mixing of genes between populations

_____ Genetic Drift   C. Changes in DNA sequence

_____ Gene Flow   D. Survival of better-suited individuals

III. The Hardy-Weinberg Principle
List three conditions required for gene frequencies to remain constant according to the Hardy-Weinberg principle:

1._____

2._____

3._____

IV. Applications of Population Genetics
Name one application of population genetics in each field:

1. Conservation: _____

_____

2. Medicine: _____

_____

3. Agriculture: _____

_____

V. True or False

_____ The gene pool is the total collection of alleles in a population.

_____ Mutations always introduce harmful changes to a population.

_____ Gene flow decreases genetic diversity in a population.

_____ The Hardy-Weinberg principle describes evolving populations.

VI. Short Answer

1. Explain how genetic diversity helps populations survive environmental

changes:_____

_____

_____

2. Describe how natural selection can change gene frequencies in a

population: _____

_____

_____

VII. In your own words, explain why studying population genetics is important:

_____

_____

_____

_____

_____

#1

How do genes and alleles contribute to the traits we see in organisms?

Think about how different versions of a gene, called alleles, can lead to different traits like eye color or blood type.

#2

Why is genetic diversity important for the survival of a population?

Reflect on how a diverse gene pool can help a population adapt to changes in the environment, like new diseases or climate changes.

#3

What are some factors that can change the frequencies of genes in a population?

Consider the role of mutations, natural selection, genetic drift, and gene flow in altering gene frequencies.

#4

How does the Hardy-Weinberg principle help scientists understand if a population is evolving?

Think about the conditions under which gene frequencies remain constant and how deviations from this can indicate evolution.

#5

In what ways can population genetics be applied in real-world situations?

Reflect on how this field of science is used in conservation, medicine, and agriculture to solve practical problems.

#6

Why might genetic drift have a larger impact on smaller populations compared to larger ones?

Think about how random changes in allele frequencies can significantly affect smaller populations more than larger ones due to fewer individuals.

19. Population Genetics - Vocabulary

TERM	DEFINITION
Population genetics	
Population	
Gene	
Allele	
Gene pool	
Genetic diversity	
Mutation	

TERM	DEFINITION
Natural selection	
Genetic drift	
Gene flow	
Hardy-Weinberg Principle	
Interbreed	
Trait	
Adaptation	

Population Genetics

```
L M B I P O F H J K W H Z P S H F Q S Z D R M X
U L R Z D P H G E N E P O O L A B O Q D M P Y B
T A Y Z M R P M L M I C I P D R D K H O Y S A Y
R X N Q P V S V L O P S X U Z D M A Q G R Y L T
H G A X M R G J O B T R G L Q Y J S A H H W L P
N G T U P X I E Z J I G Y A G W R V Y H S R E Q
X V U M U T A T I O N B L T M E R K J Z T T L G
W H R L M Y O V S F O J A I O I M V A K Q T E E
G D A X I K O H U U W P D O W N S K W V G B F N
E T L S O G Q I O O I O A N T B W L A U J R B E
N V S Y C K G R J Z H R P J R E P J E G H X J M
E R E T Q I N B D H C V T S A R D A D A I I G N
F F L Y K J V V U Z F O A Z I G M R D K B R N M
L H E G X U R Y X I S I T N T P B E Q W G G H O
O Y C Y G E N E T I C D I V E R S I T Y Y N Q D
W R T V I U N Y D O C V O G S I R I W L Z E J X
H N I X A T K N E Y G X N X M N Q U Y B F K S H
P B O C Z N K Z D A L O B A O C V I L O I Y P D
U D N F M S R D L N O U W C C I U L A H I T Q D
L F P B G J M W V J B U W P C W Q X D G R E
Q M X O G M S S W D P D O J L L W F M C M S O
I N T E R B R E E D V K G E N E T I C D R I F T
K I T S L P O P U L A T I O N G E N E T I C S S
C H U R O Q O D F N K T B U F U A G G R G I Y C
```

Hardy-Weinberg Principle	Gene flow	Genetic drift
Natural selection	Genetic diversity	Adaptation
Trait	Interbreed	Mutation
Gene pool	Allele	Gene
Population	Population genetics	

Population Genetics

Across
2. A group of individuals of the same species that live in the same area and can interbreed.
5. A random change in allele frequencies, especially impactful in small populations, where chance events can cause certain alleles to become more or less common. Genetic ____
8. The study of how genes vary within groups of organisms and how these gene frequencies change over time. (Two words)
10. A specific characteristic or feature determined by genes, like eye color or height.
13. The total collection of alleles in a population, representing all the genetic diversity available. (Two words)

14. The movement of genes between different populations through interbreeding, which introduces new alleles and increases genetic diversity. Gene ___

Down
1. The variety of alleles within a population's gene pool, which helps populations survive environmental changes. Genetic ____
3. A change in the DNA sequence that can introduce new alleles into a population; can be neutral, harmful, or beneficial.
4. A beneficial trait that becomes more common in a population due to natural selection, helping the population survive in its environment.

6. A principle used to predict how gene frequencies will behave in a non-evolving population, providing a baseline for comparing real populations. ___-Weinberg Principle
7. The process where individuals within a population mate and produce offspring, sharing their genetic material.
9. The process where individuals with traits better suited to their environment are more likely to survive and reproduce, making those traits more common over time. Natural ____
11. Different versions of a gene, such as the blue, brown, and green eye color.
12. A segment of DNA that determines specific traits, like eye color or blood type.

Mechanisms of Evolution: Causing Change

Have you ever wondered why there are so many different kinds of plants and animals on Earth? The answer lies in a fascinating process called evolution. Evolution is how life changes over time, and it's driven by several key mechanisms. Let's learn about these mechanisms in a way that helps you understand how they work.

Natural Selection: Survival of the Fittest

Mechanisms of evolution include natural selection, genetic drift, gene flow, and mutation, which collectively drive the changes in genetic variation within populations over time.

One of the most important mechanisms of evolution is natural selection. Imagine you have a group of rabbits. Some rabbits have brown fur, which helps them hide from predators in a forest. Others have white fur, which makes them easy targets. Over time, the brown rabbits are more likely to survive and have babies. These babies will also have brown fur. This process is called natural selection. It means that traits that help an organism survive are more likely to be passed on to the next generation.

Mutation: The Source of New Traits

Another key mechanism is mutation. Mutations are changes in the DNA of an organism. DNA is like a set of instructions for building and running a living thing. Sometimes, mistakes happen when DNA is copied, leading to mutations. Most mutations don't make much difference, but some can create new traits. For example, a mutation might give a rabbit slightly longer ears. If this helps the rabbit hear predators better, it's more likely to survive and pass on the long-ear trait to its offspring.

Genetic Drift: Chance Changes

Genetic drift is another way evolution can happen. Unlike natural selection, which is about survival advantages, genetic drift is all about chance. Imagine a small population of birds living on an island. One year, a storm wipes out most of the birds, purely by chance. The surviving birds might have different traits than the original population, just because of who survived the storm. Over time, these chance events can lead to significant changes in the population.

Gene Flow: Mixing Populations

Gene flow is when individuals from different populations interbreed. This mixing can introduce new traits into a population. For example, if a few birds from one island fly to another island

and start breeding with the local birds, their offspring will have a mix of traits from both populations. This can lead to new combinations of traits and increase the genetic diversity of the population.

Non-Random Mating: Choosing Partners

In many species, individuals don't choose mates randomly. This is called non-random mating. For example, peahens (female peacocks) often choose mates based on the size and color of the peacock's tail. Peacocks with larger, more colorful tails are more likely to attract mates and have offspring. This selective mating can increase the frequency of certain traits in a population.

Evolution is the gradual change in species over time through processes like natural selection and genetic variation.

Adaptation: Fitting In Better

All these mechanisms can lead to adaptation, which is when a population becomes better suited to its environment. For example, if a population of fish lives in a dark cave, individuals with better night vision are more likely to survive and reproduce. Over time, the population will adapt to life in the dark, and most of the fish will have excellent night vision.

Speciation: Forming New Species

When populations change enough, they can become so different that they no longer interbreed. This is called

speciation. For example, if a group of animals is separated by a mountain range, each group might adapt to its environment in different ways. Over thousands or millions of years, these differences can become so significant that the two groups become separate species.

Coevolution: Evolving Together

Sometimes, species evolve together in a process called coevolution. This happens when two or more species influence each other's evolution. For example, bees and flowers have evolved together. Flowers have developed bright colors and sweet nectar to attract bees, while bees have evolved to collect pollen from flowers. This mutually beneficial relationship helps both species survive and reproduce.

Evolution is a complex but fascinating process that explains the diversity of life on Earth. By understanding the mechanisms of evolution—natural selection, mutation, genetic drift, gene flow, non-random mating, adaptation, speciation, and coevolution—you can better appreciate how life changes over time. Evolution is happening all around you, even if you can't see it in real-time. Every living thing, including you, is part of this incredible journey.

20. Mechanisms of Evolution
GUIDED NOTES

I. Mechanisms of Evolution
List the eight key mechanisms of evolution discussed in the article:

1. _____   2. _____

3. _____   4. _____

5. _____   6. _____

7. _____   8. _____

II. Matching Mechanisms to Descriptions
Match each mechanism with its description:

___ Natural Selection   A. Changes in DNA that can create new traits

___ Mutation   B. Interbreeding between different populations

___ Genetic Drift   C. Becoming better suited to an environment

___ Gene Flow   D. Survival of organisms with advantageous traits

___ Non-Random Mating   E. Changes in population due to chance events

___ Adaptation   F. Choosing mates based on specific traits

___ Speciation   G. Formation of new species

___ Coevolution   H. Multiple species influencing each other's evolution

III. Examples and Explanations
Provide a brief example or explanation for each mechanism:

1. Natural Selection: _____

2. Mutation: _____

3. Genetic Drift: _____

4. Gene Flow: _____

5. Non-Random Mating: _____

6. Adaptation: _____

7. Speciation: _____

8. Coevolution: _____

IV. True or False
Mark each statement as True (T) or False (F):

_____ Evolution only occurs through natural selection.

_____ Mutations are always beneficial to an organism.

_____ Genetic drift is more significant in small populations.

_____ Gene flow can introduce new traits into a population.

_____ Non-random mating has no effect on evolution.

V. Short Answer
Answer the following questions in your own words:

1. Why is DNA important in the process of evolution?

_____

_____

2. How can a small change like longer ears in rabbits affect a population over time?

_____

_____

3. Explain how the environment plays a role in natural selection:

_____

_____

VI. Reflection
In your own words, explain why understanding evolution is important for studying life on Earth:

_____

_____

_____

#1

How does natural selection affect the traits of a population over time?

Consider how the brown rabbits in the forest are more likely to survive and reproduce compared to the white rabbits.

#2

What role do mutations play in the process of evolution?

Think about how a mutation, like longer ears in a rabbit, can create new traits that may help the organism survive better.

#3

How can genetic drift change a population, and why is it different from natural selection?

Reflect on the example of the storm affecting a small population of birds, and how chance events can lead to changes.

#4

In what ways can gene flow introduce new traits into a population?

Consider the impact of birds from one island interbreeding with birds from another island and how this increases genetic diversity.

#5

Why might non-random mating increase certain traits within a population?

Think about the example of peahens choosing peacocks with larger, more colorful tails and how this affects the traits in the next generation.

#6

How do adaptation and speciation work together to create new species?

Reflect on how a population adapting to its environment over time might eventually become so different that it forms a new species.

TERM	DEFINITION
Evolution	
Natural selection	
Mutation	
Genetic drift	
Gene flow	
Non-random mating	
Adaptation	

TERM	DEFINITION
Speciation	
Coevolution	
Trait	
DNA	
Population	
Genetic diversity	
Selective mating	

Mechanisms of Evolution

```
B V T M H Q C I K W Q M U T A T I O N L A I S L
A A X X I R Y O Q H J N V T A D A P T A T I O N
Z R O Y B Y D T C M G F F A X F V O U G D M N T
S Z L K T O A D Z A E W O Q I N O T K X N W N P
L T T N F W M B S J N L Q T V G U A N T A L W Q
L Y I R N U Y L B F E Q I V I E J B A K T L F U
S P E C I A T I O N T J N U P N T V Z L U I U O
P Y D Q N K S K V G I R C B F E R N C S R Z X Q
G D F U A M B U A Z C Y V V Q T E G H C A Q P T
N D I M H J S T T Z D O W W Y I F F W O L V G O
M P B A H N J A S I R M B S U C M V M E S A E V
H S O N H I Q N Y Q I C F R T D Y W T V E D N N
M L D N A A N H I R F Y R W K I D J A O L P E D
U J K D Z R D G B Z T P U O C V P B O L E U F M
J K P E H F G D Y X U T W K B E Q B K U C O L S
P O P U L A T I O N T C L K W R I Y B T T M O H
T R A I T X N B D X K E O X N S Y A S I I Z W O
K Y L E R O U Q K O B G D J Y I V F Z O O J Q X
O T O X Z Q B V C R K W U E P T G A R N N M M T
R D S G X I F K P P O T A A R Y J M T A U S U X
S E L E C T I V E M A T I N G C I G H J A Y H I
K E H K S C E A N O N R A N D O M M A T I N G F
S G I Y D W H M G Q I K A M S J N I M W O T F H
A Q M S C N P E V O L U T I O N N T G V H N T Z
```

Selective mating	Genetic diversity	Non-random mating
Genetic drift	Population	DNA
Trait	Coevolution	Speciation
Adaptation	Gene flow	Mutation
Natural selection	Evolution	

Mechanisms of Evolution

Across

2. The formation of new and distinct species through the process of evolution.

3. The variety of different genes within a population, which can be increased through mechanisms like gene flow. Genetic ____

5. When individuals choose mates based on certain traits, often leading to those traits becoming more common in the population. ____ mating

7. A mechanism of evolution where random chance events cause changes in the traits of a small population. Genetic ____

10. The process by which different kinds of living organisms change over time through various mechanisms.

12. A specific characteristic or feature of an organism, such as fur color or ear length.

13. A mechanism of evolution where traits that help an organism survive are more likely to be passed on to the next generation. (Two words)

14. When two or more species influence each other's evolution through mutual interactions.

Down

1. The process by which a population becomes better suited to its environment over time.

4. The transfer of genetic material between different populations through interbreeding. (Two words)

6. A group of individuals of the same species living in a particular area.

8. Changes in the DNA of an organism that can create new traits; these changes can be beneficial, neutral, or harmful.

9. When individuals choose mates based on specific traits, leading to an increase in those traits within the population. __-____ mating

11. The molecule that carries genetic information in living organisms; it acts like a set of instructions for building and running an organism.

The Circle of Life:
Ecology and Energy Flow

Have you ever wondered how plants, animals, and other living things interact with each other and their environment? This fascinating network of relationships is called ecology. Ecology helps us understand how everything in nature is connected and how energy flows through these connections. Let's learn how energy moves through ecosystems and why it's so important for all living things.

What Is Ecology?

Ecology is the study of how living things interact with each other and their environment. This includes plants, animals, bacteria, and even fungi. Everything in an ecosystem is connected, and changes in one part can affect the whole system. By studying ecology, we can understand how these connections support life on Earth.

Decomposers break down dead and decaying material. This puts nutrients into the soil for plants to use.

The Basics of Energy Flow

Energy flow in an ecosystem refers to how energy moves from one organism to another. It all starts with the sun, which provides the energy that plants need to grow. Plants use sunlight to make their own food through a process called photosynthesis. This is the first step in the energy flow process.

Producers: The Energy Makers

Plants, algae, and some bacteria are called producers because they produce their own food using sunlight. These producers form the base of the ecosystem's energy pyramid. Without them, there would be no energy for the other organisms in the ecosystem.

Consumers: The Energy Users

Consumers are organisms that cannot make their own food. There are three main types of consumers: herbivores, carnivores, and omnivores.

• Herbivores eat plants. For example, a rabbit munching on grass is a herbivore.

• Carnivores eat other animals. A lion hunting a zebra is a carnivore.

• Omnivores eat both plants and animals. Humans, who eat fruits, vegetables, and meat, are omnivores.

Consumers get their energy by eating producers or other consumers. This transfer of energy is a crucial part of the ecosystem.

Decomposers: The Recyclers

Decomposers, like fungi and bacteria, play a vital role in the energy flow of an ecosystem. They break down dead plants and animals into simpler substances. This process releases nutrients back into the soil, which plants use to grow. Decomposers ensure that nothing goes to waste and that energy continues to flow through the ecosystem.

Food Chains and Food Webs

A food chain shows the direct line of energy transfer from one organism to another. For example, a simple food chain might look like this: grass → rabbit → fox. The arrows show the direction of energy flow, from the grass to the rabbit and then to the fox.

However, in real life, ecosystems are more complex. Many animals eat more than one type of food, and they may be eaten by more than one type of predator. This creates a food web, which is a network of interconnected food chains. Food webs better represent the complexity of energy flow in an ecosystem.

Producers provide all the energy that gets passed on to the different consumers.

Energy Pyramids

An energy pyramid shows how energy decreases as it moves up through the different levels of the food chain. The bottom level of the pyramid represents the producers, which have the most energy. The next levels are the primary consumers (herbivores), followed by secondary consumers (carnivores that eat herbivores), and so on. Each level has less energy than the one below it

because some energy is lost as heat when organisms use it to survive and grow.

The Importance of Energy Flow

Understanding energy flow is crucial for several reasons. It helps us see how dependent we are on plants and other producers for our survival. It also shows the importance of each organism in maintaining a balanced ecosystem. If one part of the energy flow is disrupted, it can have a ripple effect throughout the entire ecosystem.

Human Impact on Energy Flow

Humans have a significant impact on energy flow in ecosystems. Activities like deforestation, pollution, and overfishing can disrupt the balance of energy flow, leading to negative consequences for both the environment and human health. By understanding ecology and energy flow, we can make better choices to protect our planet.

Ecology and energy flow are fundamental concepts that help us understand the connections between all living things. By learning how energy moves through ecosystems, we can appreciate the delicate balance that supports life on Earth. Every organism has a role to play, and protecting our ecosystems is essential for a healthy planet. When you see a plant, animal, or even a tiny insect, think about the vital part it plays in the circle of life.

21. Ecology and Energy Flow
GUIDED NOTES

I. What is Ecology?

Define ecology in your own words:_____

_____

II. Energy Flow Basics

1. Where does energy in an ecosystem ultimately come from?

_____

2. What process do plants use to make their own food?

_____

III. Key Players in Energy Flow

Match each term with its correct description:

___ Producers   A. Break down dead organisms and release nutrients

___ Consumers   B. Cannot make their own food

___ Decomposers   C. Make their own food using sunlight

IV. Types of Consumers

List the three main types of consumers and provide an example for each:

1. _____: Example: _____

2. _____: Example: _____

3. _____: Example: _____

V. Food Chains and Food Webs

1. Draw a simple food chain with 3 organisms:

_____ → _____ → _____

2. How is a food web different from a food chain?

_____

_____

VI. Energy Pyramids

Explain why each level of an energy pyramid has less energy than the one below it:

_____

_____

VII. True or False

_____ Decomposers are not important in energy flow.

_____ Energy increases as it moves up the food chain.

_____ Humans can impact energy flow in ecosystems.

VIII. Human Impact

List two human activities that can disrupt energy flow in ecosystems:

1. _____ 2. _____

IX. Importance of Energy Flow

In your own words, explain why understanding energy flow is crucial:

_____

_____

X. Reflection

How does learning about ecology and energy flow change your view of nature and your role in it?

_____

_____

#1

How do producers, like plants and algae, contribute to the energy flow in an ecosystem?

Think about the process of photosynthesis and how it allows producers to create their own food using sunlight.

#2

Why are decomposers important in maintaining the balance of an ecosystem?

Reflect on how decomposers recycle nutrients back into the soil and what would happen if they were not present.

#3

How do food chains and food webs illustrate the complexity of energy flow in an ecosystem?

Consider the differences between a simple food chain and a more complex food web, and how they show the connections between different organisms.

#4

What might happen to an ecosystem if a key species, such as a top predator or a primary producer, were to disappear?

Think about the ripple effect throughout the food chain and how the loss of one species can impact others.

#5

In what ways do human activities, like deforestation or pollution, disrupt the energy flow in ecosystems?

Reflect on specific examples of human impact and how they alter the natural balance of energy flow.

#6

Why is it important for humans to understand and protect the flow of energy in ecosystems?

Consider how our survival depends on healthy ecosystems and the role each organism plays in supporting life on Earth.

TERM	DEFINITION
Ecology	
Ecosystem	
Energy flow	
Photosynthesis	
Producers	
Consumers	
Herbivores	

TERM	DEFINITION
Carnivores	
Omnivores	
Decomposers	
Food chain	
Food web	
Energy pyramid	
Human impact	

Ecology & Energy Flow

```
U J X R N N X F O O D C H A I N P P K C A Q M R
G P H O T O S Y N T H E S I S Q I N W F V R N G
N K M R V E P R O D U C E R S H S R D F B H E E
M K S P S M H G B C E D M R M U X F T F R K Y M
U E W R X U L U E Q Z Z F M F M N H I J O M U O
T C C T G F D A P Q Y X K G Y A T T I L A H Z B
B O H S W H H V Q I L G M Z K N J A O A D O R E
Z S E N E R G Y P Y R A M I D I M M D B V V I B
W Y C L S S N F O O D W E B O M B N C T J T R W
I S C C V A D B N D D N V B I P E Q B Q D Z G V
W T H B Y P E W P J D S U G O A V I L O F L C Q
J E L R H N R M Z J C S D O C C U Z J L M F Z
C M D E Q N L F Q I U D E T M T A P S U X X L O
L Q O D M I L J J I W E C F F S V V O S Q H R S
K F R N O J S U G Z H Z O B I Y A E G I L A N M
B K P U A L G K J S M T M J R N O W H L U O V E
E L Y T U J Y D X K C A P N U C Z L Z W H M A E
N K N E B Z C W C L B P O J G D W R F L A N W Y
F O Q C O N S U M E R S S K N X A M C A B I X Y
D U Q O A M W R F E B H E R B I V O R E S V D S
W Y H L G M U N C E L S R F F W F U Z G P O Z B
R V C O Z F L F Y Z Q C S P O J W Q O K V R I J
A B O G Q W N E N E R G Y F L O W T V Y G E F Q
T U V Y Q J E J C C C A R N I V O R E S A S E C
```

Energy flow	Energy pyramid	Human impact
Food web	Food chain	Decomposers
Omnivores	Carnivores	Herbivores
Consumers	Producers	Photosynthesis
Ecosystem	Ecology	

Ecology & Energy Flow

Across

4. A linear sequence showing how energy is transferred from one organism to another, for example, grass → rabbit → fox. (Two words)

5. The effect of human activities, such as deforestation, pollution, and overfishing, on the balance of energy flow and the health of ecosystems. Human ____

8. Consumers that eat both plants and animals to obtain their energy, such as humans and bears.

11. Organisms that cannot make their own food and must eat other organisms to obtain energy. They include herbivores, carnivores, and omnivores.

13. The process by which plants and some bacteria use sunlight to produce their own food, forming the first step in the energy flow of an ecosystem.

14. Organisms like fungi and bacteria that break down dead plants and animals, recycling nutrients back into the soil and continuing the flow of energy in an ecosystem.

Down

1. A community of living organisms and their physical environment, interacting as a system.

2. Organisms, such as plants, algae, and some bacteria, that produce their own food using sunlight and form the base of the ecosystem's energy pyramid.

3. A graphical representation showing how energy decreases as it moves up through the different levels of the food chain, from producers to various levels of consumers. Energy ____

6. The study of how living things interact with each other and their environment, including plants, animals, bacteria, and fungi.

7. Consumers that eat plants to obtain their energy, such as rabbits and cows.

9. Consumers that eat other animals to obtain their energy, such as lions and wolves.

10. The movement of energy from one organism to another within an ecosystem, starting from the sun and moving through different trophic levels. Energy ____

12. A network of interconnected food chains that better represents the complexity of how energy flows through an ecosystem. (Two words)

Population Ecology:
Dynamics of Life in Ecosystems

Population ecology is an exciting branch of biology that explores how groups of the same species interact with each other and their environment. Whether it's a herd of deer in a forest, a school of fish in the ocean, or a colony of ants in your backyard, population ecology helps us understand the complex relationships that keep these groups thriving. Time to get into population ecology and learn why it's so important for the balance of nature.

What is Population Ecology?

Imagine a group of animals or plants living in the same area. This group is called a population. Population ecology is the study of how these populations grow, shrink, and interact with their environment. It looks at factors like the number of births and deaths, how much food is available, and how many individuals move in or out of the area. By studying these factors, scientists can learn a lot about the health of an ecosystem and how to protect it.

Key Concepts in Population Ecology

Population Size and Density: Population size is the total number of individuals in a population. Population density, on the other hand, is the number of individuals per unit area or volume. For example, if you have 100 rabbits in a 10-acre field, the population

Carrying capacity refers to how many individuals an environment can support.

density is 10 rabbits per acre. Understanding these concepts helps ecologists determine if a population is too crowded or too sparse, which can affect its survival.

Birth Rate and Death Rate: The birth rate is the number of new individuals born in a population over a certain period of time. The death rate is the number of individuals that die over the same period. If the birth rate is higher than the death rate, the population will grow. If the death rate is higher, the population will shrink. These rates are influenced by factors like food availability, predators, disease, and climate.

Immigration and Emigration: Immigration is when individuals move into a population from another area. Emigration is when individuals leave a population to move to a new area. These movements can greatly influence population size and density. For instance, if many animals migrate to a new area because of better food sources, the population in that area will increase.

Carrying Capacity: Carrying capacity is the maximum number of individuals that an environment can support without being degraded. It depends on the availability of resources like food, water, and shelter. When a population exceeds its carrying capacity, resources become limited, leading to competition, stress, and a possible decline in the population size.

Why is Population Ecology Important?

Population ecology is crucial for several reasons:

Conservation Efforts: By understanding the dynamics of populations, scientists can develop strategies to protect endangered species and manage natural resources effectively.

Disease Control: Studying population ecology helps in predicting and controlling the spread of diseases within animal and human populations.

Population density refers to how many individuals of a population are within a given area.

Agriculture: Farmers use principles of population ecology to manage crops and livestock, ensuring sustainable yields and healthy ecosystems.

Urban Planning: City planners use population data to design infrastructure that supports growing human populations without harming the environment.

Human Impact on Populations

Humans have a significant impact on populations and ecosystems. Activities like deforestation, pollution, and overfishing can drastically alter population dynamics. For example, cutting down forests destroys the habitats of many species, leading to a decline in animal populations. Pollution can cause health problems for both wildlife and humans, affecting birth and death rates.

Protecting Our Planet

Understanding population ecology helps us make better decisions to protect our planet. Simple actions like recycling, conserving water, and supporting sustainable practices can reduce our impact on the environment. By learning about the delicate balance of ecosystems, you can play a part in preserving nature for future generations.

Population ecology is a vital field of study that helps us understand the intricate relationships between species and their environments. By exploring concepts like population size, birth and death rates, and carrying capacity, we can appreciate the complexity of nature and the importance of maintaining ecological balance. Whether you're interested in wildlife conservation, agriculture, or urban development, population ecology offers valuable insights that can guide us toward a sustainable future.

22. Population Ecology
GUIDED NOTES

I. Key Terms in Population Ecology
Define the following terms:

1. Population Ecology: _____

_____

2. Population: _____

3. Population Size: _____

4. Population Density: _____

II. Key Concepts in Population Ecology
Match each concept with its definition:

____ Birth Rate

____ Death Rate

____ Immigration

____ Emigration

____ Carrying Capacity

A. Maximum number of individuals an environment can support

B. Movement of individuals into a population

C. Number of new individuals born over a period of time

D. Movement of individuals out of a population

E. Number of individuals that die over a period of time

III. Factors Affecting Population Dynamics
List four factors that can influence population size and density:

1. _____ 2. _____

3. _____ 4. _____

IV. Importance of Population Ecology
Explain how population ecology is important in each of the following areas:

1. Conservation Efforts: _____

_____

2. Disease Control: _____

_____

3. Agriculture: _____

_____

4. Urban Planning: _____

_____

V. Human Impact on Populations
Provide two examples of how human activities can affect population dynamics:

1. _____

2. _____

VI. True or False
Mark each statement as True (T) or False (F):

_____ Population ecology only studies animal populations, not plant populations.

_____ The carrying capacity is always fixed and never changes.

_____ Immigration and emigration can affect population size.

_____ If the birth rate is higher than the death rate, the population will grow.

VII. Reflection
In your own words, explain why studying population ecology is important for maintaining ecological balance:

_____

_____

_____

#1

How do birth and death rates affect the size of a population over time?

Consider how an increase in births or deaths can change the number of individuals in a population.

#2

Why is carrying capacity important for maintaining a balanced ecosystem?

Reflect on what happens when a population exceeds its carrying capacity and how it impacts the environment.

#3

What role does immigration and emigration play in the health of a population?

Think about how the movement of individuals into and out of an area can change population size and density.

#4

How can human activities like deforestation and pollution affect population ecology?

Consider the direct and indirect ways that human actions can disrupt natural populations and their habitats.

#5

Why might understanding population ecology be important for conservation efforts?

Reflect on how knowledge of population dynamics can help protect endangered species and manage natural resources.

#6

How can studying population ecology help us make better decisions for urban planning and agriculture?

Think about how insights from population ecology can guide the design of cities and farming practices to support sustainable growth.

TERM	DEFINITION
Population ecology	
Population	
Population size	
Population density	
Birth rate	
Death rate	
Immigration	

TERM	DEFINITION
Emigration	
Carrying capacity	
Ecosystem	
Conservation efforts	
Disease control	
Urban planning	
Human impact	

Population Ecology

```
P D X Y J S B T O X U U L X F D U P O R E W J N
Q J E T C W I Z B P F I M M I G R A T I O N C P
Q Q F C O H I H T A M P O P U L A T I O N X E O
G C X G M S J C W S Z M V O U S X D Y N I U Y P
Q Y L O P Q O S J Y I M H S R I S K M I Z B V U
Y M T W E C O S Y S T E M D B C Z A U F N I I L
Z B B E J E I F L L V G T M A I H Q Z E S R N A
P J P N M K H N K J P N M A N V P Z W R G T C T
R E O R D E A T H R A T E W P C S S F Z H H W I
Q G P C R W K B H K S J U M L L I Z B Q Y R F O
V T U V E C A R R Y I N G C A P A C I T Y A E N
H U L D G I E M R F D R O D P N C R N X T Y D
W D A T O Z G H O W D C D P N E Y D U U R E W E
P S T A P O B H Z J S C A R I F B D V N E G D N
C T I N A J J L J Y Z P Q Z N S J G C T F X E S
K D O D D C C X S N P I H W G X B Q T O N W K I
C O N S E R V A T I O N E F F O R T S Z H A E T
H Q E T U D B M H C V X R N R I P I A C Z I N Y
H M C J P O P U L A T I O N S I Z E H O O D M F
N Y O B M K A U R J S A X A O G F F M P D C W J
Q E L A Q C A E I E M I G R A T I O N J W M L C
K G O S Q P P A Y W N J H U M A N I M P A C T
K H G C T D T Z S U F J V C T H Z I A T U A J D
X U Y I O G R D I S E A S E C O N T R O L S I C
```

Human impact	Urban planning	Disease control
Conservation efforts	Carrying capacity	Death rate
Birth rate	Population density	Population size
Population ecology	Ecosystem	Emigration
Immigration	Population	

Population Ecology

Across

3. The number of individuals that die in a population over a specific period of time. ____ rate

6. A community of living organisms and their interactions with their environment, including both biotic (living) and abiotic (non-living) components.

8. The number of individuals per unit area or volume in a given population. Population ___

10. The practice of predicting and managing the spread of diseases within animal and human populations. Disease ____

11. The number of new individuals born in a population over a specific period of time. ____ rate

12. A group of animals or plants of the same species living in the same area.

13. The total number of individuals in a population. Population ____

14. The process of designing and organizing urban spaces, considering population data to support sustainable growth without harming the environment. Urban ____

Down

1. The maximum number of individuals that an environment can support without being degraded.

2. The effects of human activities like deforestation, pollution, and overfishing on populations and ecosystems, which can lead to changes in population dynamics and environmental degradation. Human ____

4. The movement of individuals into a population from another area.

5. The movement of individuals out of a population to a new area.

7. Strategies and actions taken to protect endangered species and manage natural resources. ____ efforts

9. The study of how groups of the same species interact with each other and their environment, focusing on factors like population growth, shrinkage, and movement. Population ____

The Dance of Matter:
Biogeochemical Cycles

Have you ever wondered how the elements that make up our world move around and support life on Earth? From the air we breathe to the food we eat, these elements are constantly cycling through our environment. These cycles are known as biogeochemical cycles, and they are essential for maintaining life on our planet. Let's learn about biogeochemical cycles and see how they work to keep everything in balance.

Precipitation is the part of the water cycle where water has condensed enough that it falls back to the planet's surface.

What Are Biogeochemical Cycles?

Biogeochemical cycles are the pathways by which elements like carbon, nitrogen, oxygen, and phosphorus travel through the Earth's atmosphere, hydrosphere (water bodies), lithosphere (land), and biosphere (living organisms). These cycles ensure that essential nutrients are recycled and made available for all living things. Without these cycles, life as we know it wouldn't be possible.

The Carbon Cycle

The carbon cycle is one of the most important biogeochemical cycles. Carbon is a key element in all living organisms and is found in the atmosphere as carbon dioxide (CO_2). Plants play a vital role in this cycle through a process called photosynthesis. They take in CO_2 from the air and use sunlight to convert it into oxygen and glucose (a type of sugar). This glucose provides energy for plants and, when animals eat plants, it becomes their energy source too.

When plants and animals die, their bodies decompose and return carbon to the soil. Some of this carbon becomes fossil fuels like coal and oil over millions of years. When humans burn these fossil fuels for energy, CO_2 is released back into the atmosphere, completing the cycle.

The Nitrogen Cycle

Nitrogen is another essential element for living organisms, as it is a major component of proteins and DNA. The nitrogen cycle involves several steps to convert nitrogen from the atmosphere into forms that plants and animals can use.

Most of the nitrogen on Earth is found in the atmosphere as nitrogen gas (N_2), which is not directly usable by most living organisms. Certain bacteria in the soil and water, known as nitrogen-fixing bacteria, can convert N_2 into ammonia (NH_3), a form that plants can absorb through their roots. Plants use this nitrogen to grow, and when animals eat the plants, they obtain the nitrogen they need.

When plants and animals die or release waste, decomposers like bacteria and fungi break down the organic matter, returning nitrogen to the soil in the form of ammonium (NH_4^+). Other bacteria convert ammonium back into nitrogen gas through a process called denitrification, releasing it into the atmosphere and completing the cycle.

The Water Cycle

The water cycle, also known as the hydrological cycle, describes how water moves through the Earth's atmosphere, surface, and underground. Water evaporates from the surface of oceans, rivers, and lakes due to the heat from the sun. This water vapor rises into the atmosphere and cools, forming clouds through condensation.

Volcanic eruptions release carbon dioxide into the atmosphere.

When the clouds become heavy with moisture, they release it as precipitation (rain, snow, sleet, or hail). This water returns to the Earth's surface, replenishing rivers, lakes, and groundwater. Plants also play a role in the water cycle through a process called transpiration, where they release water vapor from their leaves into the atmosphere.

The Phosphorus Cycle

Phosphorus is an essential element for DNA, RNA, and ATP (the energy currency of cells). Unlike carbon and nitrogen, phosphorus does not have a gaseous form and does not cycle through the atmosphere. Instead, it cycles through rocks, soil, water, and living organisms.

Phosphorus is released from rocks through a process called weathering, where wind and water break down rocks into smaller particles. Plants absorb phosphorus from the soil through their roots, and animals obtain it by eating plants. When plants and animals die, decomposers break down their bodies, returning phosphorus to the soil. Some phosphorus can also enter water bodies, where it becomes part of the sediments. Over time, these sediments can form new rocks, continuing the cycle.

Biogeochemical cycles are like the Earth's recycling system, ensuring that essential elements are continuously cycled and made available for all living things. Understanding these cycles helps us appreciate the delicate balance that supports life on our planet.

23. Biogeochemical Cycles
GUIDED NOTES

I. What Are Biogeochemical Cycles?

Define biogeochemical cycles in your own words:_____

_____

List the four spheres through which elements travel in biogeochemical cycles:

1. _____   2._____

3. _____   4._____

II. Major Biogeochemical Cycles

Match each cycle with its key characteristic:

_____ Carbon Cycle   A. Involves photosynthesis and fossil fuels

_____ Nitrogen Cycle   B. Includes evaporation and precipitation

_____ Water Cycle   C. Relies on nitrogen-fixing bacteria

_____ Phosphorus Cycle   D. Does not have a gaseous form

III. The Carbon Cycle

Name two important processes in the carbon cycle:

1. _____: Plants use CO2, sunlight, and water to produce

oxygen and glucose

2. _____: The breakdown of dead organisms, returning

carbon to the soil

How do human activities contribute to the carbon cycle?

_____

_____

IV. The Nitrogen Cycle

List the steps of the nitrogen cycle in order:

1. Nitrogen gas in atmosphere

2. _____

3. _____

4. _____

5. _____

6. Nitrogen gas returned to atmosphere

V. The Water Cycle

Name three forms of precipitation:

1. _____   2._____

3. _____

Explain the process of transpiration: _____

_____

VI. The Phosphorus Cycle

True or False:

_____ Phosphorus has a gaseous form like carbon and nitrogen.

_____ Phosphorus is released from rocks through weathering.

_____ Plants absorb phosphorus from the air through their leaves.

How does phosphorus move from living organisms back to the environment?

_____

_____

VII. Importance of Biogeochemical Cycles

In your own words, explain why biogeochemical cycles are essential for life on Earth:

_____

_____

#1

How do plants contribute to the carbon cycle?

Think about the process of photosynthesis and how plants take in carbon dioxide (CO_2) from the atmosphere and convert it into oxygen and glucose.

#2

Why is nitrogen important for living organisms?

Consider the role of nitrogen in building proteins and DNA, and how plants and animals obtain usable forms of nitrogen.

#3

What role do bacteria play in the nitrogen cycle?

Reflect on the different types of bacteria involved, such as nitrogen-fixing bacteria and decomposers, and their specific functions in converting nitrogen into usable forms.

#4

How does the water cycle help sustain life on Earth?

Think about the processes of evaporation, condensation, and precipitation, and how they ensure that water is continuously available for plants, animals, and humans.

#5

Why is the phosphorus cycle important even though phosphorus does not cycle through the atmosphere?

Consider how phosphorus is essential for DNA, RNA, and ATP, and how it cycles through rocks, soil, water, and living organisms without involving the atmosphere.

#6

How do human activities impact biogeochemical cycles, particularly the carbon cycle?

Reflect on activities such as burning fossil fuels and deforestation, and how they alter the natural balance of these cycles.

TERM	DEFINITION
Biogeochemical cycle	
Carbon cycle	
Photosynthesis	
Respiration	
Decomposition	
Fossil fuels	
Nitrogen cycle	

TERM	DEFINITION
Nitrogen fixation	
Ammonification	
Nitrification	
Denitrification	
Water cycle	
Evaporation	
Transpiration	

Biogeochemical Cycles

```
N V O E D S Q Q B N Y J T D C S T F L S D X O U
T R A N S P I R A T I O N U A U N Y I H X J G K
T C B F N R P S A C R A H R R I S V Y A H V U
N I I Y G G F A O X O I S B B S I N K M A I H I
I S O D B B Z U G S Y G N J O T W P L M X G N P
T W G Z E Y G K U H R G O J N E A R P O A Q I E
R V E L J O Y N C O T A V W C Z T Q B N K L W V
O N O T W F Z K G A Z K O G Y P E P S I S D Q F
G K C E E E T L P R I I E A C V R B X F G P Z O
E P H A B A Y C M C U G Q U L X C Z U I L I T S
N W E K R A P B F I U D W R E V Y K O C X G B S
F A M W Y B P H J B T R A E C L C V I A Y R K I
I T I R L G K G D C T Y L K C V L T N T C E U L
X E C D D A X D S Q Q A W K R K E A B I I S Q F
A R A D X E V A P O R A T I O N B I I O M P O U
T Q L Y P D N I T R I F I C A T I O N N W I A E
I T C J M E Z V I J J S Y T T B F J U H D R I L
O W Y T H T P H O T O S Y N T H E S I S B A D S
N D C N N I T R O G E N C Y C L E C L Y P T B L
X I L N E W K F T B C F T E U B R F P G H I O H
L F E A M B U E D E N I T R I F I C A T I O N R
M F J C F X M P K Z P O F Z M Y V Y F C O N D G
R D E C O M P O S I T I O N J B B A U U E N L E
D T B Q N Z M F G S S C G O X T Y U A L J I C C
```

Water cycle	Nitrogen fixation	Nitrogen cycle
Fossil fuels	Carbon cycle	Biogeochemical cycle
Transpiration	Evaporation	Denitrification
Nitrification	Ammonification	Decomposition
Respiration	Photosynthesis	

Biogeochemical Cycles

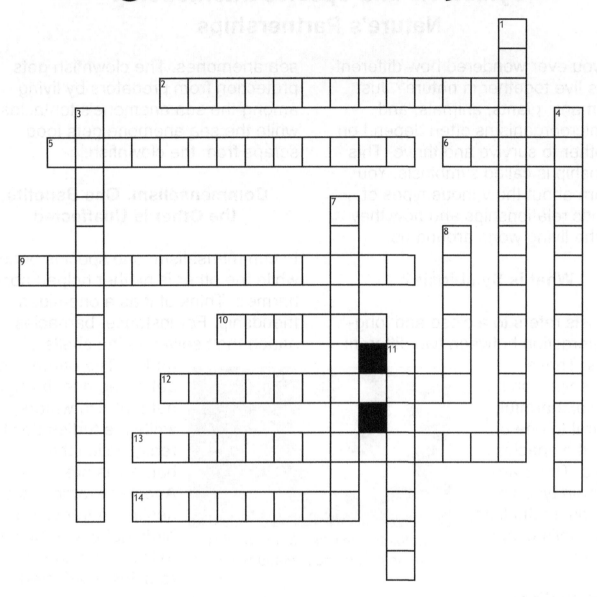

Across

2. The breakdown of dead plants and animals by decomposers like bacteria and fungi, returning essential nutrients, including carbon and nitrogen, back to the soil.

5. The process by which bacteria convert ammonium (NH4+) into nitrate (NO3-), a form of nitrogen that plants can absorb and use.

6. The continuous movement of H2O through the Earth's atmosphere, surface, and underground, involving processes like evaporation, condensation, precipitation, and transpiration. ____ cycle

9. The process by which plants use sunlight to convert carbon dioxide and water into glucose (a type of sugar) and oxygen, playing a crucial role in the carbon cycle.

10. Natural fuels such as coal and oil formed from the remains of ancient plants and animals over millions of years, which release carbon dioxide when burned. ____ fuels

12. The process by which water changes from a liquid to a gas (water vapor) due to heat from the sun, part of the water cycle.

13. The conversion of organic nitrogen (from dead plants and animals) into ammonium (NH4+) by decomposers.

14. The series of processes by which nitrogen is converted into different chemical forms and moves between the atmosphere, soil, and living organisms. ____ cycle

Down

1. The process by which bacteria convert nitrate (NO3-) back into nitrogen gas (N2), releasing it into the atmosphere and completing the nitrogen cycle.

3. The natural pathways by which essential elements like carbon, nitrogen, oxygen, and phosphorus move through the Earth's atmosphere, hydrosphere, lithosphere, and biosphere. ____ cycle

4. The process by which plants release water vapor from their leaves into the atmosphere, contributing to the water cycle.

7. The process by which living organisms, including plants and animals, convert glucose and oxygen into energy, releasing carbon dioxide back into the atmosphere.

8. The process by which carbon is exchanged between the atmosphere, oceans, soil, and living organisms, mainly through photosynthesis, respiration, decomposition, and combustion. ____ cycle

11. The process by which certain bacteria in the soil and water convert nitrogen gas (N2) from the atmosphere into ammonia (NH3), a form that plants can use. Nitrogen ____

Symbiosis and Species Interactions: Nature's Partnerships

Have you ever wondered how different species live together in nature? Just like humans, plants, animals, and even microorganisms often depend on each other to survive and thrive. This relationship is called symbiosis. You will learn about the various types of symbiotic relationships and how they affect the living world around us.

What is Symbiosis?

Symbiosis refers to a close and long-term interaction between two different species. These relationships can be beneficial, harmful, or neutral to one or both of the species involved. There are three main types of symbiosis: mutualism, commensalism, and parasitism.

Mutualism is when both species benefit from their relationship.

Mutualism: When Both Partners Benefit

In mutualism, both species involved benefit from the relationship. It's like a win-win situation. For example, bees and flowers have a mutualistic relationship. Bees get nectar from flowers, which they use to make honey. In return, bees help flowers by spreading their pollen, allowing them to reproduce. Another example is the relationship between clownfish and sea anemones. The clownfish gets protection from predators by living among the sea anemone's tentacles, while the sea anemone gets food scraps from the clownfish.

Commensalism: One Benefits, the Other is Unaffected

In commensalism, one species benefits while the other is neither helped nor harmed. Think of it as a one-sided friendship. For instance, barnacles attach themselves to the shells of turtles. The barnacles get a free ride through nutrient-rich waters, while the turtles don't really notice the barnacles are there. Another example is birds nesting in trees. The birds get a safe place to live, while the tree remains unaffected.

Parasitism: One Benefits at the Expense of the Other

Parasitism is a relationship where one species benefits while the other is harmed. The benefiting species is called the parasite, and the harmed species is the host. For example, ticks are parasites that feed on the blood of mammals, including humans. The ticks get nourishment, but the host can suffer from blood loss and diseases transmitted by the ticks. Another example is the mistletoe plant, which attaches itself to trees and shrubs to take water and nutrients, often weakening or killing the host plant.

Other Types of Species Interactions

Besides symbiosis, there are other types of interactions between species that are crucial to ecosystems.

Predation: This is when one species, the predator, hunts and eats another species, the prey. For example, lions hunt zebras for food. Predation helps control the population of prey species and can lead to evolutionary changes.

Competition: When two species compete for the same resources, such as food, water, or shelter, it's called competition. This can happen within the same species or between different species. For instance, plants in a forest compete for sunlight. Competition can limit the growth of species and affect their population sizes.

Amensalism: In this type of interaction, one species is harmed while the other remains unaffected. For example, when a large tree blocks sunlight from smaller plants below, the small plants may die, but the large tree is unaffected.

Parasitism is one organism benefits while the other is harmed.

Why Are These Interactions Important?

Understanding species interactions is essential because they shape ecosystems and affect biodiversity. Biodiversity refers to the variety of life in an area, and it's crucial for the health of our planet. Symbiotic relationships can enhance the survival and reproduction of species, making ecosystems more resilient to changes.

For example, coral reefs are incredibly diverse ecosystems because of the mutualistic relationship between coral and algae. The algae live inside the coral and provide it with food through photosynthesis, while the coral provides the algae with a protected environment and nutrients.

Symbiosis and other species interactions are fascinating aspects of biology that show how interconnected life is on Earth. By studying these relationships, you can better understand the delicate balance of ecosystems and the importance of preserving biodiversity. Think about this the next time you observe a bee pollinating a flower or a bird nesting in a tree that these tiny interactions play a big role in the web of life.

24. Symbiosis and Species Interactions
GUIDED NOTES

I. What is Symbiosis?

Define symbiosis: _____

_____

List the three main types of symbiosis:

1. _____   2._____

3. _____

II. Types of Symbiosis

Match each type of symbiosis with its definition:

_____ Mutualism   A. One species benefits, the other is harmed

_____ Commensalism   B. Both species benefit

_____ Parasitism   C. One species benefits, the other is unaffected

III. Examples of Symbiotic Relationships

Provide an example for each type of symbiosis:

1. Mutualism: _____

2. Commensalism: _____

3. Parasitism: _____

IV. Other Types of Species Interactions

List three other types of species interactions mentioned in the article:

1. _____   2._____

3. _____

V. Definitions

Define the following terms:

1. Predation: _____

_____

2. Competition: _____

_____

3. Amensalism: _____

_____

VI. True or False

_____ In mutualism, only one species benefits from the relationship.

_____ Parasitism always results in the immediate death of the host.

_____ Competition can occur between members of the same species.

_____ Biodiversity refers to the variety of life in an area.

VII. Short Answer

1. Explain why understanding species interactions is important for ecosystems:

_____

_____

2. Describe how coral reefs demonstrate a mutualistic relationship:

_____

_____

VIII. Reflection

In your own words, explain how the concept of symbiosis relates to your everyday life or the world around you:

_____

_____

_____

#1

How do mutualistic relationships benefit both species involved?

Think about the example of bees and flowers and how each species gains something essential from the other.

#2

Why is commensalism considered a one-sided friendship?

Reflect on how barnacles benefit from attaching to turtles without affecting the turtles.

#3

What are the negative impacts of parasitic relationships on the host species?

Consider the example of ticks and how they harm their hosts by feeding on their blood and possibly transmitting diseases.

#4

How does predation help control the population of prey species?

Think about how predators like lions hunting zebras can influence the number of zebras in an ecosystem.

#5

In what ways can competition between species limit their growth and affect their populations?

Consider how plants in a forest compete for sunlight and how this competition might limit the growth of some plants.

#6

Why is understanding species interactions important for preserving biodiversity?

Reflect on how symbiotic relationships contribute to the health and resilience of ecosystems, making them better able to withstand changes.

TERM	DEFINITION
Symbiosis	
Mutualism	
Commensalism	
Parasitism	
Predation	
Competition	
Amensalism	

TERM	DEFINITION
Host	
Parasite	
Ecosystem	
Biodiversity	
Photosynthesis	
Nectar	
Evolutionary changes	

Symbiosis & Species Interactions

```
Z H O S T R R E K C O M M E N S A L I S M O Q T
H E H X W M I P W N P K W T C Z P E I T L C C Y
O R X E W L X N P E A W Y O F M G P K F F A X H
Q C R C X R N U L N Q F J T L I A J C W F M Q F
N O M T Y Z Q O J M Y K J K I P L O Z U A E N E
F M W L B E D A C W H J X Y L L Y I H Z N M M V
R P B Z R C B I O D I V E R S I T Y Y X D S H O
W E T Y E O I A Z Q A A F T V B P V S V J A W L
D T S G T S H A L H N U J H P F K I M W B L O U
U I I W R Y K E V O L U T I O N A R Y I H I W T
I T R A H S D I F N V T P R E D A T I O N S I I
S I Q S X T Z D A T O I H Y N V Q W R W V M R O
T O S S H E V T T J O S O S P S N Y R O E A O N
Z N O Q O M F L L R D X T C J Q M R G D D H H A
G G Y Z E W X V G N J W O V K S U F S T Q V Z R
H X O X L G C T A C Y U S J E I T N V H U O A Y
Y L G Z V E D H A Q K N Y A V B U E P Y T Z E C
J A P A R A S I T E K K N G I Z A C S D B I Z H
Z E K M N Z R Y H U Y P T S J Q L T T S U T G A
Q S B E C O B F Q H E R H T I L I A F E H I I N
V X H D Y W Z N R M K T E X F E S R X B B Z J G
W L P A R A S I T I S M S V T O M Y A K T L Y E
I R E S Y M B I O S I S I J M L B Q S M N F P S
W S C E R D U P D C F U S X F H H F I G X Q Q E
```

Evolutionary changes	Nectar	Photosynthesis
Biodiversity	Ecosystem	Parasite
Host	Amensalism	Competition
Predation	Parasitism	Commensalism
Mutualism	Symbiosis	

Symbiosis & Species Interactions

Across

3. An interaction where one species is harmed while the other remains unaffected, such as a large tree blocking sunlight from smaller plants.

7. A community of interacting species and their physical environment, which can be shaped by symbiotic relationships.

10. When two species compete for the same resources, such as food, water, or shelter, which can limit the growth of species, like plants competing for sunlight in a forest.

11. An interaction where one species, the predator, hunts and eats another species, the prey, such as lions hunting zebras.

12. Adaptations that occur in species over time, often influenced by interactions like predation and competition, leading to survival and reproduction advantages. _____ changes

13. The variety of life in an area, which is crucial for the health of our planet and can be affected by species interactions.

14. A close and long-term interaction between two different species that can be beneficial, harmful, or neutral to one or both species involved.

Down

1. A symbiotic relationship where one species benefits at the expense of the other, like ticks feeding on the blood of mammals.

2. The species that benefits in a parasitic relationship, like a tick feeding on a mammal.

4. The process by which plants and some other organisms use sunlight to synthesize foods from carbon dioxide and water, important in mutualistic relationships like that between coral and algae.

5. A sugary fluid produced by flowers that attracts pollinators like bees, playing a key role in mutualistic relationships.

6. A type of symbiotic relationship where one species benefits while the other is neither helped nor harmed, such as barnacles attaching to turtles.

8. A type of symbiotic relationship where both species involved benefit from the interaction, like bees and flowers.

9. The species that is harmed in a parasitic relationship, like a mammal hosting ticks.

Nature's Way of Rebuilding Ecosystems

Have you ever wondered what happens to a forest after a fire or how a barren land turns into a lush meadow? This process is called ecological succession. It's nature's way of rebuilding and transforming ecosystems over time. Understanding ecological succession helps you appreciate how resilient and dynamic nature really is.

What is Ecological Succession?

A climax community is a stable community of plants and animals.

Ecological succession is the process by which the structure of a biological community evolves over time. There are two main types of succession: primary and secondary. Both types show how nature can recover and rebuild, but they start from different points.

Primary Succession: Starting from Scratch

Primary succession occurs in lifeless areas where there is no soil, such as after a volcanic eruption or on a newly formed sand dune. Here's how it works:

1. Bare Rock Stage: It all begins with bare rock. No soil, no plants, just solid rock.

2. Pioneer Species: The first to arrive are pioneer species like lichen and moss. These tough organisms can live on rocks and start breaking them down into smaller particles.

3. Soil Formation: As the pioneer species grow and die, they decompose and add organic material to the rock particles, gradually forming soil.

4. Grasses and Small Plants: Once there's enough soil, grasses and small plants start to grow, adding more organic material to the soil.

5. Shrubs and Fast-Growing Trees: Over time, shrubs and fast-growing trees like birch and aspen move in, creating more shade and further enriching the soil.

6. Climax Community: Finally, a stable community of plants and animals, known as the climax community, develops. This could be a dense forest or any other mature ecosystem depending on the region.

Secondary Succession: Rebuilding After Disturbance

Secondary succession happens in areas where an existing community has been disturbed but soil and some organisms still remain. Examples include areas after a forest fire, flood, or human activities like farming. Here's the process:

1. Disturbance: A disturbance such as a fire, storm, or human activity clears out a large portion of the ecosystem.

2. Soil Remains: Unlike primary succession, the soil remains intact, and seeds, roots, and microorganisms are often still present.

3. Pioneer Species: Fast-growing plants, such as weeds and grasses, are the first to colonize the disturbed area. They help stabilize the soil and prevent erosion.

4. Intermediate Species: Once the pioneer species establish themselves, shrubs and small trees start to grow, providing habitats for animals and other plants.

5. Climax Community: Eventually, the ecosystem reaches a stable state again, with a diverse range of plants and animals. This mature community is known as the climax community.

Why is Ecological Succession Important?

Ecological succession is vital for several reasons:

Biodiversity: It promotes biodiversity by creating new habitats and opportunities for different species to thrive.

Ecosystem Recovery: It allows ecosystems to recover from disturbances, ensuring the survival of plants and animals.

Soil Formation: In primary succession, it helps in the formation of soil, which is essential for plant growth.

Nutrient Cycling: It plays a role in nutrient cycling, helping to maintain the balance of nutrients in the soil.

Real-Life Examples of Ecological Succession

Mount St. Helens: After the volcanic eruption in 1980, scientists observed primary succession as life slowly returned to the barren landscape.

Abandoned Farmland: When farmland is abandoned, secondary succession occurs as grasses, shrubs, and trees gradually take over, turning it back into a forest over decades.

Coral Reefs: After a disturbance like a hurricane, coral reefs undergo secondary succession as new corals and marine life recolonize the damaged area.

Ecological succession is a fascinating and essential process that demonstrates nature's resilience and ability to adapt. By understanding how ecosystems rebuild and evolve, you can better appreciate the complexity and beauty of the natural world. Next time you see a forest, meadow, or even an empty lot, think about the incredible journey of ecological succession that brought it to life.

Ecological succession is how a biological community develops or recovers from different circumstances.

25. Ecological Succession
GUIDED NOTES

I. Types of Ecological Succession
List the two main types of ecological succession:

1. _____   2. _____

II. Primary Succession Stages
Order the stages of primary succession by numbering them 1-6:

_____ Shrubs and Fast-Growing Trees

_____ Bare Rock Stage

_____ Grasses and Small Plants

_____ Pioneer Species

_____ Climax Community

_____ Soil Formation

III. Secondary Succession
Fill in the blanks to describe secondary succession:

1. Starts after a _____ in an existing community

2. Unlike primary succession, _____ remains intact

3. First to colonize: _____ species (e.g., weeds and grasses)

4. Next stage: _____ species (shrubs and small trees)

5. Final stage: _____ community

IV. Importance of Ecological Succession

Match each benefit with its description:

_____ Biodiversity   A. Helps maintain balance of nutrients in soil

_____ Ecosystem Recovery   B. Creates new habitats for different species

_____ Soil Formation   C. Allows ecosystems to recover from
                                     disturbances

_____ Nutrient Cycling   D. Essential for plant growth in primary
                                     succession

V. Real-Life Examples

Identify the type of succession for each example:

1. Mount St. Helens after volcanic eruption: _____ succession

2. Abandoned farmland turning into forest: _____ succession

3. Coral reef recovering after a hurricane: _____ succession

VI. True or False

_____ Ecological succession only occurs after major natural disasters.

_____ Primary succession starts with bare rock and no soil.

_____ The climax community is the first stage of ecological succession.

_____ Secondary succession occurs faster than primary succession.

VII. In your own words, explain why understanding ecological succession is important:

_____

_____

VIII. Vocabulary

Define the following terms:

1. Ecological Succession:

_____

_____

2. Pioneer Species:

_____

_____

3. Climax Community:

_____

_____

#1

How do pioneer species contribute to the process of primary succession?

Think about how pioneer species like lichen and moss create soil from bare rock and how this helps other plants grow.

#2

What are the main differences between primary and secondary succession?

Reflect on the starting conditions of each type of succession, such as the presence or absence of soil and existing organisms.

#3

Why is biodiversity important in the context of ecological succession?

Consider how creating new habitats during succession allows different species to thrive and how this contributes to a healthy ecosystem.

#4

How does secondary succession help ecosystems recover after disturbances like fires or floods?

Think about the role of remaining soil, seeds, and roots in the quick recovery of plants and animals after a disturbance.

#5

Why is soil formation crucial in primary succession, and how does it occur?

Reflect on the role of pioneer species in breaking down rocks and adding organic material to form soil, which is essential for supporting plant life.

#6

Can you think of any real-life examples of ecological succession in your local area?

Look around your community for places where you can observe succession, such as abandoned lots, recovering forests, or areas affected by natural disasters.

TERM	DEFINITION
Ecological succession	
Primary succession	
Secondary succession	
Pioneer species	
Bare rock stage	
Soil formation	
Climax community	

TERM	DEFINITION
Disturbance	
Nutrient cycling	
Biodiversity	
Ecosystem recovery	
Intermediate species	
Mount St. Helens	
Coral reefs	

Ecological Succession

```
E C O L O G I C A L S U C C E S S I O N Y T V H
P W X X B A R E R O C K S T A G E W U Y L Z J P
E C O S Y S T E M R E C O V E R Y Z D Z Y P O U
C L L S Z C X J H T W W X U C A U C C H C R L P
M I B S Z O B Z B D Y C C X N I T E A P S I T I
O M Q V W R O C H K N C O B Z H J C D X E M P O
T A E S I A I Q V V U P W Z K G J N I W C A I N
R X J G S L B L O E T X W U B X B A S U O R X E
Q C N I R R D S F V R O D S O M B X T S N Y E E
T O K B Y E D C F Y I M T E X M L B U O D S V R
W M C B I E B N M E E Y F F D A Z J R X A U D S
J M W H L F O J P V N X J E E C M S B Z R C F P
M U F C J S U I Y R T U L H G I G R A C Y C W E
P N D T K Q L U B D C A Q M U S E B N U S E Z C
Q I P T X S A B N I Y K E V Y I U T C E U S P I
S T F B G K M I K C C A P N R Q Z M E U C S W E
W Y G R N X U X J R L V Q V V O Z A T R C I I S
P U D S F D I T Z B I X P L A Q D C A A E O V X
X D U T W A V M O H N D X Y U F N H A D S N J G
B A R F N D X I F C G B B I O D I V E R S I T Y
O H T T I N T E R M E D I A T E S P E C I E S N
P O N L Z H W G P K T Y F M L P E N S D O X V A
U S O I L F O R M A T I O N E M D W Q P N O Y H
J M O U N T S T H E L E N S X A F X A J L H L P
```

Coral reefs	Mount St Helens	Intermediate species
Ecosystem recovery	Nutrient cycling	Climax community
Soil formation	Bare rock stage	Pioneer species
Secondary succession	Primary succession	Ecological succession
Biodiversity	Disturbance	

Ecological Succession

Across

2. The first organisms to colonize a barren environment in primary succession, such as lichen and moss, which help to break down rock and form soil. ____ species

4. A type of ecological succession that occurs in areas where an existing community has been disturbed but soil and some organisms still remain. ____ succession

5. A stable and mature community of plants and animals that emerges at the end of ecological succession, representing a balanced ecosystem. ____ community

9. The initial stage of primary succession where the environment consists solely of bare rock with no soil or plants. ___ ___ stage

10. An example of primary succession observed after the 1980 volcanic eruption, where scientists studied the gradual return of life to the barren landscape. Mount St. ____

12. The process by which an ecosystem regains its structure, function, and species diversity after a disturbance, often through secondary succession. Ecosystem ____

13. An event such as a fire, flood, or human activity that disrupts an existing ecosystem, often initiating secondary succession.

14. The process during primary succession where organic material from decomposing pioneer species combines with rock particles to create soil. Soil ____

Down

1. Plants and animals that colonize an area after pioneer species during succession, often including shrubs and small trees. ____ species

3. The process by which nutrients are recycled within an ecosystem, playing a vital role in maintaining the balance of nutrients in the soil during succession. Nutrient ____

6. An example of secondary succession, where new corals and marine life recolonize a reef after disturbances like hurricanes, helping the ecosystem recover. Coral ___

7. The variety of plant and animal species within an ecosystem, which increases during ecological succession as new habitats are created.

8. The process by which the structure of a biological community evolves over time, involving stages of species colonization and ecosystem development. ____ succession

11. A type of ecological succession that occurs in lifeless areas where there is no soil, starting from bare rock or other barren environments. ____ succession

Your greatest superpower is your ability to choose one thought over another.

Choose positive thoughts over negative to live your very best life.

Our Lessons On:
TeachersPayTeachers (TPT)
https://www.teacherspayteachers.com/store/3andb

Our Workbooks On:
Amazon
https://amzn.to/3ygpsvk

Answer Keys

I. What is Biology?

Define biology in your own words:
Biology is the study of living organisms and their interactions with the environment.

II. Key Areas of Biology

Match each area of biology with its description:

1. Genetics   C. Study of how traits are passed from parents to offspring
2. Evolution   D. Process through which species change over time through natural selection
3. Ecology   A. Study of how organisms interact with each other and their environment
4. Physiology   B. Study of how living organisms function

III. The Building Blocks of Life: Cells

List three common features of cells:
1. Cell Membrane
2. Nucleus
3. Cytoplasm

IV. Genetics

Explain what genes are and their importance:
Genes are segments of DNA that determine specific traits. They are important because they explain how characteristics are inherited and why we might look similar to our parents. Genes also help us understand genetic disorders and how they can be passed down through generations.

V. Evolution

Who proposed the theory of natural selection? Charles Darwin

Briefly explain the concept of natural selection:
Natural selection is the process where organisms with favorable traits are more likely to survive and reproduce, passing these traits to future generations. Over time, this leads to changes in species and the development of new ones.

VI. Ecology

What is an ecosystem? Provide an example:
An ecosystem is a community of living organisms interacting with their physical surroundings. Examples could include forests, oceans, or deserts.

VII. Physiology

What does physiology study? Give an example:
Physiology studies how living organisms function, examining the physical and chemical processes that occur within organisms to keep them alive. An example is studying how the human heart, lungs, and brain work together to sustain life.

VIII. True or False

True   All living organisms are made up of cells.

False   DNA is stored in the cell membrane. (Correct: DNA is stored in the nucleus)

False   Ecology only studies plants and animals, not their environment. (Correct: Ecology studies organisms and their environment)

True   Evolution explains the diversity of life on Earth.

IX. Short Answer

Name two ways biology is important in the real world:
Answers may vary, but could include:
1. Developing new medical treatments
2. Enhancing crop production
3. Protecting endangered species
4. Understanding and addressing environmental issues

X. Reflection

In your own words, explain why studying biology is valuable:
Answers will vary, but should touch on points such as understanding the natural world, addressing global challenges, potential career opportunities, and gaining appreciation for the complexity of life.

What Is Biology?

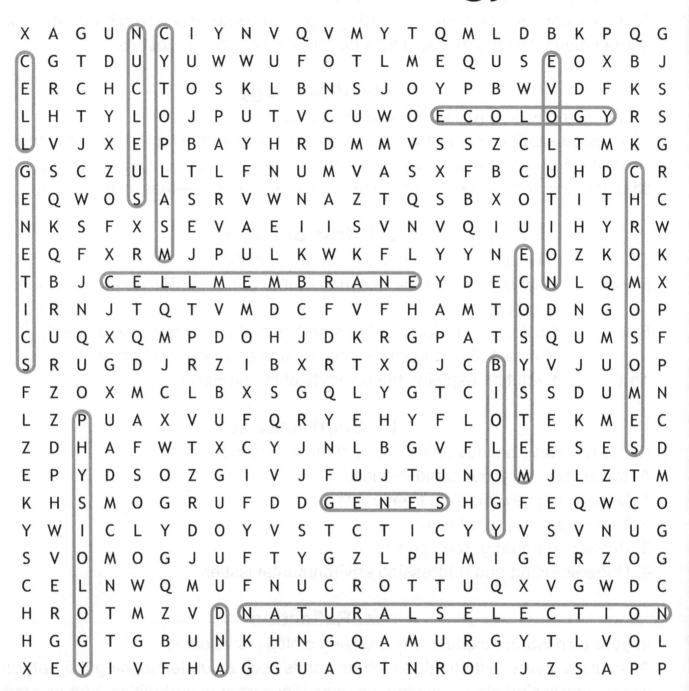

Natural selection
Ecosystem
Genes
Genetics
Cell

Cell membrane
Ecology
Chromosomes
Cytoplasm
Biology

Physiology
Evolution
DNA
Nucleus

What Is Biology?

Across

5. Segments of DNA that determine specific traits, such as eye color or height.

8. The protective barrier that surrounds a cell and controls what enters and exits the cell. Cell _____

9. The study of how traits are passed from parents to offspring through genes.

10. The study of how organisms interact with each other and their environment.

12. A community of living organisms interacting with their physical surroundings, such as a forest, ocean, or desert.

13. The process through which species of organisms change over time through natural selection.

14. The jelly-like substance inside a cell where various cell activities occur.

Down

1. The control center of a cell that contains genetic material (DNA).

2. The theory proposed by Charles Darwin that suggests organisms with favorable traits are more likely to survive and reproduce. Natural _____

3. The study of how living organisms function, including the physical and chemical processes that keep them alive.

4. Structures within cells that contain DNA and organize genetic information.

6. The molecule that carries genetic information in all living organisms.

7. The basic unit of life in all living organisms.

11. The branch of science that deals with the study of living organisms and their interactions with the environment.

I. Introduction

What is the main question this article explores?
What makes something alive? / What characteristics define life?

II. Eight Characteristics of Life

List the eight main characteristics of life discussed in the article:

1. Organization and Cells
2. Metabolism
3. Homeostasis
4. Growth and Development
5. Reproduction
6. Response to Stimuli
7. Adaptation Through Evolution
8. Energy Use

III. Details about Each Characteristic

1. Organization and Cells

Define cells: The basic units of life, like tiny factories performing vital functions
Single-celled organism example: Bacteria
Multi-celled organism example: Humans

2. Metabolism

Definition of metabolism: The set of life-sustaining chemical reactions that occur in living organisms
Two main processes of metabolism:
 a. Anabolism: building up
 b. Catabolism: breaking down

3. Homeostasis

Definition: The process of maintaining a stable internal environment
Example from the text: Body shivers when cold or sweats when hot

4. Growth and Development

Difference between growth and development:
Growth: An increase in size and number of cells
Development: The process by which organisms change and mature over time
Example of development from the text: A seed grows into a plant, or a caterpillar develops into a butterfly

5. Reproduction

Two types of reproduction:
 a. Sexual
 b. Asexual
Example of each:
 a. Humans reproduce sexually
 b. Bacteria can reproduce asexually by splitting into two identical cells

6. Response to Stimuli

Why is this ability important? It helps organisms survive and thrive

Two examples from the text:
 1. Plants grow towards light
 2. Animals move away from danger

7. Adaptation Through Evolution

Definition of evolution: Changes in the genetic makeup of a population over many generations
Example from the text: The long necks of giraffes evolved to help them reach leaves high in trees

8. Energy Use

Why do living organisms need energy? To perform their life functions
How do plants obtain energy? Through photosynthesis using sunlight
How do animals obtain energy? By eating plants or other animals

IV. True or False

Mark each statement as True (T) or False (F):

T   All living organisms are made up of cells.
F   Metabolism only involves breaking down substances.
T   Homeostasis is the ability to maintain a stable internal environment.
F   Only animals can respond to stimuli.
F   Evolution occurs within a single organism's lifetime.

V. Reflection

In your own words, explain why understanding the characteristics of life is important for studying biology:

Answers may vary, but should touch on points such as:
It helps us distinguish between living and non-living things
It provides a framework for understanding how organisms function and survive
It allows us to appreciate the complexity and diversity of life
It forms the foundation for more advanced biological concepts
It helps us understand how life sustains itself and evolves over time

Characteristics of Life

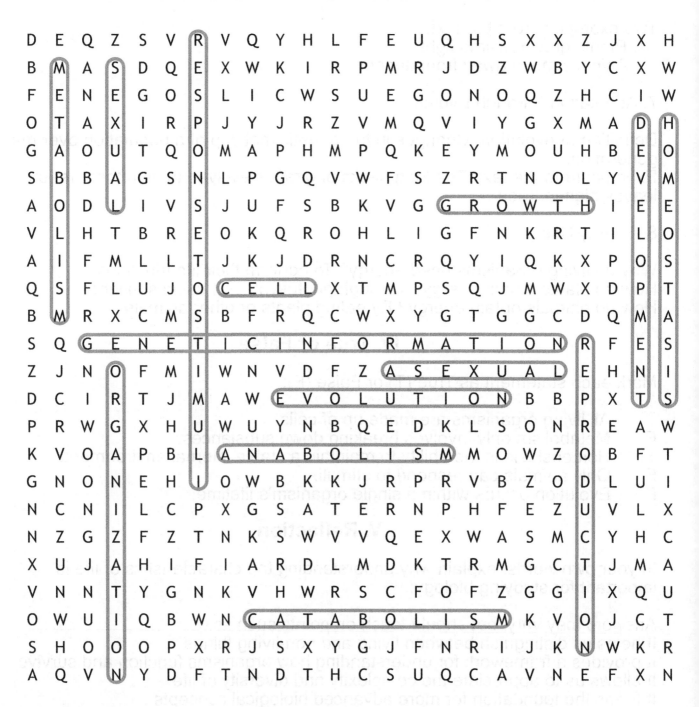

Response to stimuli   Genetic information   Evolution

Asexual   Sexual   Reproduction

Development   Growth   Homeostasis

Catabolism   Anabolism   Metabolism

Organization   Cell

Characteristics of Life

Across

4. The hereditary material that guides growth, development, and reproduction in organisms. ____ information

9. The production of offspring from a single parent, resulting in identical genetic copies. ____ reproduction

10. The increase in size and number of cells in an organism.

11. The ability of an organism to maintain a stable internal environment despite external changes.

13. The ability of organisms to react to environmental changes for survival and thriving. Response to ____

14. The process by which an organism changes and matures over time.

Down

1. The set of life-sustaining chemical reactions in organisms, including anabolism and catabolism.

2. The structured arrangement of cells into tissues, organs, and systems in multicellular organisms.

3. The biological process of creating new organisms, either sexually or asexually.

5. The process of breaking down complex molecules into simpler ones, releasing energy.

6. The process of adaptation and change in organisms over generations, leading to new traits that enhance survival.

7. The process of building up complex molecules from simpler ones, essential for growth and repair.

8. The basic unit of life, functioning like a tiny factory to perform vital functions.

12. The production of offspring through the combination of genetic material from two parents. ____ reproduction

I. The Importance of Water

List four key reasons why water is crucial for living organisms:

1. Solvent Properties (Universal solvent, dissolves many substances)
2. Temperature Regulation (High heat capacity, helps maintain stable body temperature)
3. Chemical Reactions (Many reactions occur in water, water helps break down substances)
4. Transport (Main component of blood, carries oxygen and nutrients)

II. Macromolecules

Match each macromolecule with its primary function:

Carbohydrates -   B. Main source of energy
Lipids -   D. Store energy and make up cell membranes
Proteins -   C. Building blocks of the body
Nucleic Acids -   A. Store and transmit genetic information

III. Types of Macromolecules

For each macromolecule, provide its basic building block:

Carbohydrates: Sugar molecules
Lipids: Fatty acids and glycerol
Proteins: Amino acids
Nucleic Acids: Nucleotides

IV. Water and Macromolecules Interaction

Explain how water interacts with macromolecules in these processes:

1. Hydration and Reactions: Water dissolves macromolecules so they can participate in chemical reactions. For example, enzymes (proteins) need water to function properly.

2. Transport and Nutrients: Water carries macromolecules throughout the body. Blood, which is mostly water, transports glucose (a carbohydrate) to cells for energy.

3. Cell Structure and Function: Water maintains the shape and structure of cells and their components. Proteins and lipids in cell membranes rely on water to keep cells flexible and functional.

V. Real-Life Applications

Write one way understanding water and macromolecules applies to each field:

1. Nutrition: Understanding which foods provide essential macromolecules can help in making healthier food choices and maintaining a balanced diet.

2. Medicine: Many medicines are designed to interact with macromolecules like proteins and nucleic acids, which helps in understanding how treatments work.

3. Environmental Science: Understanding water's role in biology highlights the importance of protecting water sources and preventing water pollution.

VI. True or False

True	Water makes up about 70% of the human body.
False	There are five main types of macromolecules. (Correct answer: There are four main types)
True	Proteins are made of amino acids.
True	Nucleic acids include DNA and RNA.

VII. In your own words, explain why learning about water and macromolecules is important for understanding biology:

Answers will vary, but should touch on how water and macromolecules are fundamental to life processes. Students might mention that understanding these concepts helps explain how cells function, how the body processes nutrients, or how biological systems maintain themselves. They might also note the relevance to fields like medicine, nutrition, or environmental science.

Water & Macromolecules

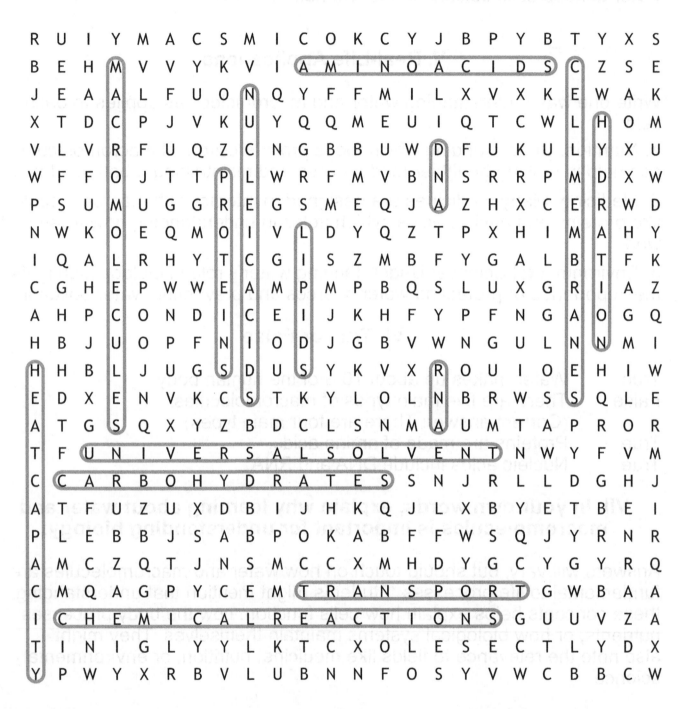

Universal solvent

Cell membranes

DNA

Lipids

Transport

Heat capacity

Hydration

Amino acids

Carbohydrates

Chemical reactions

Nucleic acids

RNA

Proteins

Macromolecules

Water & Macromolecules

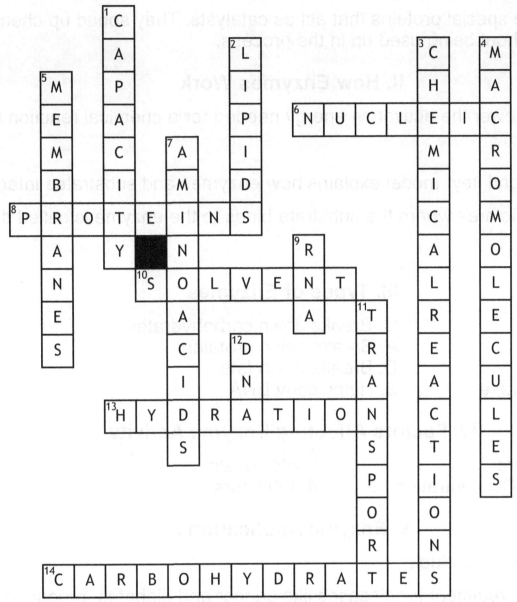

Across

6. Macromolecules that store and transmit genetic information, including DNA and RNA, made of nucleotides. ____ acids

8. Macromolecules that are the building blocks of the body, making up muscles, enzymes, and hormones, and composed of amino acids.

10. A property of water that allows it to dissolve many substances, making it essential for cells to use nutrients, minerals, and chemicals efficiently. Universal ____

13. The process of water helping to dissolve macromolecules so they can participate in chemical reactions, necessary for enzymes to function properly.

14. Macromolecules that serve as the body's main source of energy, found in foods like bread, pasta, and fruits, and made of sugar molecules.

Down

1. The ability of water to absorb and release heat slowly, helping to regulate body temperature and maintain stability. Heat ____

2. Macromolecules, also known as fats, that store energy, make up cell membranes, and provide insulation and protection for organs, made of fatty acids and glycerol.

3. Processes in the body, such as digestion and energy production, that occur in water, where water molecules help break down and transport substances. (Two words)

4. Large, complex molecules essential for life, including carbohydrates, lipids, proteins, and nucleic acids.

5. Structures made of lipids and proteins that rely on water to maintain their shape and flexibility, essential for cell function. Cell ____

7. The building blocks of proteins, with 20 different types that combine in various ways to form proteins. (Two words)

9. A type of nucleic acid involved in protein synthesis and the transmission of genetic information, composed of nucleotides.

11. The role of water in carrying oxygen and nutrients to cells and removing waste products, primarily through the blood.

12. A type of nucleic acid that contains genetic information essential for growth, development, and reproduction, composed of nucleotides.

I. What Are Enzymes?

Enzymes are special proteins that act as catalysts. They speed up chemical reactions without being used up in the process.

II. How Enzymes Work

1. Enzymes lower the activation energy needed for a chemical reaction to occur.

2. The "lock and key" model explains how enzymes and substrates interact.

3. The specific area where the substrate binds to the enzyme is called the active site.

III. Types of Enzymes

Amylase -   C. Breaks down carbohydrates
Protease -   A. Breaks down proteins
Lipase -   D. Breaks down fats
DNA Polymerase -   B. Helps copy DNA

IV. Factors Affecting Enzyme Activity

1. Temperature   2. pH Levels
3. Substrate Concentration   4. Inhibitors

V. Enzyme Applications

Possible answers include:

1. Medicine: Treatment for diseases like cancer and diabetes, production of insulin

2. Food Industry: Making cheese, bread, and yogurt

3. Household Products: Laundry detergents for breaking down stains

VI. True or False

False -   Enzymes are not used up in the chemical reactions they catalyze.

False -   Each enzyme typically works on a specific substrate.

True -   The shape of an enzyme is important for its function.

False -   Enzymes work best at specific temperatures, typically around 37°C for human enzymes.

VII. Short Answer

1. Explanation of the "Lock and Key" model: The enzyme (lock) has a specific shape that only allows certain substrates (keys) to fit into its active site. When the substrate fits, it forms an enzyme-substrate complex, allowing the reaction to occur.

2. Importance of enzymes in living organisms: Enzymes are crucial because they speed up chemical reactions necessary for life processes. Without enzymes, these reactions would be too slow to sustain life.

VIII. Reflection

Answers will vary, but should touch on points such as:

Enzymes are fundamental to understanding how living organisms function

Knowledge of enzymes helps us comprehend biological processes like digestion and growth

Enzyme applications in medicine, food industry, and household products demonstrate their practical importance in everyday life

Understanding enzymes can lead to advancements in treating diseases and developing new technologies

Enzymes

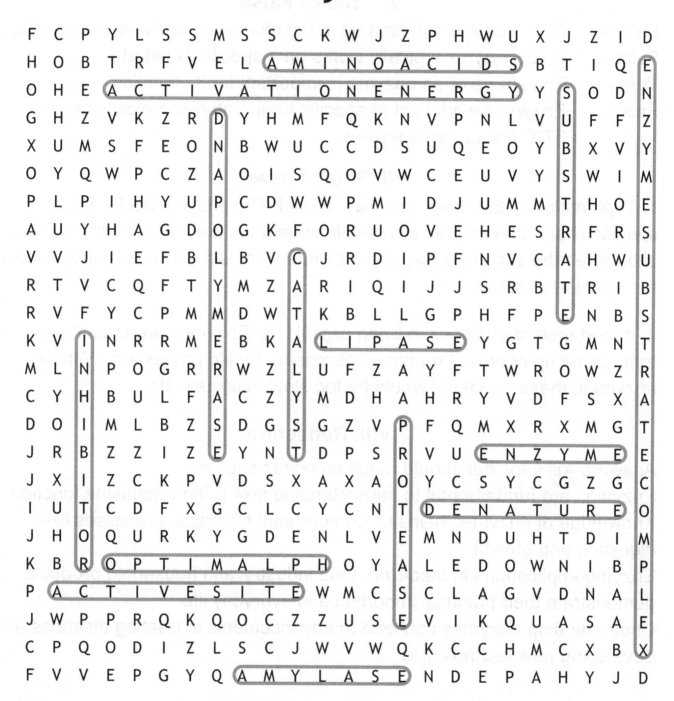

F C P Y L S S M S S C K W J Z P H W U X J Z I D
H O B T R F V E L A M I N O A C I D S B T I Q E
O H E A C T I V A T I O N E N E R G Y Y S O D N
G H Z V K Z R D Y H M F Q K N V P N L V U F F Z
X U M S F E O N B W U C C D S U Q E O Y B X V Y
O Y Q W P C Z A O I S Q O V W C E U V Y S W I M
P L P I H Y U P C D W W P M I D J U M M T H O E
A U Y H A G D O G K F O R U O V E H E S R F R S
V V J I E F B L B V C J R D I P A F N V C A H W U
R T V C Q F T Y M Z A R I Q I J J S R B T R I B
R V F Y C P M D W T K B L L G P H F P E N B S
K V I N R R M E B K A L I P A S E Y G T G M N T
M L N P O G R R W Z L U F Z A Y F T W R O W Z R
C Y H B U L F A C Z Y M D H A H R Y V D F S X A
D O I M L B Z S D G S G Z V P F Q M X R X M G T
J R B Z Z I Z E Y N T D P S R V U E N Z Y M E E
J X I Z C K P V D S X A X A O Y C S Y C G Z G C
I U T C D F X G C L C Y C N T D E N A T U R E O
J H O Q U R K Y G D E N L V E M N D U H T D I M
K B R O P T I M A L P H O Y A L E D O W N I B P
P A C T I V E S I T E W M C S C L A G V D N A L
J W P P R Q K Q O C Z Z U S E V I K Q U A S A E
C P Q O D I Z L S C J W V W Q K C C H M C X B X
F V V E P G Y Q A M Y L A S E N D E P A H Y J D

Optimal pH	DNA polymerase	Enzyme-substrate complex
Activation energy	Inhibitor	Lipase
Protease	Amylase	Denature
Active site	Substrate	Amino acids
Catalyst	Enzyme	

Enzymes

Across

2. The minimum amount of energy required to start a chemical reaction, which enzymes help to lower. ____ energy

5. The building blocks of proteins, including enzymes, which are made up of long chains of these molecules. (Two words)

8. The process by which an enzyme loses its shape and function due to factors like high temperature or extreme pH levels.

10. A special protein that acts as a catalyst to speed up chemical reactions without being consumed in the process.

11. An enzyme found in saliva that helps break down carbohydrates into simpler sugars.

12. The specific pH level at which an enzyme works best, varying from enzyme to enzyme. ____ pH

13. Enzymes that break down proteins into amino acids; found in the stomach and intestines.

14. The specific molecule that an enzyme interacts with during a chemical reaction, fitting into the enzyme's active site like a key into a lock.

Down

1. A molecule that can slow down or stop enzyme activity by blocking the active site or altering the enzyme's shape.

3. An enzyme that breaks down fats into fatty acids and glycerol, produced in the pancreas and active in the small intestine.

4. An enzyme that assists in copying DNA during cell division, ensuring genetic information is passed on accurately. DNA ____

6. The region on an enzyme where the substrate binds and the chemical reaction takes place. (Two words)

7. This forms when an enzyme binds to its substrate, facilitating the chemical reaction. Enzyme-substrate ____

9. A substance that increases the rate of a chemical reaction without being used up or altered in the process.

Chapter 4 Answer Key
GUIDED NOTES

I. Cell Theory

List the three main ideas of cell theory:

1. All living things are made of one or more cells.
2. The cell is the basic unit of life.
3. All cells come from pre-existing cells.

II. Types of Cells

There are two major categories of cells. Name them:

1. Prokaryotic cells
2. Eukaryotic cells

A. Prokaryotic Cells

List three key features of prokaryotic cells:

1. No nucleus
2. Simple structure (lack many specialized structures or organelles)
3. Small size

B. Eukaryotic Cells

List three important characteristics of eukaryotic cells:

1. Have a nucleus
2. Contain organelles (specialized structures)
3. Larger size (compared to prokaryotic cells)

III. Specialized Cells

Match each specialized cell type with its function:

Red blood cells   C. Carry oxygen in the body

Nerve cells   A. Transmit signals in the body

Muscle cells   B. Enable movement

Plant cells   D. Make their own food through photosynthesis

IV. Cell Structures

Name two structures found in plant cells that are not typically found in animal cells:

1. Cell wall   2. Chloroplasts

V. True or False

Mark each statement as True (T) or False (F):

T   All living things are made of one or more cells.
F   Prokaryotic cells have a nucleus.
T   Eukaryotic cells can form multicellular organisms.
T   All cells come from pre-existing cells.

VI. Short Answer

1. Explain why cells are considered the basic unit of life:
   Cells are considered the basic unit of life because they are the smallest structures that can carry out all the functions necessary for an organism to survive. They perform all essential life processes such as growth, reproduction, and responding to the environment.

2. Describe one way that studying cells can benefit society:
   Studying cells can benefit society in several ways, such as:
   Understanding diseases at a cellular level, leading to new treatments
   Developing new medicines
   Improving agricultural practices
   Advancing biotechnology and genetic engineering

VII. Reflection

In your own words, explain why understanding cell theory and different types of cells is important for your science education:
   (Answers will vary, but should touch on ideas such as:)
   Understanding cell theory and different types of cells is crucial for science education because it provides a foundation for understanding all living organisms. It helps explain how life functions at its most basic level, which is essential for further study in biology, medicine, and related fields. This knowledge allows us to comprehend complex biological processes, diseases, and the interconnectedness of all life forms.

Cell Theory & Types Of Cells

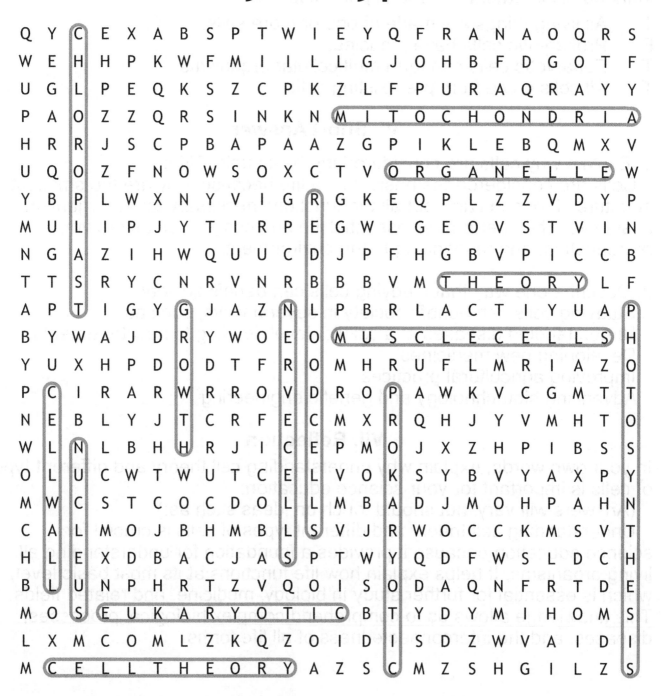

Muscle cells

Cell theory

Cell wall

Organelle

Prokaryotic

Nerve cells

Growth

Chloroplast

Nucleus

theory

Red blood cells

Photosynthesis

Mitochondria

Eukaryotic

Cell Theory & Types Of Cells

Across
6. A rigid structure found in plant cells that provides support and protection. (Two words)

7. Cells that transmit signals throughout the body, allowing for communication between the brain and other parts of the body. ____ cells

10. The control center of a eukaryotic cell that contains the cell's genetic material (DNA).

11. Organelles in eukaryotic cells that produce energy through cellular respiration.

13. An organelle found in plant cells that carries out photosynthesis, converting light energy into chemical energy.

14. The process by which chloroplasts in plant cells convert sunlight, carbon dioxide, and water into glucose and oxygen.

Down
1. Cells that contract and relax to enable movement and support body functions. ____ cells

2. A complex cell with a nucleus and organelles, found in plants, animals, fungi, and protists. ____ cell

3. The principle that all living things are made of cells, cells are the basic unit of life, and new cells come from pre-existing cells. Cell ____

4. The smallest unit of life that can perform all life processes; cells can be unicellular or multicellular.

5. Specialized cells that carry oxygen from the lungs to the rest of the body and return carbon dioxide to the lungs. __ ___ cells

8. A simple, small cell without a nucleus, typically found in bacteria and archaea. ____ cell

9. Specialized structures within a cell that perform specific functions, such as mitochondria and chloroplasts.

12. The process by which organisms increase in size and number of cells, largely driven by cell division and replication.

I. Introduction

Cells are the basic units of life and contain smaller structures called organelles.

II. Cell Organelles and Their Functions

Nucleus -   C
Mitochondria -   A
Ribosomes -   E
Endoplasmic Reticulum -   F
Golgi Apparatus -   D
Lysosomes -   B
Vacuoles -   G

III. Organelle Details

1. Nucleus: Often called the brain of the cell, it contains DNA which holds instructions for making proteins.

2. Mitochondria: Known as the powerhouses of the cell because they generate energy that the cell can use.

3. Ribosomes: These can be found floating freely in the cytoplasm or attached to the endoplasmic reticulum.

4. Endoplasmic Reticulum (ER):
   Rough ER: Covered with ribosomes and helps in production and packaging of proteins.

Smooth ER: Involved in making lipids and breaking down toxic substances.

5. Golgi Apparatus: Ensures that cellular products get to where they need to go, similar to a postal service.

6. Lysosomes: Contain enzymes that digest unwanted substances, acting like the cell's janitors.

7. Vacuoles: In plant cells, they are large and central, while in animal cells, they are smaller.

8. Cytoplasm: The jelly-like substance that fills the inside of the cell, mostly made of water.

IV. True or False

False
True
False
True
False

V. Short Answer

(Answers may vary, but should include ideas such as):
Understanding cell organelles is important for comprehending life at the microscopic level because it helps us appreciate the complexity of cells, which are the building blocks of all living things. Knowing the functions of different organelles allows us to understand how cells carry out vital processes like energy production, protein synthesis, and waste management. This knowledge forms the foundation for understanding more complex biological systems and processes.

Cell Organelles & Functions

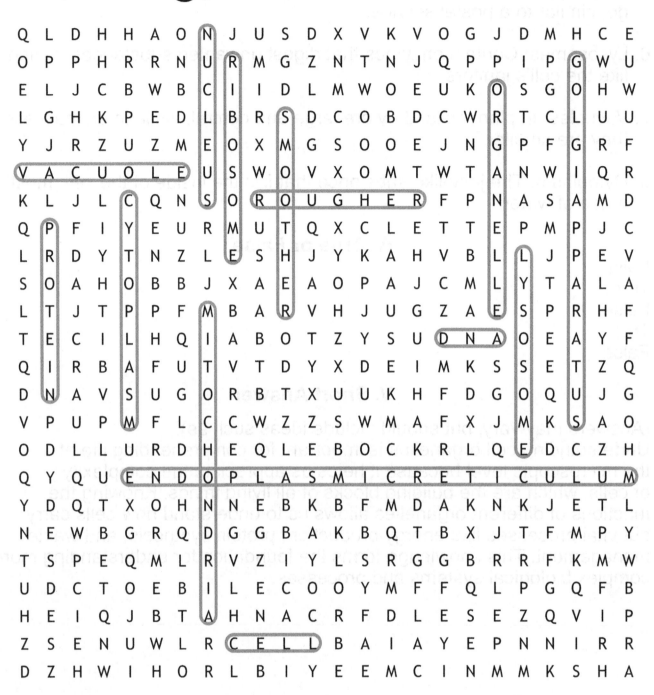

```
Q L D H H A O N J U S D X V K V O G J D M H C E
O P P H R R N U R M G Z N T N J Q P P I P G W U
E L J C B W B C I I D L M W O E U K O S G O H H
L G H K P E D L B R S D C O B D C W R T C L U U
Y J R Z U Z M E O X M G S O O E J N G P F G R F
V A C U O L E U S W O V X O M T W T A N W I Q R
K L J L C Q N S O R O U G H E R F P N A S A M D
Q P F I Y E U R M U T Q X C L E T T E P M P J C
L R D Y T N Z L E S H J Y K A H V B L J P E V
S O A H O B B J X A E A O P A J C M L Y T A L A
L T J T P P F M B A R V H J U G Z A E S P R H F
T E C I L H Q I A B O T Z Y S U D N A O E A Y F
Q I R B A F U T V T D Y X D E I M K S S E T Z Q
D N A V S U G O R B T X U U K H F D G O Q U J G
V P U P M F L C C W Z Z S W M A F X J M K S A O
O D L L U R D H E Q L E B O C K R L Q E D C Z H
Q Y Q U E N D O P L A S M I C R E T I C U L U M
Y D Q T X O H N N E B K B F M D A K N K J E T L
N E W B G R Q D G G B A K B Q T B X J T F M P Y
T S P E Q M L R V Z I Y L S R G G B R R F K M W
U D C T O E B I L E C O O Y M F F Q L P G Q F B
H E I Q J B T A H N A C R F D L E S E Z Q V I P
Z S E N U W L R C E L L B A I A Y E P N N I R R
D Z H W I H O R L B I Y E E M C I N M M K S H A
```

Golgi apparatus	Smooth ER	Rough ER
Endoplasmic reticulum	Protein	Cytoplasm
Vacuole	Lysosome	Ribosome
Mitochondria	DNA	Nucleus
Organelle	Cell	

Cell Organelles & Functions

Across

4. Deoxyribonucleic acid, the molecule that carries the genetic instructions for life, found within the nucleus of a cell.

8. The cleanup crew of the cell, containing enzymes that break down waste materials and cellular debris.

9. The part of the ER studded with ribosomes, involved in protein production and packaging. ____ endoplasmic reticulum

10. The basic unit of life, containing various organelles that each have specific functions necessary for its survival and operation.

12. The cell's shipping department, which modifies, sorts, and packages proteins and lipids for distribution within or outside the cell. ____ apparatus

13. A tiny structure where proteins are synthesized; these can be free in the cytoplasm or attached to the endoplasmic reticulum.

14. The part of the ER that lacks ribosomes and is involved in lipid production and detoxification processes. ____ endoplasmic reticulum

Down

1. A storage organelle that holds water, nutrients, and waste products; large and central in plant cells, smaller in animal cells.

2. Known as the powerhouses of the cell, these organelles generate energy by converting nutrients into usable cellular energy.

3. A network of membranous tubules within the cell, involved in the production, folding, and transport of proteins (rough ER) and lipids (smooth ER). ____ reticulum

5. A specialized structure within a cell that performs a distinct function, much like different departments in a factory.

6. A molecule produced by ribosomes that is essential for building cell structures and carrying out various cellular functions.

7. The control center of the cell, containing DNA, which holds the genetic instructions for making proteins and managing cell activities.

11. The jelly-like substance inside the cell that surrounds organelles and provides a medium for their movement and interaction.

I. What is the Cell Cycle?

Define the cell cycle in your own words:
A series of events that cells go through as they grow and divide

Main purpose of the cell cycle: To create two identical daughter cells from one parent cell

II. The Stages of the Cell Cycle

List the four main stages of the cell cycle:
1. G1 (Gap 1)
2. S (Synthesis)
3. G2 (Gap 2)
4. M (Mitosis)

III. Matching

Match each phase with its description:

G1 Phase -   C. Cell grows and prepares for DNA replication
S Phase -   A. DNA duplication occurs
G2 Phase -   D. Cell produces proteins necessary for cell division
M Phase -   B. Cell division takes place

IV. Fill in the Blanks

1. During the S phase, the cell duplicates its DNA.
2. The M phase is also known as mitosis.
3. Mitosis has its own stages: prophase, metaphase, anaphase, and telophase.
4. The process where the entire cell divides is called cytokinesis.

V. Short Answer

Explain the role of checkpoints in the cell cycle:
Checkpoints act as quality control, ensuring the cell is ready to move to the next stage. They check for errors and can pause the cycle to fix issues or trigger cell death if necessary. Checkpoints help prevent diseases like cancer by controlling cell division.

VI. True or False

False   The cell cycle is only important for growth and development.
True   Checkpoints in the cell cycle help prevent diseases like cancer.
True   All the cells in your body originated from a single fertilized egg cell.
False   The G1 phase occurs after DNA replication.

VII. Importance of the Cell Cycle

List three reasons why the cell cycle is important:
1. Growth and Development
2. Tissue Repair and Regeneration
3. Maintenance of Tissues

VIII. In your own words, explain how the cell cycle relates to tissue repair and regeneration:

The cell cycle is crucial for tissue repair and regeneration because it allows the body to produce new cells to replace damaged or injured ones. When you get a cut or injury, the cell cycle activates to create new cells, helping the wound heal and restoring the damaged tissue to its original state.

IX. Reflection

How does understanding the cell cycle help you appreciate your body's functions? (2-3 sentences)
Answers may vary, but should touch on the following points:
Understanding the cell cycle helps appreciate the complexity of bodily processes
It explains how the body grows, heals, and maintains itself
It illustrates the constant activity happening at a cellular level to keep us healthy

Cell Cycle

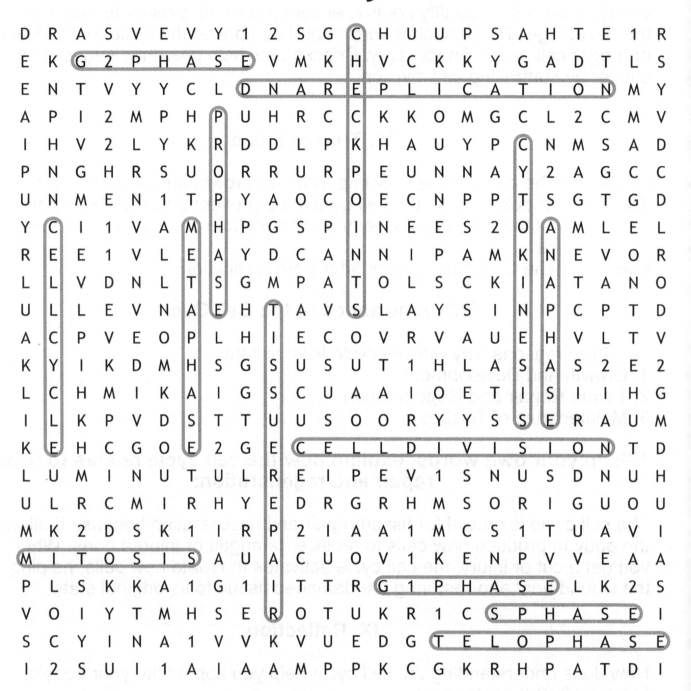

Tissue repair

Checkpoints

Anaphase

Mitosis

G1 Phase

Cell division

Cytokinesis

Metaphase

G2 Phase

Cell cycle

DNA replication

Telophase

Prophase

S Phase

Cell Cycle

Across
2. Built-in mechanisms in the cell cycle that ensure each stage is completed correctly before the cell moves to the next stage.

8. The process of copying the cell's DNA during the S phase, ensuring each daughter cell gets an identical set of genetic material. DNA ____

11. The overall process where a single cell divides to form two new, identical daughter cells. Cell ____

12. The stage of mitosis where nuclear membranes start to form around each set of chromosomes, and the cell begins to split.

13. A series of events that cells go through as they grow and divide, ensuring the production of two identical daughter cells from one parent cell. (Two words)

14. The stage of the cell cycle where the cell duplicates its DNA, ensuring each daughter cell receives a complete set of genetic instructions. _ ____

Down
1. The final part of cell division where the cytoplasm divides, resulting in two separate daughter cells.

3. The process where the cell cycle produces new cells to replace damaged or old cells, aiding in the healing of injuries. Tissue ____

4. The stage after DNA replication, where the cell continues to grow and produces proteins necessary for cell division. __ ____

5. The first stage of mitosis where the chromosomes condense, and the nuclear envelope begins to break down.

6. The stage of mitosis where sister chromatids are pulled apart to opposite ends of the cell.

7. The first stage of the cell cycle, where the cell grows and carries out normal functions while preparing for DNA replication. __ ____

9. The stage of mitosis where chromosomes align in the center of the cell, ensuring equal separation to each daughter cell.

10. The stage where the cell's nucleus and then the entire cell divide, resulting in two identical daughter cells.

I. What is Photosynthesis?

Define photosynthesis in your own words:

Photosynthesis is a process used by plants, algae, and some bacteria to convert light energy from the sun into chemical energy stored as glucose.

Break down the word "photosynthesis":

1. "Photo" means: light

2. "Synthesis" means: putting together

II. Ingredients for Photosynthesis

List the four main ingredients needed for photosynthesis:

1. Sunlight

2. Water (H_2O)

3. Carbon Dioxide (CO_2)

4. Chlorophyll

III. The Photosynthesis Equation

Fill in the blanks in the photosynthesis equation:

$$6CO_2 + 6H_2O \rightarrow C_6H_{12}O_6 + 6O_2$$

IV. Two Stages of Photosynthesis

Match each stage with its description:

Light-Dependent Reactions   B. Splits water molecules and stores energy in ATP and NADPH

Calvin Cycle   A. Converts carbon dioxide into glucose

V. Importance of Photosynthesis

List four reasons why photosynthesis is important:

1. Provides food for plants

2. Produces oxygen for organisms to breathe

3. Supports ecosystems by forming the base of the food chain

4. Regulates atmospheric gases (absorbs CO_2, releases O_2)

VI. Photosynthesis in Daily Life

Explain how photosynthesis affects your daily life:
Possible answer: Photosynthesis affects my daily life by providing the food I eat, the oxygen I breathe, and even contributing to the fossil fuels used for energy. It also helps maintain a balanced environment by regulating atmospheric gases.

VII. True or False

False Photosynthesis only occurs in plants.
True The Amazon rainforest produces about 20% of the world's oxygen.
False Fossil fuels are unrelated to photosynthesis.

VIII. Fun Facts

Write two interesting facts about photosynthesis that you learned:

1. Some plants can perform photosynthesis underwater, using dissolved carbon dioxide.
2. Algae in the oceans perform more photosynthesis than all the land plants combined.

IX. In your own words, explain why learning about photosynthesis is important:

Possible answer: Learning about photosynthesis is important because it helps us understand how life on Earth is sustained. It explains how plants produce food and oxygen, which are essential for most life forms. Understanding photosynthesis also helps us appreciate the interconnectedness of ecosystems and the importance of plants in maintaining a balanced environment.

Photosynthesis

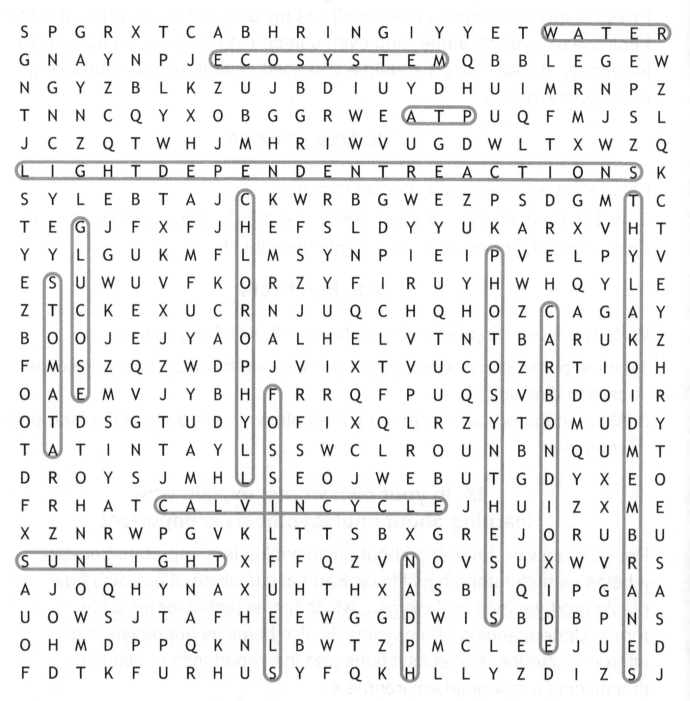

Fossil fuels

Calvin cycle

ATP

Carbon dioxide

Glucose

Ecosystem

Light-dependent reactions

Thylakoid membranes

Water

Photosynthesis

Stomata

NADPH

Chlorophyll

Sunlight

Photosynthesis

Across

3. An essential ingredient for photosynthesis, absorbed by plant roots from the soil.

7. Tiny openings on the surface of leaves that allow for the exchange of gases, including the intake of carbon dioxide and release of oxygen.

10. Structures within the chloroplasts where the light-dependent reactions of photosynthesis occur. ____ membranes

11. The primary energy source for photosynthesis, providing the light energy needed to drive the process.

13. The process by which plants, algae, and some bacteria convert light energy from the sun into chemical energy stored in glucose.

14. The first stage of photosynthesis, occurring in the thylakoid membranes, where sunlight excites electrons to split water molecules, releasing oxygen and storing energy in ATP and NADPH. ____ ____ reactions

Down

1. A gas taken from the air by plants through tiny openings on the leaves called stomata, used in the photosynthesis process. (Two words)

2. The green pigment in plant leaves that captures sunlight and is crucial for converting light energy into chemical energy.

4. Energy sources like coal and oil, formed from the remains of ancient plants that stored energy from photosynthesis millions of years ago. (Two words)

5. The second stage of photosynthesis, occurring in the stroma of the chloroplasts, where ATP and NADPH are used to convert carbon dioxide into glucose; also known as the light-independent reactions. ____ cycle

6. A community of living organisms and their physical environment, where photosynthesis supports the food chain by providing energy and oxygen.

8. An energy-carrying molecule produced during the light-dependent reactions, used in the Calvin cycle to help convert carbon dioxide into glucose.

9. An energy-rich molecule produced during the light-dependent reactions, used alongside ATP in the Calvin cycle to synthesize glucose.

12. A type of sugar produced during photosynthesis that plants use as food to grow, reproduce, and carry out life functions.

I. What is Cellular Respiration?

Define cellular respiration in your own words:
Cellular respiration is the process by which cells convert glucose (sugar) into ATP (energy) that the cell can use.

What does ATP stand for, and what is its role in the cell?
ATP stands for Adenosine Triphosphate. It serves as the energy currency of the cell, powering various cellular activities and processes.

II. The Three Stages of Cellular Respiration

List the three main stages of cellular respiration:
1. Glycolysis
2. Krebs Cycle
3. Electron Transport Chain (ETC)

III. Stage 1: Glycolysis

1. Where does glycolysis occur in the cell?
   In the cytoplasm of the cell

2. What does the word "glycolysis" mean?
   Sugar splitting

3. True or False: Glycolysis requires oxygen.
   False

IV. Stage 2: The Krebs Cycle

1. Where does the Krebs cycle take place?
   In the mitochondria

2. What is another name for the Krebs cycle?
   Citric acid cycle

3. Name two important molecules produced during the Krebs cycle:
   a) NADH
   b) FADH2

V. Stage 3: Electron Transport Chain (ETC)

1. Where does the ETC occur in the cell?
   In the inner membrane of the mitochondria

2. What is the main function of the ETC?
   To produce the majority of ATP

3. How is ATP produced in this stage?
   High-energy electrons are passed along a series of proteins, creating a hydrogen ion gradient. As hydrogen ions flow back across the membrane through ATP synthase, ATP is generated.

VI. Importance of Cellular Respiration

List three reasons why cellular respiration is important for living organisms:
1. Provides energy for muscle contraction
2. Supplies energy for brain function
3. Powers all biological processes in the body

VII. Key Terms

Match each term with its correct definition:

Glucose   D. The type of sugar broken down in cellular respiration
Mitochondria   C. Where the Krebs cycle and ETC occur
ATP   A. The energy currency of the cell
Glycolysis   B. The first stage of cellular respiration

VIII. Reflection

In your own words, explain how understanding cellular respiration helps you appreciate the complexity of living organisms:
Answers will vary, but should reflect an understanding of how cellular respiration demonstrates the intricate processes occurring at the cellular level to sustain life. Students might mention the multiple stages involved, the efficiency of energy production, or how this process connects to other body systems (e.g., respiratory, digestive).

Cellular Respiration

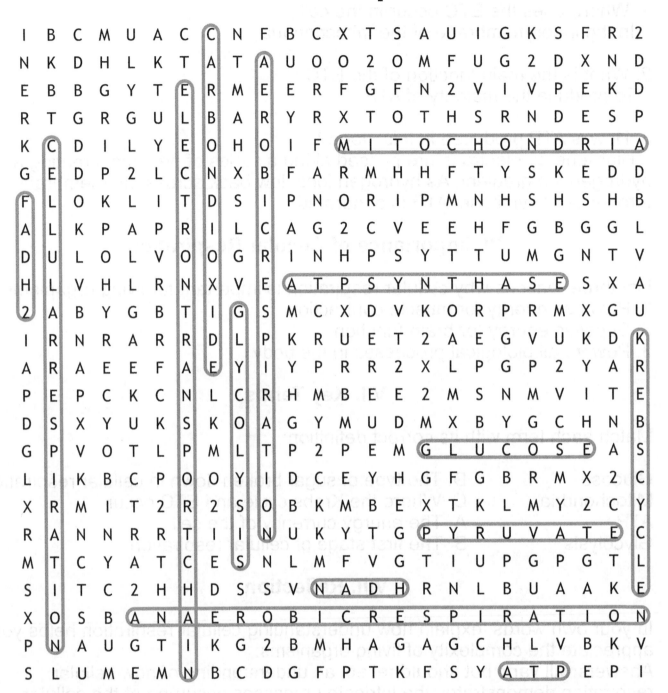

Aerobic respiration

Anaerobic respiration

FADH2

NADH

ATP

ATP synthase

Cellular respiration

Krebs cycle

Pyruvate

Glucose

Electron transport chain

Carbon dioxide

Mitochondria

Glycolysis

Cellular Respiration

Across
3. A type of sugar that is a primary energy source for cells, broken down during cellular respiration to produce ATP.
6. A compound formed from the splitting of glucose during glycolysis, which then enters the Krebs cycle.
7. A waste product released during the Krebs cycle, exhaled by the lungs during breathing. (Two words)
8. The first stage of cellular respiration, occurring in the cytoplasm, where glucose is split into two molecules of pyruvate, producing a small amount of ATP and NADH.
9. A molecule that carries high-energy electrons produced during glycolysis and the Krebs cycle to the Electron Transport Chain.
12. The process by which cells convert glucose into adenosine triphosphate (ATP), providing energy for all cellular activities. Cellular ____
13. The organelles in the cell known as the "powerhouses," where the Krebs cycle and Electron Transport Chain occur.
14. A protein in the inner mitochondrial membrane that uses the flow of hydrogen ions to generate ATP from ADP. ATP ____

Down
1. A type of respiration that does not require oxygen, such as glycolysis. ____ respiration
2. The final stage of cellular respiration, taking place in the inner mitochondrial membrane, where most ATP is produced through the movement of high-energy electrons and hydrogen ions. ____ ____ chain
4. The second stage of cellular respiration, occurring in the mitochondria, where pyruvate is broken down to produce carbon dioxide, NADH, FADH2, and a small amount of ATP.
5. A type of respiration that requires oxygen, involving the Krebs cycle and Electron Transport Chain. ____ respiration
10. The energy currency of the cell, used to power various functions within the body.
11. A molecule similar to NADH that carries high-energy electrons to the Electron Transport Chain.

I. Types of Cellular Respiration

1. Aerobic respiration
2. Anaerobic respiration

II. Aerobic Respiration

1. oxygen
2. mitochondria
3. a. Glycolysis
   b. Krebs Cycle
   c. Electron Transport Chain

III. Steps of Aerobic Respiration

1. B
2. A
3. C

IV. Anaerobic Respiration

1. Lactic Acid Fermentation
2. Alcoholic Fermentation

V. Compare and Contrast

Feature	Aerobic Respiration	Anaerobic Respiration
Oxygen requirement	Requires oxygen	Does not require oxygen
Location in the cell	Mitochondria	Cytoplasm
ATP yield per glucose	Up to 38 ATP	2 ATP

VI. True or False

False
True
False
True

VII. Fill in the Blanks

1. adenosine triphosphate
2. lactic acid buildup
3. oxygen

VIII. Short Answer

Possible answer: Both aerobic and anaerobic respiration are important for the human body because they provide energy in different situations. Aerobic respiration is more efficient and is used when oxygen is available, providing energy for most of our daily activities. Anaerobic respiration, while less efficient, is crucial during intense physical activities when oxygen supply is limited, allowing muscles to continue functioning and providing quick bursts of energy.

IX. In your own words

Possible answer: Learning about cellular respiration is important for understanding how our bodies function because it explains how we get energy from the food we eat. This knowledge helps us understand why we need to breathe, why exercise affects our bodies the way it does, and how our diet impacts our energy levels. It also provides a foundation for understanding many biological processes and health-related topics.

Aerobic & Anaerobic Respiration

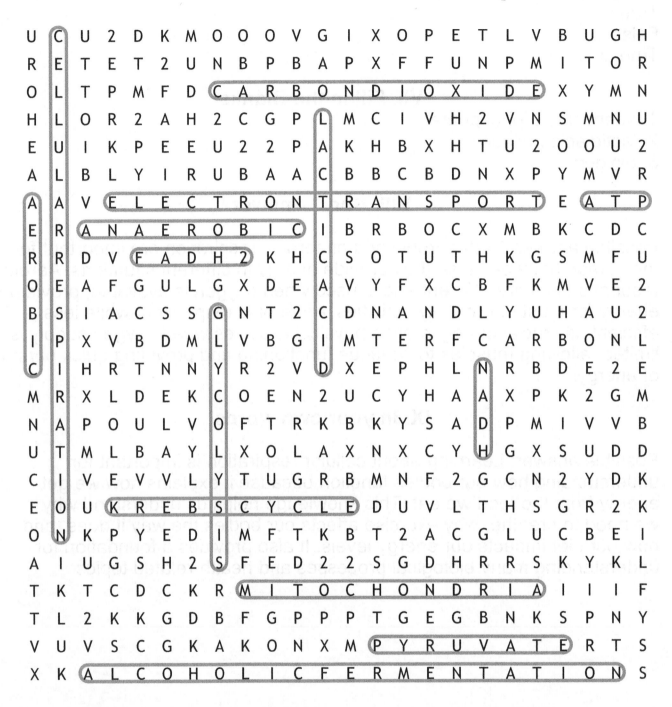

Carbon dioxide

Cellular respiration

FADH2

Glycolysis

Aerobic

Alcoholic fermentation

Pyruvate

NADH

Mitochondria

ATP

Krebs Cycle

Lactic acid

Electron transport

Anaerobic

Aerobic & Anaerobic Respiration

Across
2. A three-carbon molecule produced during glycolysis from the breakdown of glucose, which can be further processed in respiration.

4. The process by which cells convert food into energy, stored in the form of ATP, to power various cellular activities. Cellular ____

5. The first step in cellular respiration where one molecule of glucose is broken down into two molecules of pyruvate, producing a small amount of ATP and NADH.

7. A type of anaerobic respiration in muscle cells where pyruvate is converted into lactic acid, regenerating NAD+ and allowing glycolysis to continue. ___ ___ fermentation

9. A type of cellular respiration that does not require oxygen, occurring in the cytoplasm, and used during low oxygen conditions. ____ respiration

11. A type of cellular respiration that requires oxygen to produce energy, mainly occurring in the mitochondria. ____ respiration

14. Organelles in cells known as the powerhouse, where aerobic respiration and most ATP production occur.

Down
1. A sequence of proteins in the inner mitochondrial membrane that uses electrons from NADH and FADH2 to produce a significant amount of ATP. ____ ____ chain

3. A series of chemical reactions in the mitochondria that further break down pyruvate, producing NADH, FADH2, and carbon dioxide. ____ Cycle

6. A type of anaerobic respiration in yeast and some bacteria where pyruvate is converted into ethanol and carbon dioxide, regenerating NAD+. ____ fermentation

8. The primary energy-carrying molecule in cells, used to fuel a wide range of cellular functions.

10. A waste product released during the Krebs cycle and alcoholic fermentation, expelled from the body during exhalation. ____ dioxide

12. An energy-carrying molecule produced during glycolysis and the Krebs cycle, used in the electron transport chain to generate ATP.

13. Another energy-carrying molecule produced during the Krebs cycle, also used in the electron transport chain to generate ATP.

I. What is Fermentation?

Define fermentation in your own words:

Fermentation is a natural process where microorganisms like bacteria and yeast convert sugars into other substances, such as acids, gases, or alcohol, usually in the absence of oxygen.

II. Types of Fermentation

List and briefly describe the two main types of fermentation:

1. Alcoholic Fermentation: Carried out by yeast, produces alcohol and carbon dioxide from sugars.

2. Lactic Acid Fermentation: Performed by certain bacteria, converts sugars into lactic acid.

III. The Science of Fermentation

Match each equation to the correct type of fermentation:

$C_6H_{12}O_6 \rightarrow 2C_2H_5OH + 2CO_2$ B. Alcoholic Fermentation
$C_6H_{12}O_6 \rightarrow 2C_3H_6O_3$ A. Lactic Acid Fermentation

IV. Importance of Fermentation

Explain three reasons why fermentation is important:

1. Food Preservation: Fermentation inhibits the growth of harmful bacteria, keeping food safe to eat for longer periods.

2. Nutritional Benefits: Fermented foods contain probiotics that are good for gut health and boost the immune system.

3. Energy Production: Fermentation helps muscles produce energy during intense exercise when oxygen is low.

V. Fermented Foods

Name four common foods or beverages that rely on fermentation:

1. Bread   2. Yogurt   3. Pickles   4. Cheese

(Note: Wine, beer, sauerkraut, and kimchi are also acceptable answers)

VI. True or False

False Fermentation only occurs in the presence of oxygen.

True Yeast is responsible for alcoholic fermentation.

True Lactic acid fermentation gives yogurt its tangy taste.

False Fermentation cannot occur in the human body.

VII. Fill in the Blanks

1. Fermentation is carried out by microorganisms like bacteria and yeast.

2. During intense exercise, muscles may switch to lactic acid fermentation when oxygen is low.

3. The carbon dioxide produced during fermentation helps bread rise.

4. Fermented foods are loaded with beneficial bacteria known as probiotics.

VIII. Short Answer

Explain how fermentation was used for food preservation before refrigeration:
Fermentation produces acids and alcohols that inhibit the growth of harmful bacteria. This keeps the food safe to eat for longer periods, allowing people to preserve food without refrigeration.

IX. In your own words, explain why learning about fermentation is important for high school students:

(Answers will vary, but may include:)
Learning about fermentation helps students understand important biological processes, the science behind common foods, and the role of microorganisms in our daily lives. It connects chemistry, biology, and practical applications, demonstrating how scientific concepts apply to real-world situations. Understanding fermentation can also promote healthier food choices and appreciation for traditional food preparation methods.

Fermentation

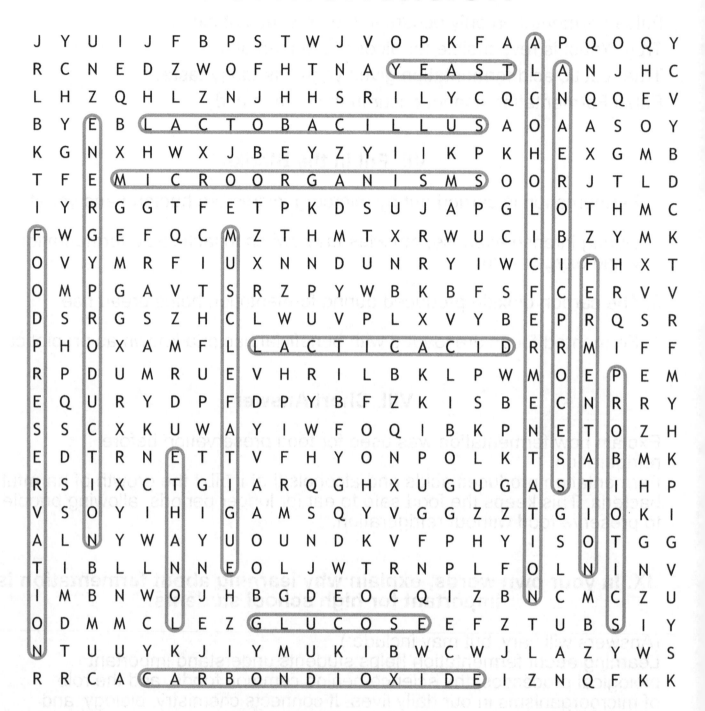

Lactic acid

Food preservation

Glucose

Ethanol

Microorganisms

Muscle fatigue

Alcoholic fermentation

Probiotics

Lactobacillus

Fermentation

Energy production

Anaerobic process

Carbon dioxide

Yeast

Fermentation

Across

2. The "burn" felt in muscles during intense exercise, caused by lactic acid fermentation when muscles run out of oxygen. Muscle ____
3. A type of alcohol produced during alcoholic fermentation.
8. A type of fermentation where bacteria convert sugars into lactic acid, found in foods like yogurt and sauerkraut and also occurs in muscles during intense exercise. ____ ____ fermentation
10. A type of sugar that is broken down during fermentation to produce energy.
12. The process of keeping food safe to eat for longer periods, often achieved through fermentation by producing acids and alcohols that inhibit harmful bacteria. Food ____
13. A type of bacteria involved in lactic acid fermentation, producing lactic acid from sugars.
14. Beneficial bacteria found in fermented foods that aid digestion and boost the immune system.

Down

1. A gas produced during fermentation that helps bread rise and gives beverages their fizz. (Two words)
4. The process by which cells generate energy, including through fermentation when oxygen levels are low. Energy ____
5. A type of fermentation where yeast converts sugars into alcohol and carbon dioxide, used in making beverages like wine and beer. ____ fermentation
6. Tiny living organisms like bacteria and yeast that are involved in processes like fermentation.
7. A natural process where microorganisms like bacteria and yeast convert sugars into substances such as acids, gases, or alcohol, often in the absence of oxygen.
9. A process that occurs in the absence of oxygen, such as fermentation. ____ process
11. A type of fungus used in alcoholic fermentation to convert sugars into alcohol and carbon dioxide.

Chapter 11 Answer Key

GUIDED NOTES

I. What is DNA?

1. DNA stands for: Deoxyribonucleic acid
2. DNA is found in: The cells of all living organisms
3. Describe what DNA looks like inside a cell: Long, twisted strands coiled up tightly to fit inside the cell's nucleus

II. The Structure of DNA

Match each part of DNA with its description:

Double helix -   B. Twisted ladder shape
Sides of the ladder -   A. Made of sugar and phosphate molecules
Rungs of the ladder -   C. Nitrogenous bases
Nitrogenous bases -   D. Adenine (A), Thymine (T), Cytosine (C),
                                   Guanine (G)

III. Base Pairing

Fill in the correct base pair:

1. Adenine (A) pairs with: Thymine (T)
2. Cytosine (C) pairs with: Guanine (G)

IV. DNA Replication

List the three steps of DNA replication in order:

1. Unwinding the Helix
2. Pairing Up
3. Forming New Strands

V. Protein Synthesis

Name and briefly describe the two main steps in protein synthesis:

1. Transcription: DNA is copied into messenger RNA (mRNA) in the nucleus

2. Translation: mRNA is read by ribosomes in the cytoplasm to assemble

   amino acids into a protein

VI. Importance of DNA

List three fields where understanding DNA is important and give one example for each:

1. Field: Medicine Example: Understanding genetic diseases and developing new treatments
2. Field: Forensics Example: DNA fingerprinting to solve crimes
3. Field: Agriculture Example: Creating crops that are more resistant to pests and diseases

VII. True or False

DNA is the same in all living organisms.   False

The structure of DNA is a single straight line.   False

DNA contains instructions for making proteins.   True

DNA replication creates two identical copies, each with
one old and one new strand.   True

VIII. In your own words, explain why DNA is called the "blueprint of life":

Answers may vary, but should include concepts such as:

DNA contains all the instructions needed for an organism to grow, develop, and reproduce

It determines an individual's characteristics

DNA guides the processes that keep life thriving

It stores and transmits genetic information accurately

Structure & Function of DNA and RNA

```
L E N D S A P Y F L U E R K H I E U R W N N N L T P W P K P M
H W L C F P U X W W V G Y W V D U S E D I P X O W P N T Q O J
I W Y G J I V U B Y M R K O R K M Y W B B I E N P U N Y G R A
S Q P K A I T T H C Y O B I C A O S R M N V A M S T U B C T M
G E V C I J R F S I B Q F J O P Z L G W G B P L G K C Y P C S
C B Z C X L D O Q P W T O K M I Z H Q U C Z V Y M H L Z O C U
M J D X J H D U U L I R N T H D O U B L E H E L I X E X I F H
L W M M Z J B D J L K A H J J P U M M R Z F O Z H X U K R Z Z
H D Z L K C K E Z Q D N U U D J Y D Z S R B P R E U S P P C S
Y N Y X L C O D O N A S G K R F L Z B G T B Q R A N O H Q W U
M M A X Y L B W A D C L M P V G M W N H H L S L R U F M R N G
S E M I C O N S E R V A T I V E R E P L I C A T I O N R G G A
S W Z D H L I X B L G T O T P R O T E I N S Y N T H E S I S R
W J C S E P F M T G P I A Q D T Y G Y P B H W U V Z R K M W P
S L T F X Q C Z M S K O R I H T O I R L F U R D A W K J Y I H
E F R B A A Z K F C F N B B R U X S E M C K O S F O Z C K X O
M O A R E V E Y Q F L Y G C U A K Q P T Z H L B X V U D W M S
I G N D N A K I S R Q D B P A A P Z L U W O M L P Q X N G Y P
C F S A J D R R O D E M A W O B C Z I F X B B M R M I X X E H
O W C A P R R U N S P S S Y L B H F C C X Y V B J D Y C D W A
N S R K V R X I R T R G E A C A I N A G G Q H L O P P N I R T
S C I L X G L J U B N S P D D Z Q S T L I G K D J U X T U U E
E P P D L V D W I B J I A P U O Q Q I N Z N H K P Z Q H V J B
R F T S N I D G K U N N I W T Z V Y O L U L O N N M J F U M A
V D I G F I Q F L W O X R J X G G N S H Q A Z T Q O E U X C
A D O N E A C K X J O D I C U F E H K T K I F K R C K K G T K
T Z N O W K V N N L V A N A U T R G A Q Q G D R N N W T B X B
I F J Q E G P F R G C P G A E X F H Y O R R N A B P J N K O
V J Z R E W T F X U E O K M T N W G V L U Z G R J V U E N D
E L H U D F L L A M J S R V R O T C X M T E P N P X R N F D E
E N I T R O G E N O U S B A S E S P T D H X G A Z N B O F V W
```

Semi-conservative replication	Base pairing	Nitrogenous bases
Sugar-phosphate backbone	Protein synthesis	tRNA
Codon	mRNA	Translation
Transcription	Replication	Double helix
Nucleus	DNA	

Structure & Function of DNA and RNA

Across
6. The molecules that form the rungs of the DNA ladder; includes adenine (A), thymine (T), cytosine (C), and guanine (G). _____ bases

10. The process by which the genetic code carried by mRNA is read by a ribosome to assemble amino acids into a protein.

11. The sides of the DNA ladder, made up of alternating sugar and phosphate molecules. Sugar-phosphate _____

13. The process of copying a section of DNA into messenger RNA (mRNA), which carries the genetic code out of the nucleus.

14. The twisted ladder-like structure of DNA, consisting of two long strands that run in opposite directions. (Two words)

Down
1. The process of making proteins from the genetic code in DNA, involving transcription and translation. Protein _____

2. A method of DNA replication where each new DNA molecule consists of one old strand and one new strand. _____-_____ replication

3. The specific pairing of nitrogenous bases in DNA; adenine pairs with thymine, and cytosine pairs with guanine. _____ pairing

4. The process by which DNA makes a copy of itself during cell division, ensuring that each new cell receives an exact copy of the DNA.

5. A set of three bases on the mRNA that corresponds to a specific amino acid.

7. The molecule that contains the genetic instructions for the development, functioning, growth, and reproduction of all living organisms.

8. The molecule that carries the genetic instructions from DNA in the nucleus to the ribosome in the cytoplasm.

9. The molecule that brings the correct amino acids to the ribosome during protein synthesis.

12. The membrane-bound structure within a cell that contains the DNA.

I. DNA Basics

1. What does DNA stand for? Deoxyribonucleic acid
2. DNA is composed of two long strands that form a double helix

List the four types of nucleotides in DNA:

1. Adenine (A) 3. Cytosine (C)
2. Thymine (T) 4. Guanine (G)

II. Importance of DNA Replication

Explain in your own words why DNA replication is important:

DNA replication ensures that each new cell produced during growth or repair has the same genetic information as the original cell. This process is fundamental to life because, without it, organisms couldn't grow, develop, or reproduce.

III. Steps of DNA Replication

Match each step with its description:

Initiation -	C
Unzipping the DNA -	A
Building the New Strands -	B
Leading and Lagging Strands -	F
Proofreading and Error Correction -	E
Termination -	D

IV. Enzymes Involved in DNA Replication

Name the enzyme responsible for each function:

1. Unwinds the double helix: Helicase
2. Adds new nucleotides and performs proofreading: DNA Polymerase
3. Synthesizes short RNA primer: Primase
4. Joins Okazaki fragments: DNA Ligase
5. Prevents DNA from becoming too tightly coiled: Topoisomerase

V. True or False

DNA replication ensures that each new cell has different genetic information from the original cell. False

The leading strand is synthesized in short segments called Okazaki fragments. False

DNA polymerase follows base-pairing rules: A with T and C with G. True

Errors during replication can lead to mutations and genetic disorders. True

VI. Short Answer

1. Describe the structure of DNA: DNA is composed of two long strands that form a double helix, resembling a twisted ladder. The rungs of this ladder are made up of pairs of nucleotides (A, T, C, G) that pair up specifically: A with T and C with G.

2. Explain what is meant by "semi-conservative replication": Semi-conservative replication refers to the process where each new DNA molecule consists of one original strand and one newly synthesized strand.

3. Why is accurate DNA replication critical? Accurate DNA replication is critical for maintaining the integrity of an organism's genetic information. Errors during replication can lead to mutations, which can cause diseases or other genetic disorders.

VII. In your own words, explain why understanding DNA replication is important for high school students:

Answers may vary, but should touch on points such as: understanding how our bodies grow and repair themselves, appreciating the complexity of life at a molecular level, gaining insight into genetic diseases, and building a foundation for further study in biology or genetics.

DNA Replication

```
P R E J G T E E P I T T U S L Y E C X B F U N M M D L H U S X
L E P U X U O R D N A R E P L I C A T I O N M Y U B B P T E R
R P Q W Q T D E U A E U R T B O K F G Q T T R I W J O I O B Y
P L F U C E F G U L V O Q K L K H T Q U F Z V J L V F K P M M
K I T S J J D C L S V F Q X U S H O W Z J E I I S F O O H S
L C W Z M J V O I B Y Z O N I F Z B N I F T Q S E I R G I H
M A W S Z X O S D P J H Q L V P Z B A E M J M I W V F D S T D
X T D W Y Q Y J G Y X S B N D Y U Q R X D W X Y A X R F O B C
A I V H B V V R Y R H K G C C R Q P S Z H D T W E O W K M B K
P O O H B S B J U H B O Z W Q L A G G I N G S T R A N D E L Y
Q N E W Y Q S W J M E J T H Z K Q H I P Y J Q S S T O E R K Z
A F F M Q H Q A G S E W D O X Q X U B U D D S J R K Q J A W T
A O A S A R O K A Z A K I F R A G M E N T S Q W F U I Y S C J
T R K I Q N A Y L E A D I N G S T R A N D K E E F E J Z E E O
Y K X I X R U S P S U U Z S W M M A A Y T E P Q B B D E K I
X V R W X W M U P A F W F H R O Y Y Q W E P I F L K X J B Z L
J V Y P W L J D Z F L D A I Z V Z Y M J L K Q R O U R Z T S E
P B M R W F J N G L I X T O A C C C Z W S P Y Z H A X H X M D
D H N I N D T A K I N C C R L K I N R P G D W Y E L Z W G C M
V D U M N H P L D P D A O B B N I E Z A A J M B L R H Z D C F
W J C A S E M I C O N S E R V A T I V E R E P L I C A T I O N
Q D L S S C C G R I W E X R L K G G S B X C Y V C J W L S N V
N E E R G A A Q J W B L E X O C C H K R D G A A H Q E T G W
R A O L J Y S D O U B L E H E L I X J Q F D K S Z C O Y T I
B E T A W Z Q E Y S X R M Q C L U Y G R G I H Z E E K C L N B
H I I G M B Y U T J L F F J Z A K X C D J S A Y G K V L T Q
A Q D J F N A S S S K S U S L P A C P V B E H Y G W V Q P B S
T F E Z M T B Z C G X K J S D N A P O L Y M E R A S E J C W N
D L S U R Q J U Y Y O N Y D E D Q V J R C J L F A C B C T E S
V R T Y K D S R W L K R S A H G B N K V W A K K L P G O E J
P K W Y B D N K Q I P J J R X S Y G H F W J S G B X L E M U M
```

Semi-conservative replication	DNA ligase	Okazaki fragments
Lagging strand	Leading strand	DNA polymerase
Replication fork	DNA replication	Topoisomerase
Primase	Helicase	Double helix
Nucleotides	DNA	

DNA Replication

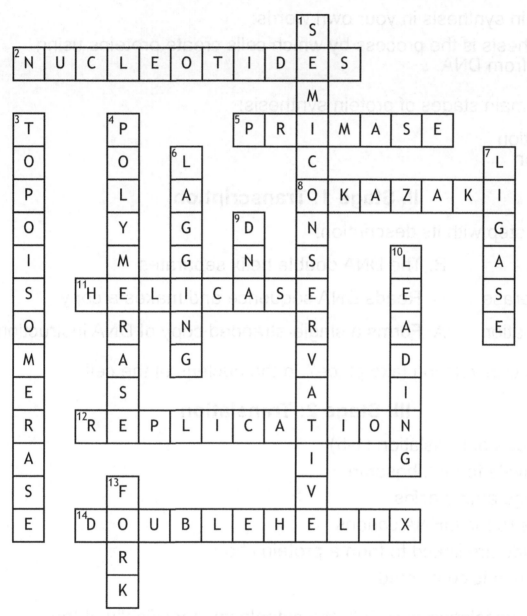

Across

2. The building blocks of DNA, consisting of adenine (A), thymine (T), cytosine (C), and guanine (G), which pair up in specific ways (A with T and C with G).

5. The enzyme that synthesizes a short RNA primer to provide a starting point for DNA polymerase.

8. Short segments of DNA synthesized on the lagging strand during replication. _____ fragments

11. The enzyme that unwinds the double helix and separates the DNA strands during replication.

12. The process by which DNA makes an exact copy of itself before cell division. DNA _____

14. The twisted ladder-like structure of DNA formed by two strands of nucleotides. (Two words)

Down

1. The method of DNA replication where each new DNA molecule consists of one original strand and one newly synthesized strand. ___-___ replication

3. The enzyme that prevents the DNA from becoming too tightly coiled during replication.

4. The enzyme that adds new nucleotides to the template strand and proofreads the new DNA strand for errors. DNA _____

6. The DNA strand that is synthesized in short segments, called Okazaki fragments, opposite to the direction of the replication fork. _____ strand

7. The enzyme that joins Okazaki fragments together to create a continuous DNA strand. DNA ___

9. The molecule that carries the genetic instructions for life, composed of two long strands forming a double helix.

10. The DNA strand that is synthesized continuously in the direction of the replication fork. _____ strand

13. The point where the two DNA strands separate to allow replication. Replication _____

Chapter 13 Answer Key
GUIDED NOTES

I. What is Protein Synthesis?

Define protein synthesis in your own words:

Protein synthesis is the process by which cells create proteins using instructions from DNA.

List the two main stages of protein synthesis:

1. Transcription
2. Translation

II. Stage 1: Transcription

Match each step with its description:

DNA Unzips -   B. The DNA double helix separates

RNA Polymerase -   C. Reads DNA sequence and makes a copy

mRNA Formation -   A. Forms a single-stranded copy of DNA instructions

Where does transcription take place? In the nucleus of the cell

III. Stage 2: Translation

Order the steps of translation (1-5):
1. mRNA travels to the ribosome
2. tRNA brings amino acids
3. Ribosome reads mRNA codons
4. Amino acids are linked to form a protein chain
5. Protein chain is completed

Where does translation occur? In the cytoplasm, specifically at the ribosomes

IV. Key Terms

Define the following terms:
1. Amino acids: The building blocks of proteins
2. Codons: Three-letter sequences on mRNA that code for specific amino acids

318 | 25x: Biology © 2024 3andB.com

3. Anticodons: Three-letter sequences on tRNA that match specific codons
4. Ribosomes: Cellular structures where proteins are assembled

V. Importance of Protein Synthesis

List four types of proteins and their functions:
1. Enzymes: Speed up chemical reactions in the body
2. Hormones: Send signals between different parts of the body
3. Antibodies: Help fight off infections as part of the immune system
4. Structural proteins: Give structure to skin, bones, and muscles (e.g., collagen)

VI. True or False

False	Protein synthesis occurs only in the nucleus.
True	mRNA carries genetic information from DNA to ribosomes.
True	tRNA molecules carry amino acids to the ribosome.
False	The genetic code is different for every living organism.

VII. Fun Facts

Write down two interesting facts about protein synthesis:
1. A single ribosome can add up to 20 amino acids to a protein chain every second.
2. The genetic code used in protein synthesis is nearly universal among all living organisms.

VIII. In your own words, explain why understanding protein synthesis is important for your body's health:

Understanding protein synthesis is important because proteins are involved in nearly every function of our bodies. They are essential for growth, repair, and maintaining overall health. Knowing how proteins are made helps us appreciate the complexity of our bodies and understand how nutrition, exercise, and other factors can affect our health at a cellular level.

Protein Synthesis

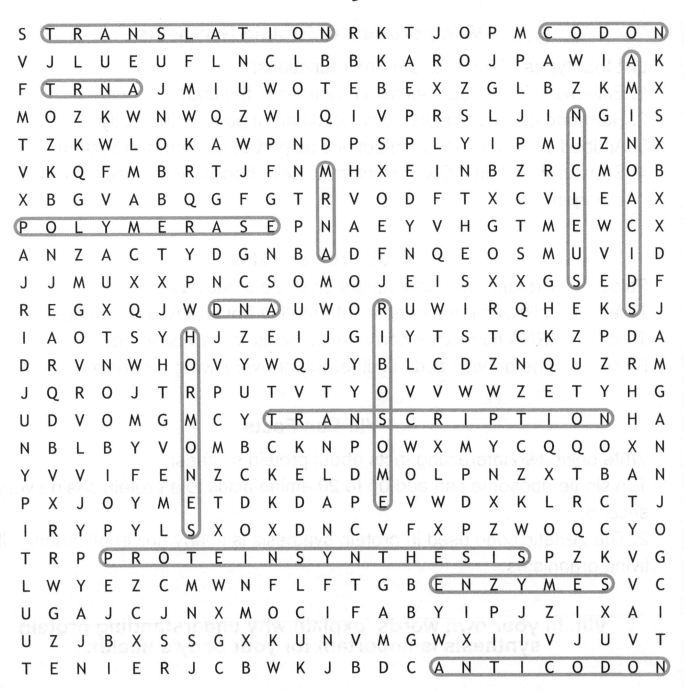

Protein synthesis

Anticodon

Ribosome

DNA

Transcription

Hormones

Codon

mRNA

Nucleus

Amino acids

Enzymes

tRNA

polymerase

Translation

Protein Synthesis

Across

6. The process by which cells create proteins, essential for almost every function in the body. Protein ____

7. The control center of the cell where transcription takes place, containing the cell's DNA.

9. A single-stranded copy of DNA's instructions that carries the genetic code to the ribosomes.

12. The cell's protein-making factory where translation occurs and proteins are assembled.

13. The molecule that carries genetic instructions for making proteins.

14. The first stage of protein synthesis, where DNA instructions are copied into messenger RNA (mRNA).

Down

1. Proteins that speed up chemical reactions in the body, such as digesting food.

2. Proteins that send signals between different parts of the body to regulate various functions.

3. The second stage of protein synthesis, where mRNA is used to assemble amino acids into a protein.

4. The enzyme that reads the DNA sequence and makes a copy of it called mRNA during transcription. RNA ____

5. The building blocks of proteins that are linked together during protein synthesis. (Two words)

8. A three-letter code on tRNA that matches a codon on mRNA, ensuring the correct amino acid is added to the protein chain.

10. The molecule that carries amino acids to the ribosome during translation, matching them to the mRNA codons.

11. A sequence of three nucleotides on mRNA that corresponds to a specific amino acid.

I. What is Meiosis?

Define meiosis in your own words:
Meiosis is a type of cell division that reduces the number of chromosomes by half, creating four unique daughter cells (gametes) with a unique combination of genes.

List two key differences between meiosis and mitosis:
1. Meiosis produces four daughter cells, while mitosis produces two.
2. Meiosis results in genetically diverse haploid cells, while mitosis produces identical diploid cells.

II. The Two Stages of Meiosis

Fill in the blanks:

Meiosis occurs in two main stages: Meiosis I and Meiosis II.

III. Meiosis I: Reducing Chromosome Number

Match each phase with its description:

Prophase I   -   D. Chromosomes condense and crossing over occurs
Metaphase I -   A. Chromosomes align in the middle of the cell
Anaphase I   -   B. Homologous chromosomes are pulled apart
Telophase I   -   C. Cell splits into two haploid cells

IV. Meiosis II: Creating Four Unique Cells

List the four phases of Meiosis II in order:
1. Prophase II
2. Metaphase II
3. Anaphase II
4. Telophase II

V. Importance of Meiosis

Explain three reasons why meiosis is important:
1. Genetic Diversity: Meiosis introduces genetic variation through crossing over and random assortment of chromosomes.
2. Reproduction: Meiosis is essential for sexual reproduction by producing gametes with the correct number of chromosomes.
3. Evolution and Adaptation: Genetic diversity from meiosis helps populations adapt to changing environments.

VI. Key Terms

Match each term with its definition:

Chromosome - C. Structure made of DNA containing genetic information

Gametes - D. Reproductive cells (sperm and eggs)

Haploid - A. Cells with half the usual number of chromosomes

Homologous - E. Pairs of chromosomes, one from each parent Chromosomes

Crossing - B. Exchange of genetic material between chromosomes Over

VII. True or False

Meiosis produces four identical daughter cells.   False
Crossing over occurs during Prophase I.   True
Meiosis is necessary for asexual reproduction.   False
Genetic diversity is a result of meiosis.   True

VIII. In your own words, explain why understanding meiosis is important for high school students:

Answers may vary, but should touch on points such as:
- Understanding how genetic traits are passed down
- Appreciating the source of genetic diversity
- Grasping a fundamental process in biology and reproduction
- Connecting meiosis to concepts of evolution and adaptation
- Preparing for further studies in biology, genetics, or related fields

Meiosis

```
U C F M A B V Y R P F T P M G O D K S Z M G U V L B U N Q Z U
F E I P T K L H T P Z T I O F K M E M X Q R F E Y Q Z T M C E
H U K S O G Z A E T K B H G G C H R O M O S O M E C I A R K Z
Y Y T W L D K J L B J A B W A Z I T S J M Y O R H G Y G K U W
D N C Q K Z D V O O V S R E N U U B W C B I U A W P E H B I V
A N B E H Q H U P C U T F I B U M H C F A O R K M Y O O P O X
D H N J Y C F K H W A S F M P B Z O O N B N B Z A V Q C U L
N S N B B P F U A W X D E B E Q T E X H A W E E K K C R M N C
O A P R O P H A S E I I Q I C E T A H P D W N W H K B Q U N
I E R H N T F N E Y I N Z Z O U A S R G H Z C S K D K G V P U
T F R H G L U O I V C D M Z S U C Y R X A G X T K L G I W S P
U X G N A O N L I K P O V X I T I X F G S J Q M J J Q V H T L
I U X C M X T X A E X S P L S F Z Q Q C E F N A D E O T A C I
P M W H E G B U N O M E T A P H A S E I I R O E X L B K P U V
E E C V T C X S D C Y F P C I V Q U A C I T E G H P H U L R A
H T O E E E H R C D B G E C R O S S I N G O V E R M B C O B B
P A B A S C C V Y D P P H O D O B N E V V K Y A W K Z Q I F X
K P A I K N H X T O N D O B O T K J G X E S D F U J O O D V B
X H Y J J K K K O X Q Z U O R S Y G Y E I K E R Z O U U E L G
A A H G V U O M K B N O D B F F C Z V X Y G B O I G I C I V U
L S U L W L Q G I I S X J D S I E R X A J G X C S V N U R D M
S E R T Z W F L N U M F G P G B Q B X B W Q K T O Z C Q D E K
J I B I W A Q L E I P G T J K F C K K N J K V M U T P Z J H B
U I I F E I L F S N H O M O L O G O U S C H R O M O S O M E S
H U L C B U R J I M Q W Y X M Z V L R G O H N F N D D D L A D
P E D E D Y J W S K H S V K S N A C K R S M W U W B A O O U H
U V D W B E I C Z A P R O P H A S E I V U Y J C K D D R A J D
C P B M O K O F Q B D O E W Y R R X W W T T O F H F E F P K P
P Y J B I G P G D H S S E W Z S A Q E I H P D U I P M J J M A
J N P A N A P H A S E I Q U Z E G O X W X C E Y O D M X G L A
T E L O P H A S E I A N D C Y T O K I N E S I S J H S J T K N
```

Telophase II and cytokinesis	Anaphase II	Metaphase II
Prophase II	Telophase I and cytokinesis	Anaphase I
Metaphase I	Prophase I	Crossing over
Homologous chromosomes	Haploid	Gametes
Chromosome	Meiosis	

Meiosis

Across

2. The final phase of Meiosis II, where each of the two haploid cells divides again, resulting in four unique haploid daughter cells. ___ II and cytokinesis

3. The first phase of Meiosis I, where chromosomes condense, homologous chromosomes pair up to form tetrads, and crossing over occurs. ____ I

8. The phase of Meiosis I where tetrads align in the middle of the cell, and spindle fibers attach to the chromosomes. ____ I

10. Pairs of chromosomes, one from each parent, that are similar in shape, size, and genetic content. ____ chromosomes

12. The final phase of Meiosis I, where the cell splits into two haploid cells, each with half the original number of chromosomes. Telophase I and ____

13. Reproductive cells (sperm in males and eggs in females) produced by meiosis, each containing half the usual number of chromosomes.

14. A structure made of DNA and proteins that contains genetic information necessary for the development and function of an organism.

Down

1. The phase of Meiosis II where chromosomes line up in the middle of each haploid cell, and spindle fibers attach to the centromeres of the sister chromatids. ____ II

4. The phase of Meiosis II where spindle fibers pull sister chromatids apart, moving them to opposite ends of the cell. ____ II

5. The exchange of genetic material between homologous chromosomes during Prophase I of meiosis, resulting in new combinations of genes. ____ over

6. A type of cell division that reduces the number of chromosomes by half, creating four unique daughter cells called gametes.

7. A cell that has one set of chromosomes, which is half the number of chromosomes found in a typical body cell.

9. The first phase of Meiosis II, where chromosomes condense again in the two new haploid cells. ____ II

11. The phase of Meiosis I where spindle fibers pull homologous chromosomes to opposite ends of the cell, while sister chromatids remain together. ____ I

I. Key Concepts

1. Inheritance: The process through which genetic information is passed from parents to their offspring.
2. Genes: Structures that contain genetic information and are found on chromosomes.
3. Chromosomes: Structures inside cells that contain genes.
4. DNA: The molecule that carries genetic instructions for life.

II. DNA and Genes

1. DNA stands for: Deoxyribonucleic acid
2. Humans have 46 chromosomes in each cell (23 from each parent).
3. DNA is described as a recipe book that contains all the instructions needed to build and maintain your body. Each gene is like a specific recipe or set of instructions within that book.

III. Alleles and Traits

1. Alleles are different versions of genes.
2. Table:

Type of Allele	Description
Dominant	Tend to show up more often; "bossy" ones
Recessive	Quieter and only show up when you have two copies

3. Example: If you inherit a dominant allele for brown eyes from one parent and a recessive allele for blue eyes from the other, you will have brown eyes. You need two recessive alleles to have blue eyes.

IV. Punnett Squares

1. Punnett squares are simple charts used to predict how traits are inherited.
2. The purpose is to see how different combinations of alleles can result in different traits and predict the likelihood of inheriting particular traits.

V. Gregor Mendel

1. Gregor Mendel was a monk who loved gardening and conducted experiments with pea plants.
2. Mendel studied how traits are passed down through generations in pea plants.
3. Mendel's work is important because it discovered the basic principles of inheritance and laid the foundation for modern genetics.

VI. Genetic Disorders

Type of Disorder	Example	How it's Inherited
Recessive	Cystic fibrosis	Need two copies of the faulty gene
Dominant	Huntington's disease	Only one copy of the faulty gene needed

VII. Nature vs. Nurture

1. Environmental factors like diet, lifestyle, and exposure to different environments can influence how genes are expressed.
2. Example: A person might have a genetic predisposition to be tall, but without proper nutrition while growing up, they might not reach their full height potential.

VIII. Modern Genetics

Two advancements in modern genetics:
1. DNA sequencing
2. Genetic testing

Inheritance

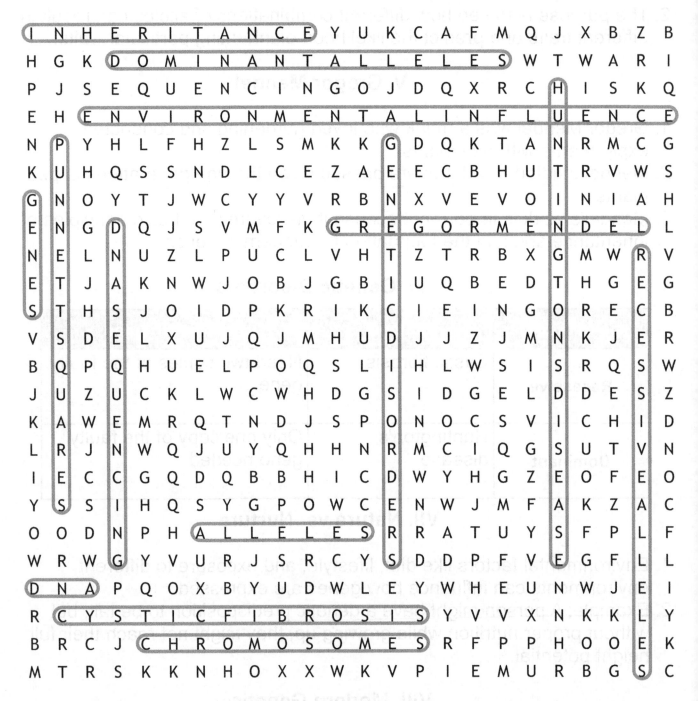

I	N	H	E	R	I	T	A	N	C	E	Y	U	K	C	A	F	M	Q	J	X	B	Z	B
H	G	K	D	O	M	I	N	A	N	T	A	L	L	E	L	E	S	W	T	W	A	R	I
P	J	S	E	Q	U	E	N	C	I	N	G	O	J	D	Q	X	R	C	H	I	S	K	Q
E	H	E	N	V	I	R	O	N	M	E	N	T	A	L	I	N	F	L	U	E	N	C	E
N	P	Y	H	L	F	H	Z	L	S	M	K	K	G	D	Q	K	T	A	N	R	M	C	G
K	U	H	Q	S	S	N	D	L	C	E	Z	A	E	E	C	B	H	U	T	R	V	W	S
G	N	O	Y	T	J	W	C	Y	Y	V	R	B	N	X	V	E	V	O	I	N	I	A	H
E	N	G	D	Q	J	S	V	M	F	K	G	R	E	G	O	R	M	E	N	D	E	L	L
N	E	L	N	U	Z	L	P	U	C	L	V	H	T	Z	T	R	B	X	G	M	W	R	V
E	T	J	A	K	N	W	J	O	B	J	G	B	I	U	Q	B	E	D	T	H	G	E	G
S	T	H	S	J	O	I	D	P	K	R	I	K	C	I	E	I	N	G	O	R	E	C	B
V	S	D	E	L	X	U	J	Q	J	M	H	U	D	J	J	Z	J	M	N	K	J	E	R
B	Q	P	Q	H	U	E	L	P	O	Q	S	L	I	H	L	W	S	I	S	R	Q	S	W
J	U	Z	U	C	K	L	W	C	W	H	D	G	S	I	D	G	E	L	D	D	E	S	Z
K	A	W	E	M	R	Q	T	N	D	J	S	P	O	N	O	C	S	V	I	C	H	I	D
L	R	J	N	W	Q	J	U	Y	Q	H	H	N	R	M	C	I	Q	G	S	U	T	V	N
I	E	C	C	G	Q	D	Q	B	B	H	I	C	D	W	Y	H	G	Z	E	O	F	E	O
Y	S	S	I	H	Q	S	Y	G	P	O	W	C	E	N	W	J	M	F	A	K	Z	A	C
O	O	D	N	P	H	A	L	L	E	L	E	S	R	R	A	T	U	Y	S	F	P	L	F
W	R	W	G	Y	V	U	R	J	S	R	C	Y	S	D	D	P	F	V	E	G	F	L	L
D	N	A	P	Q	O	X	B	Y	U	D	W	L	E	Y	W	H	E	U	N	W	J	E	I
R	C	Y	S	T	I	C	F	I	B	R	O	S	I	S	Y	V	V	X	N	K	K	L	Y
B	R	C	J	C	H	R	O	M	O	S	O	M	E	S	R	F	P	P	H	O	O	E	K
M	T	R	S	K	K	N	H	O	X	X	W	K	V	P	I	E	M	U	R	B	G	S	C

DNA sequencing

Cystic fibrosis

Punnett squares

Alleles

Genes

Environmental influence

Genetic disorders

Recessive alleles

DNA

Inheritance

Huntington's disease

Gregor Mendel

Dominant alleles

Chromosomes

Inheritance

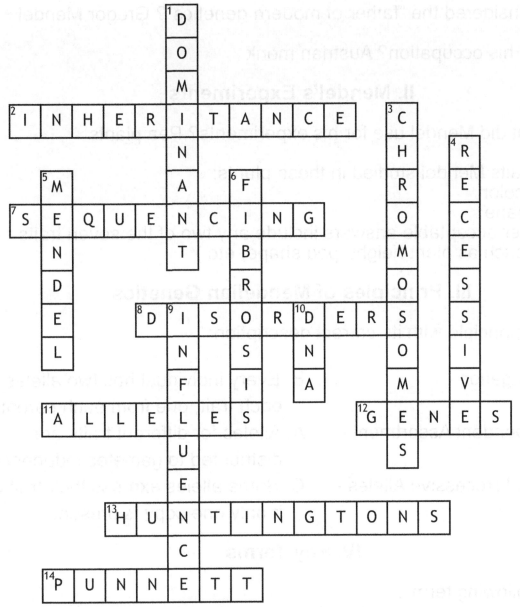

Across

2. The process through which genetic information is passed from parents to their offspring.

7. Advanced techniques used by scientists to read the genetic code and understand more about how genes work, leading to breakthroughs in various fields. DNA ____

8. Conditions caused by mutations or changes in DNA, which can be inherited in a dominant or recessive manner. Genetics ____

11. Different versions of a gene that can lead to variations in traits.

12. Structures found on chromosomes that contain the instructions for the development and functioning of living organisms.

13. A dominant genetic disorder that requires only one copy of the faulty gene to be present for the condition to develop. ____ disease

14. Simple charts used by scientists to predict the likelihood of inheriting particular traits based on different combinations of alleles. ___ squares

Down

1. Alleles that tend to show up more often and mask the presence of recessive alleles. ____ alleles

3. Thread-like structures located inside cells that carry genetic information in the form of genes.

4. Alleles that are only expressed when two copies are present, one from each parent. ____ alleles

5. A scientist and monk who conducted experiments with pea plants and discovered the basic principles of inheritance, laying the foundation for modern genetics. Gregor ____

6. A recessive genetic disorder that requires two copies of the faulty gene to be present for the condition to develop. Cystic ____

9. The role that factors like diet, lifestyle, and exposure to different environments play in influencing how genes are expressed. Environmental

____

10. The molecule that carries the genetic instructions for life, acting like a recipe book for building and maintaining an organism's body.

I. Key Figures in Genetics

1. Who is considered the "father of modern genetics"? Gregor Mendel

2. What was his occupation? Austrian monk

II. Mendel's Experiments

1. What plant did Mendel use for his experiments? Pea plants

2. List two traits Mendel studied in these plants:
   a. Flower color
   b. Seed shape
   (Note: Other acceptable answers include any two of the seven traits mentioned, such as plant height, pod shape, etc.)

III. Principles of Mendelian Genetics

Match each principle with its correct description:

Law of Segregation -   B. Every individual has two alleles for each trait, one from each parent

Law of Independent Assortment -   A. Alleles for different traits are distributed to gametes independently

Dominant and Recessive Alleles -   C. Some alleles express their trait even if only one copy is present

IV. Key Terms

Define the following terms:

1. Allele: A version of a gene

2. Gamete: A reproductive cell (sperm or egg)

3. Punnett square: A grid used to predict the possible genetic outcomes of a cross between two parents

V. Real-World Applications

Name one real-world application of Mendelian genetics for each field:

1. Medicine: Identifying and understanding the inheritance patterns of genetic diseases

2. Agriculture: Breeding plants or animals with desirable traits (e.g., higher crop yields, disease resistance)

3. Forensics: DNA analysis for solving crimes or identifying individuals

VI. True or False

False Mendel conducted his experiments with sunflowers.

False The inheritance of one trait affects the inheritance of another trait.

True A Punnett square helps predict the likelihood of traits in offspring.

VII. Short Answer

Explain why Mendel chose pea plants for his experiments:

Mendel chose pea plants because they have easily observable traits and can be quickly and easily bred. Pea plants also have distinct varieties with clear differences in certain characteristics, making them ideal for studying inheritance patterns.

VIII. In your own words, explain why learning about Mendelian genetics is important:

(Answers will vary, but should touch on some of the following points)** Learning about Mendelian genetics is important because it helps us understand how traits are inherited from parents to offspring. This knowledge has wide-ranging applications, from medicine and agriculture to forensics. It allows us to better understand genetic diseases, breed more resilient crops and livestock, and even solve crimes. On a personal level, it helps us understand why we have certain physical characteristics and can inform decisions about health and family planning.

Mendelian Genetics

```
B L T X G L K K C D U J E Y K O Y F W O P I H U W N F X E L E
S A E Y D B I N D W T Q B O A C R O S S P O L L I N A T I O N
C W X F C S Q L R M O N X F Y Q T Q W K U D Q H S J P S D V L
T O R C O V O B N K M O A J L P G V T S B O B K D U N A V A E
T F X Y R M B Q P O C G T O D M T J M O F M U A M K W S Z T R
E S H K S F J T U C Y T C N X X E G V L Q I D L K C U R Y J E
T E C N Z C P K A B V U E A N Y C I S F Q N X L D T Q Y L P C
Y G I B T X F Y I L O G U T X I Z D K U T A T E X Q P D Z B E
C R R C I R B P V N C J C W V B S P H E D N I L O B M E I O S
S E V H T I X Q U A B I P M Y B Z W S L L T M E O T V X J U S
Q G S K R O W S I B E D A W D D B X K Y E A A S K J Y N D N I
T A Q R Y M Q B L S S I N Z Y J N F J M E L V C G E M N Q V V
S T H R K W J F U U K M O H E R E D I T Y L Q F U P Y U Q Q E
Q I M G U M R W W D R D W I A D R G J U P E L W V W S T A T A
Q O M D D V B B T G G Z Z W H G V L Y C J L V U D N W G U M L
E N P K X M C H B Q W F R R E L T I I A Z E R M U C U B R G L
N G E N E T I C S L F H K M A Z A T V Y C S V H N H O V F H E
N A G H D L K T T I R G X C A X O F S H Q B U X O Y Y T S D L
H A I Q S X W F R N K Y Y J N J M X L O B K O M V I Q M D G E
T V G T M T D Y A E P L W N L J R Y D G R E G O R M E N D E L
Z A T C O A G B I O U H H G R Z Y U P U N N E T T S Q U A R E
Q R W U G U I W T T L W U X F I G O V E R F C C H R I O J F A
I I B Z Y G J N F R R C N Q H F Z N U J G C D W Z S Q K C L Q
L A W O F I N D E P E N D E N T A S S O R T M E N T L X H Q Z
M T B H L W W A P R W F D E Z W M P O W M Q Y J I V L S A G
T I B P T F I E E X K E Y P T J Y P S S T C D P Z C I V H S A
V O Y C E F F C F B D N U U T S E W U O V F G B N G A O B M
P N D Z A W J K U B D E H U Z A L G D S M D Z Q B H S G P E E
F G E F O T G C X H K T T L Z Z X F X D U J B C C J D J B A T
C P F S K L I I A J A K M E N D E L I A N G E N E T I C S I E
T Q F A G P R E D Q F T S E R M X B Z Y V W S B H Y E Z F P S
```

Punnett square	Recessive allele	Dominant allele
Law of Independent Assortment	Law of Segregation	Mendelian genetics
variation	Heredity	Gametes
Trait	Cross-pollination	Alleles
Gregor Mendel	Genetics	

Mendelian Genetics

Across

7. A diagram used to predict the genetic outcome of a cross between two individuals, showing all possible allele combinations in their offspring. ____ square

9. An allele that expresses its trait even if only one copy is present; it masks the effect of a recessive allele. ____ allele

10. Different versions of a gene that determine specific traits, with each individual inheriting two alleles for each trait, one from each parent.

11. An allele that only expresses its trait when two copies are present; its effect is masked by a dominant allele. ____ allele

12. The diversity in gene frequencies among individuals in a population, which contributes to differences in traits. Genetic ____

13. A specific characteristic of an organism that can be inherited, such as flower color or seed shape.

14. A principle that describes how alleles for different traits are distributed to gametes independently, meaning the inheritance of one trait does not affect another. Law of ___ ____

Down

1. The study of how traits are inherited through generations, based on the principles established by Gregor Mendel. ___ genetics

2. An Austrian monk known as the "father of modern genetics" for his research on pea plants and the inheritance of traits. (Two words)

3. The process of transferring pollen from one plant to the stigma of another plant to produce seeds with varying traits.

4. A principle stating that alleles for a trait separate during the formation of gametes, so each gamete carries only one allele for each trait. Law of ___

5. Reproductive cells (sperm and egg) that carry alleles from each parent and combine during fertilization.

6. The branch of biology that studies heredity and the variation of inherited characteristics.

8. The passing of traits from parents to offspring through genes.

I. What is a Mutation?

Define mutation in your own words:
A mutation is a change in the DNA sequence of an organism.

Compare DNA to a: very long book written in a special code

II. Types of Mutations

List and briefly describe the three main types of mutations:

1. Point Mutations
   Description: A single nucleotide in the DNA sequence is changed

2. Insertions and Deletions
   Description: Nucleotides are added or removed in the DNA sequence

3. Frameshift Mutations
   Description: Insertions or deletions change the way the DNA sequence is read

III. Causes of Mutations

List three ways mutations can occur:

1. Naturally during DNA replication in cell division
2. UV radiation from the sun
3. Exposure to certain chemicals or viruses

IV. Effects of Mutations

Fill in the blanks:

1. Some mutations have little or no effect.
2. Beneficial mutations can give an organism an advantage in its environment.
3. Harmful mutations can lead to diseases.

V. Mutations and Evolution

Explain how mutations contribute to evolution:
Mutations create genetic diversity, allowing populations to adapt to changing environments. Beneficial mutations can spread through a population over time, helping a species survive and thrive.

VI. Real-Life Examples of Mutations

Match each mutation example with its description:

1. Blue Eyes -

2. Antibiotic Resistance -

3. Peppered Moths -

B. Caused by a mutation affecting iris pigmentation

C. Makes bacteria survive antibiotic treatment

A. Helped moths blend in during Industrial Revolution

VII. Studying Mutations

Name one method scientists use to study mutations:
DNA sequencing

VIII. True or False

All mutations are harmful to organisms. False
Mutations play a crucial role in evolution. True
DNA sequencing can help identify mutations. True

IX. In your own words, explain why understanding mutations is important:

Answers may vary, but should touch on points such as:

Understanding genetic diversity and evolution

Helping to develop treatments for genetic diseases

Gaining insights into antibiotic resistance

Exploring the variety of life on Earth

Advancing our knowledge of genetics and biology

Mutations

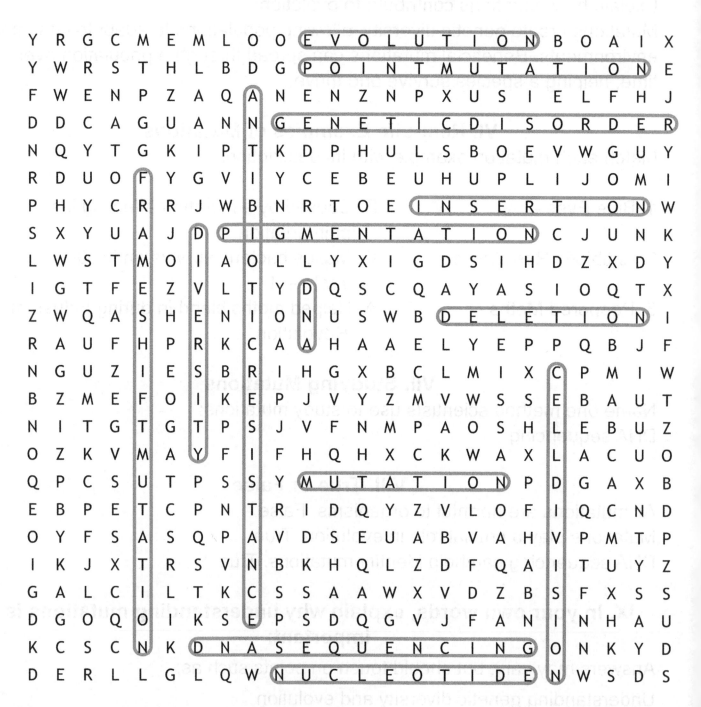

Antibiotic resistance

Cell division

Pigmentation

diversity

DNA

DNA sequencing

Frameshift mutation

Evolution

Insertion

Mutation

Genetic disorder

Point mutation

Deletion

Nucleotide

Mutations

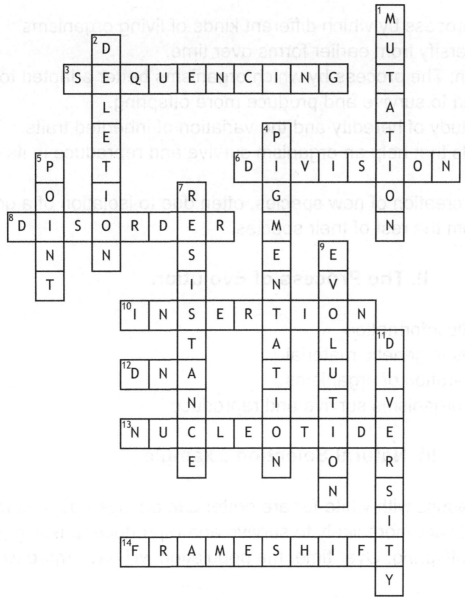

Across
3. A technique used by scientists to read the DNA code and identify mutations. DNA ____

6. The process by which a cell replicates its DNA and divides into two new cells. Cell ____

8. A disease caused by a mutation in one or more genes, such as cystic fibrosis or sickle cell anemia. Genetic ____

10. A type of mutation where one or more nucleotides are added to the DNA sequence.

12. The molecule that carries the genetic instructions for living organisms, composed of nucleotides.

13. The building blocks of DNA, consisting of a sugar, a phosphate group, and a nitrogenous base.

14. A mutation caused by insertions or deletions that change the way the DNA sequence is read, often leading to significant changes in the protein produced. ____ mutation

Down
1. A change in the DNA sequence of an organism, which can affect how the organism develops and functions.

2. A type of mutation where one or more nucleotides are removed from the DNA sequence.

4. The coloring of an organism's tissues, such as the iris of the eye, which can be affected by genetic mutations.

5. A type of mutation where a single nucleotide in the DNA sequence is changed. ____ mutation

7. A phenomenon where bacteria develop mutations that allow them to survive treatment with antibiotics. Antibiotic ____

9. The process by which populations change over time through variations in their genetic material, often influenced by mutations.

11. The variation in DNA sequences among individuals in a population, which is important for evolution and adaptation. Genetic ____

I. Key Concepts

1. Evolution: The process by which different kinds of living organisms develop and diversify from earlier forms over time.
2. Natural Selection: The process by which organisms better adapted to their environment tend to survive and produce more offspring.
3. Genetics: The study of heredity and the variation of inherited traits.
4. Adaptation: Traits that help an organism survive and reproduce in its environment.
5. Speciation: The creation of new species, often due to isolation of a group of organisms from the rest of their species.

II. The Process of Evolution

1. B. Carries genetic information
2. A. Small changes in genetic material
3. D. The next generation of organisms
4. C. Better suited organisms survive and reproduce

III. Natural Selection Example

In a snowy area, rabbits with white fur are better camouflaged against the snow. These rabbits are more likely to survive and reproduce, passing on their traits to their offspring. Over time, the population will have more white-furred rabbits.

IV. Adaptations

Examples may include:
1. Physical: Long neck of a giraffe, shape of a bird's beak
2. Behavioral: Hunting in packs

V. Speciation

A possible explanation:
A population of birds gets separated by a mountain range. Over time, the isolated groups develop different traits due to their specific environments. One group might develop longer beaks for eating insects, while the other develops shorter beaks for eating seeds. Eventually, these differences become so significant that the two groups can no longer interbreed, resulting in two distinct species.

VI. Examples of Evolution in Action

1. Peppered moth: Before the Industrial Revolution, light-colored moths were common as they blended with lichen-covered trees. As pollution increased and trees darkened with soot, dark-colored moths became more common because they were better camouflaged against the darkened trees.

2. Antibiotic resistance in bacteria: When antibiotics are used, some bacteria may have mutations that make them resistant. These resistant bacteria survive and reproduce, leading to a population that can no longer be killed by the antibiotic.

VII. True or False

False (Evolution occurs over long periods, sometimes taking millions of years)
False (Mutations can be beneficial, neutral, or harmful)
True
False (Adaptations can be physical or behavioral)

VIII. Reflection

Answers will vary, but may include points such as:
- Understanding how life on Earth has changed and adapted over time
- Appreciating the diversity of life and how it came to be
- Recognizing the ongoing nature of evolution and its impact on current issues (e.g., antibiotic resistance)
- Gaining insights into the interconnectedness of life and the environment

Evolution & Natural Selection

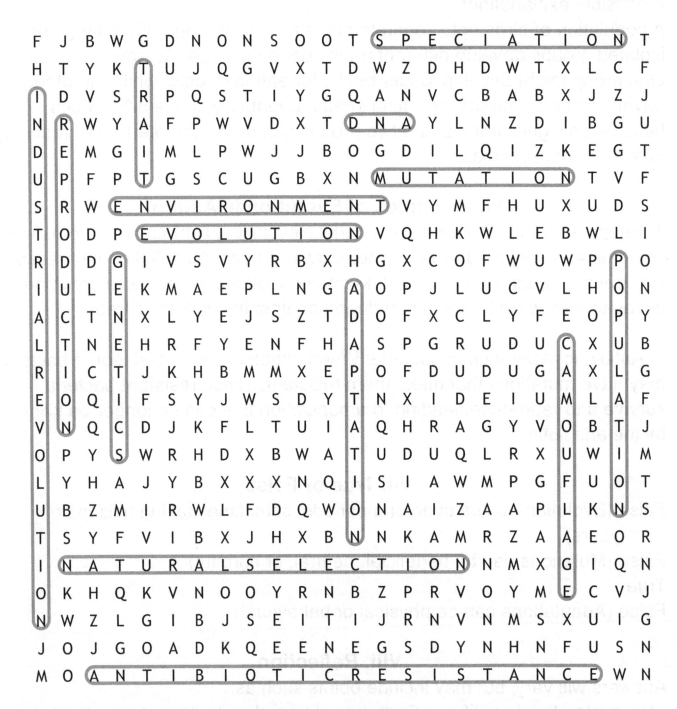

Antibiotic resistance

Population

Trait

Adaptation

Natural selection

Industrial revolution

Reproduction

DNA

Mutation

Evolution

Environment

Camouflage

Speciation

Genetics

Evolution & Natural Selection

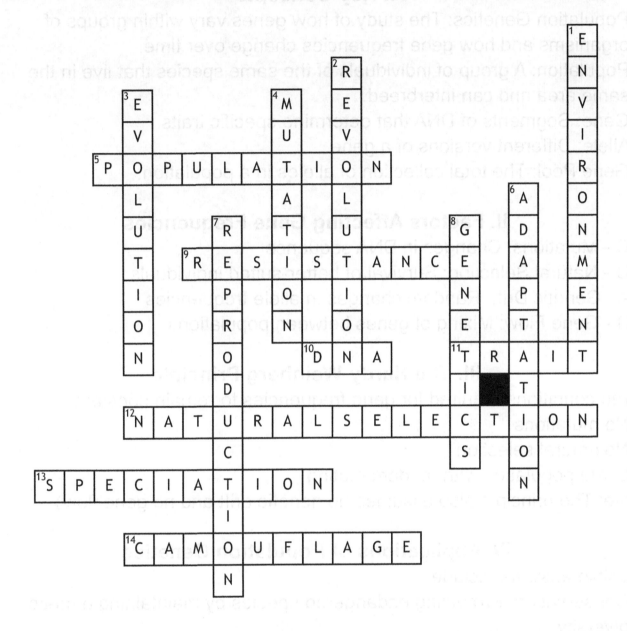

Across

5. A group of individuals of the same species living in a particular area.

9. The ability of bacteria to survive and reproduce despite being exposed to antibiotics, often due to mutations. Antibiotic ____

10. The molecule that carries genetic information in living organisms.

11. A characteristic or feature of an organism, such as eye color or leaf shape, that can be passed from one generation to the next.

12. The process by which organisms better adapted to their environment tend to survive and produce more offspring. (Two words)

13. The formation of new and distinct species through evolutionary processes, often due to geographic isolation.

14. An adaptation that allows an organism to blend into its surroundings to avoid predators.

Down

1. The surrounding conditions in which an organism lives, including natural elements and other living things.

2. A period of major industrialization and pollution that significantly impacted the environment and species like the peppered moth. Industrial ____

3. The process by which different kinds of living organisms develop and diversify from earlier forms over long periods of time.

4. A change in the DNA sequence that can introduce new traits to an organism.

6. A trait that helps an organism survive and reproduce in its environment.

7. The biological process by which new individual organisms are produced.

8. The study of heredity and the variation of inherited traits in living organisms.

I. Key Concepts

1. Population Genetics: The study of how genes vary within groups of organisms and how gene frequencies change over time.
2. Population: A group of individuals of the same species that live in the same area and can interbreed.
3. Gene: Segments of DNA that determine specific traits.
4. Allele: Different versions of a gene.
5. Gene Pool: The total collection of alleles in a population.

II. Factors Affecting Gene Frequencies

1. C - Mutations: Changes in DNA sequence
2. D - Natural Selection: Survival of better-suited individuals
3. A - Genetic Drift: Random changes in allele frequencies
4. B - Gene Flow: Mixing of genes between populations

III. The Hardy-Weinberg Principle

Three conditions required for gene frequencies to remain constant:
1. No mutations
2. No natural selection
3. Large population with random mating
(Note: The principle also assumes no genetic drift and no gene flow)

IV. Applications of Population Genetics

Possible answers include:
1. Conservation: Protecting endangered species by maintaining genetic diversity
2. Medicine: Tracking the spread of genetic diseases and developing treatments
3. Agriculture: Breeding plants and animals with desirable traits

V. True or False

True

False (Mutations can be neutral, harmful, or beneficial)

False (Gene flow typically increases genetic diversity)

False (The Hardy-Weinberg principle describes non-evolving populations)

VI. Short Answer

1. Genetic diversity helps populations survive environmental changes by:
   Providing a variety of traits that may be advantageous in new conditions
   ncreasing the likelihood that some individuals will have traits suited to
survive new challenges (e.g., diseases, climate changes)
   Allowing the population to adapt more quickly to changing environments

2. Natural selection can change gene frequencies in a population by:
   Favoring individuals with traits that are better suited to the environment
   These individuals are more likely to survive and reproduce
   Over time, the alleles for beneficial traits become more common in the
      population
   Less advantageous traits may become less common or disappear

VII. Importance of studying population genetics:

Answers may vary but should touch on points such as:

Understanding how species evolve and adapt to their environments

Helping conserve endangered species

Developing better medical treatments and understanding genetic diseases

Improving agricultural practices and crop yields

Gaining insights into human history and migration patterns

Population Genetics

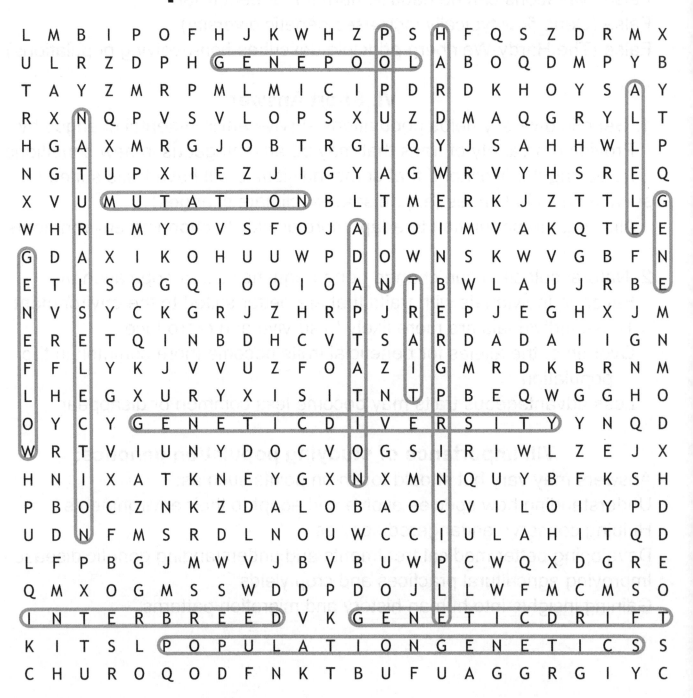

Hardy-Weinberg Principle

Natural selection

Trait

Gene pool

Population

Gene flow

Genetic diversity

Interbreed

Allele

Population genetics

Genetic drift

Adaptation

Mutation

Gene

Population Genetics

Across
2. A group of individuals of the same species that live in the same area and can interbreed.

5. A random change in allele frequencies, especially impactful in small populations, where chance events can cause certain alleles to become more or less common. Genetic ____

8. The study of how genes vary within groups of organisms and how these gene frequencies change over time. (Two words)

10. A specific characteristic or feature determined by genes, like eye color or height.

13. The total collection of alleles in a population, representing all the genetic diversity available. (Two words)

14. The movement of genes between different populations through interbreeding, which introduces new alleles and increases genetic diversity. Gene ____

Down
1. The variety of alleles within a population's gene pool, which helps populations survive environmental changes. Genetic ____

3. A change in the DNA sequence that can introduce new alleles into a population; can be neutral, harmful, or beneficial.

4. A beneficial trait that becomes more common in a population due to natural selection, helping the population survive in its environment.

6. A principle used to predict how gene frequencies will behave in a non-evolving population, providing a baseline for comparing real populations. ____-Weinberg Principle

7. The process where individuals within a population mate and produce offspring, sharing their genetic material.

9. The process where individuals with traits better suited to their environment are more likely to survive and reproduce, making those traits more common over time. Natural ____

11. Different versions of a gene, such as the blue, brown, and green eye color.

12. A segment of DNA that determines specific traits, like eye color or blood type.

I. Mechanisms of Evolution

1. Natural Selection
2. Mutation
3. Genetic Drift
4. Gene Flow
5. Non-Random Mating
6. Adaptation
7. Speciation
8. Coevolution

II. Matching Mechanisms to Descriptions

1. Natural Selection -   D. Survival of organisms with advantageous traits
2. Mutation -   A. Changes in DNA that can create new traits
3. Genetic Drift -   E. Changes in population due to chance events
4. Gene Flow -   B. Interbreeding between different populations
5. Non-Random Mating -   F. Choosing mates based on specific traits
6. Adaptation -   C. Becoming better suited to an environment
7. Speciation -   G. Formation of new species
8. Coevolution -   H. Multiple species influencing each other's evolution

III. Examples and Explanations

(Answers may vary, but should include key points similar to these)

1. Natural Selection: Brown rabbits surviving better in a forest environment due to camouflage.
2. Mutation: A change in DNA giving rabbits longer ears, potentially improving their hearing.
3. Genetic Drift: A storm wiping out most birds on an island, changing the population's traits by chance.
4. Gene Flow: Birds from one island breeding with birds on another island, introducing new traits.
5. Non-Random Mating: Peahens choosing peacocks with larger, more colorful tails.
6. Adaptation: Cave fish developing better night vision over time.

7. Speciation: Animal populations separated by a mountain range evolving into different species.
8. Coevolution: Bees and flowers evolving together, benefiting each other.

IV. True or False

1. False
2. False
3. True
4. True
5. False

V. Short Answer

(Answers may vary but should include key points similar to these)

1. DNA is important because it contains the instructions for building and running living organisms. Mutations in DNA can create new traits that may be passed on to offspring.

2. A small change like longer ears in rabbits can affect a population over time if it provides a survival advantage. Rabbits with longer ears might hear predators better, survive more often, and pass this trait to their offspring, gradually increasing the frequency of long ears in the population.

3. The environment plays a crucial role in natural selection by determining which traits are advantageous. Organisms with traits that are well-suited to their environment are more likely to survive and reproduce, passing these beneficial traits to future generations.

VI. Reflection

(Answers will vary, but should touch on points similar to these)

Understanding evolution is important for studying life on Earth because it explains the diversity of life and how species change over time. It helps us understand how organisms adapt to their environments, how new species form, and how different species interact and influence each other. This knowledge is crucial for fields like biology, ecology, and medicine, and helps us better understand and protect the natural world.

Mechanisms of Evolution

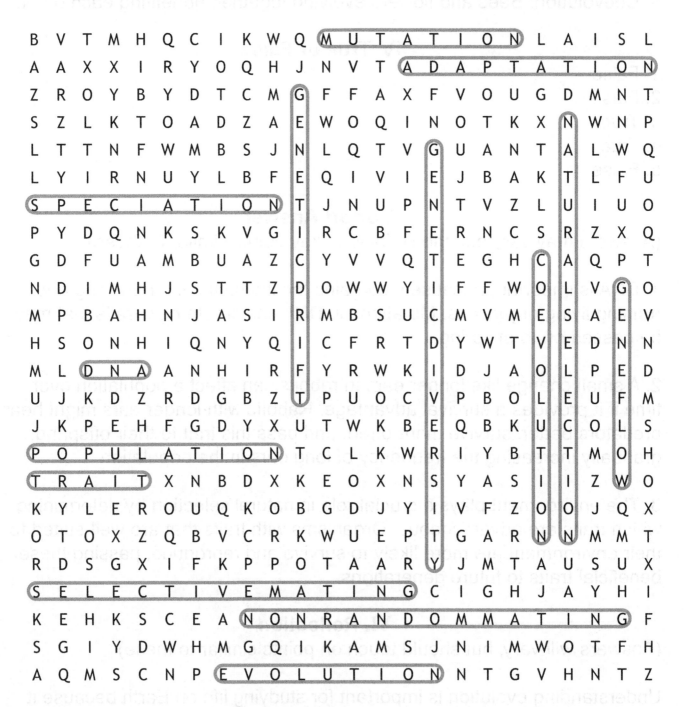

Selective mating | Genetic diversity | Non-random mating
Genetic drift | Population | DNA
Trait | Coevolution | Speciation
Adaptation | Gene flow | Mutation
Natural selection | Evolution

Mechanisms of Evolution

Across

2. The formation of new and distinct species through the process of evolution.

3. The variety of different genes within a population, which can be increased through mechanisms like gene flow. Genetic ____

5. When individuals choose mates based on certain traits, often leading to those traits becoming more common in the population. ____ mating

7. A mechanism of evolution where random chance events cause changes in the traits of a small population. Genetic ____

10. The process by which different kinds of living organisms change over time through various mechanisms.

12. A specific characteristic or feature of an organism, such as fur color or ear length.

13. A mechanism of evolution where traits that help an organism survive are more likely to be passed on to the next generation. (Two words)

14. When two or more species influence each other's evolution through mutual interactions.

Down

1. The process by which a population becomes better suited to its environment over time.

4. The transfer of genetic material between different populations through interbreeding. (Two words)

6. A group of individuals of the same species living in a particular area.

8. Changes in the DNA of an organism that can create new traits; these changes can be beneficial, neutral, or harmful.

9. When individuals choose mates based on specific traits, leading to an increase in those traits within the population. __-____ mating

11. The molecule that carries genetic information in living organisms; it acts like a set of instructions for building and running an organism.

I. What is Ecology?

Ecology is the study of how living things interact with each other and their environment.

II. Energy Flow Basics

1. Where does energy in an ecosystem ultimately come from?
   The sun

2. What process do plants use to make their own food?
   Photosynthesis

III. Key Players in Energy Flow

Producers -   C. Make their own food using sunlight

Consumers -   B. Cannot make their own food

Decomposers -   A. Break down dead organisms and release nutrients

IV. Types of Consumers

1. Herbivores: Example: Rabbit
2. Carnivores: Example: Lion
3. Omnivores: Example: Human

V. Food Chains and Food Webs

1. Example of a simple food chain:
   Grass → Rabbit → Fox

2. How is a food web different from a food chain?

   A food web is a network of interconnected food chains, showing multiple feeding relationships in an ecosystem, while a food chain shows a single, direct line of energy transfer.

VI. Energy Pyramids

Each level of an energy pyramid has less energy than the one below it because some energy is lost as heat when organisms use it to survive and grow.

VII. True or False

False - Decomposers are important in energy flow.
False - Energy decreases as it moves up the food chain.
True - Humans can impact energy flow in ecosystems.

VIII. Human Impact

Two human activities that can disrupt energy flow in ecosystems (any two of these):
1. Deforestation
2. Pollution
3. Overfishing

IX. Importance of Energy Flow

Understanding energy flow is crucial because it helps us see how all organisms in an ecosystem are interconnected and dependent on each other. It shows the importance of each organism in maintaining a balanced ecosystem and how disruptions can affect the entire system.

X. Reflection

Answers will vary, but should demonstrate an understanding of the interconnectedness of nature and the student's place within it.

Ecology & Energy Flow

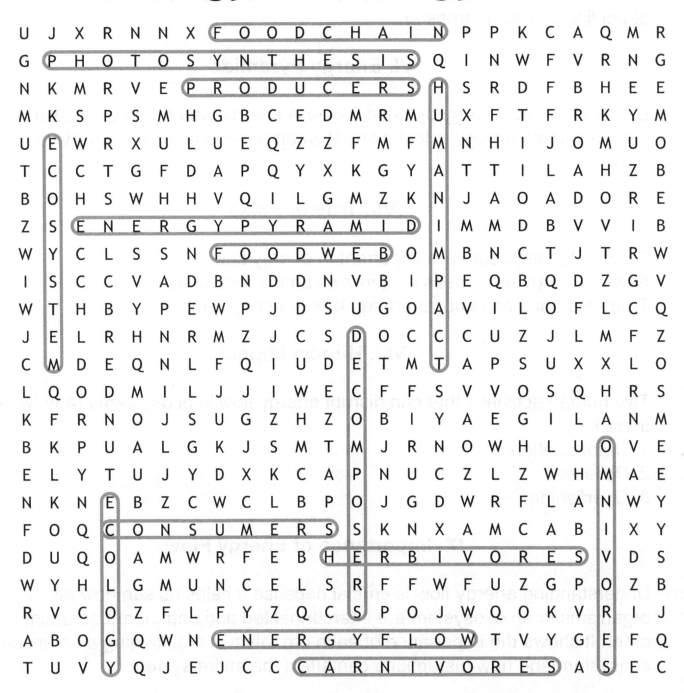

Energy flow

Food web

Omnivores

Consumers

Ecosystem

Energy pyramid

Food chain

Carnivores

Producers

Ecology

Human impact

Decomposers

Herbivores

Photosynthesis

Ecology & Energy Flow

Across

4. A linear sequence showing how energy is transferred from one organism to another, for example, grass → rabbit → fox. (Two words)

5. The effect of human activities, such as deforestation, pollution, and overfishing, on the balance of energy flow and the health of ecosystems. Human ____

8. Consumers that eat both plants and animals to obtain their energy, such as humans and bears.

11. Organisms that cannot make their own food and must eat other organisms to obtain energy. They include herbivores, carnivores, and omnivores.

13. The process by which plants and some bacteria use sunlight to produce their own food, forming the first step in the energy flow of an ecosystem.

14. Organisms like fungi and bacteria that break down dead plants and animals, recycling nutrients back into the soil and continuing the flow of energy in an ecosystem.

Down

1. A community of living organisms and their physical environment, interacting as a system.

2. Organisms, such as plants, algae, and some bacteria, that produce their own food using sunlight and form the base of the ecosystem's energy pyramid.

3. A graphical representation showing how energy decreases as it moves up through the different levels of the food chain, from producers to various levels of consumers. Energy ____

6. The study of how living things interact with each other and their environment, including plants, animals, bacteria, and fungi.

7. Consumers that eat plants to obtain their energy, such as rabbits and cows.

9. Consumers that eat other animals to obtain their energy, such as lions and wolves.

10. The movement of energy from one organism to another within an ecosystem, starting from the sun and moving through different trophic levels. Energy ____

12. A network of interconnected food chains that better represents the complexity of how energy flows through an ecosystem. (Two words)

Chapter 22 Answer Key
GUIDED NOTES

I. Key Terms in Population Ecology

1. Population Ecology: The study of how populations grow, shrink, and interact with their environment.
2. Population: A group of individuals of the same species living in the same area.
3. Population Size: The total number of individuals in a population.
4. Population Density: The number of individuals per unit area or volume.

II. Key Concepts in Population Ecology

1. Birth Rate - C. Number of new individuals born over a period of time
2. Death Rate - E. Number of individuals that die over a period of time
3. Immigration - B. Movement of individuals into a population
4. Emigration - D. Movement of individuals out of a population
5. Carrying Capacity - A. Maximum number of individuals an environment can support

III. Factors Affecting Population Dynamics

Possible answers include:
1. Food availability
2. Predators
3. Disease
4. Climate
5. Habitat availability
6. Competition for resources

IV. Importance of Population Ecology

1. Conservation Efforts: Helps develop strategies to protect endangered species and manage natural resources effectively.
2. Disease Control: Aids in predicting and controlling the spread of diseases within animal and human populations.
3. Agriculture: Helps manage crops and livestock, ensuring sustainable yields and healthy ecosystems.
4. Urban Planning: Assists in designing infrastructure that supports growing human populations without harming the environment.

V. Human Impact on Populations

Possible answers include:
1. Deforestation destroys habitats, leading to a decline in animal populations.
2. Pollution can cause health problems for wildlife and humans, affecting birth and death rates.
3. Overfishing can drastically reduce marine populations.
4. Urban development can fragment habitats and disrupt ecosystems.

VI. True or False

1. False - Population ecology studies both animal and plant populations.
2. False - Carrying capacity can change based on environmental conditions and resource availability.
3. True - Immigration and emigration can affect population size.
4. True - If the birth rate is higher than the death rate, the population will grow.

VII. Reflection

A good answer should mention the importance of understanding population dynamics for:
Maintaining biodiversity
Ensuring sustainable use of natural resources
Predicting and mitigating environmental changes
Informing conservation efforts and environmental policies
Understanding the interconnectedness of species within ecosystems

Population Ecology

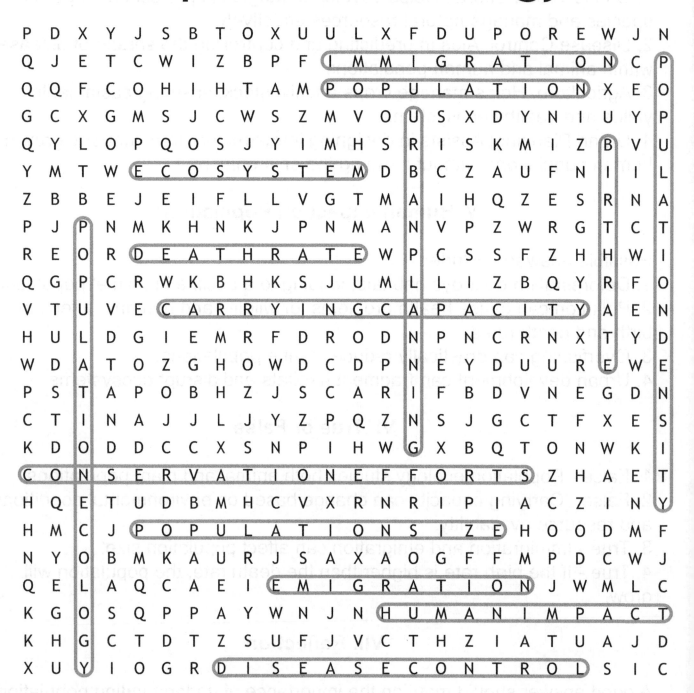

Human impact

Conservation efforts

Birth rate

Population ecology

Immigration

Urban planning

Carrying capacity

Population density

Ecosystem

Population

Disease control

Death rate

Population size

Emigration

Population Ecology

Across

3. The number of individuals that die in a population over a specific period of time. ____ rate

6. A community of living organisms and their interactions with their environment, including both biotic (living) and abiotic (non-living) components.

8. The number of individuals per unit area or volume in a given population. Population ___

10. The practice of predicting and managing the spread of diseases within animal and human populations. Disease ____

11. The number of new individuals born in a population over a specific period of time. ____ rate

12. A group of animals or plants of the same species living in the same area.

13. The total number of individuals in a population. Population ____

14. The process of designing and organizing urban spaces, considering population data to support sustainable growth without harming the environment. Urban ____

Down

1. The maximum number of individuals that an environment can support without being degraded.

2. The effects of human activities like deforestation, pollution, and overfishing on populations and ecosystems, which can lead to changes in population dynamics and environmental degradation. Human ____

4. The movement of individuals into a population from another area.

5. The movement of individuals out of a population to a new area.

7. Strategies and actions taken to protect endangered species and manage natural resources. ____ efforts

9. The study of how groups of the same species interact with each other and their environment, focusing on factors like population growth, shrinkage, and movement. Population ____

I. What Are Biogeochemical Cycles?

Define biogeochemical cycles in your own words:
Biogeochemical cycles are the pathways by which elements like carbon, nitrogen, oxygen, and phosphorus travel through the Earth's different spheres, ensuring that essential nutrients are recycled and made available for all living things.

List the four spheres through which elements travel in biogeochemical cycles:
1. Atmosphere
2. Hydrosphere
3. Lithosphere
4. Biosphere

II. Major Biogeochemical Cycles

Match each cycle with its key characteristic:
1. Carbon Cycle - A. Involves photosynthesis and fossil fuels
2. Nitrogen Cycle - C. Relies on nitrogen-fixing bacteria
3. Water Cycle - B. Includes evaporation and precipitation
4. Phosphorus Cycle - D. Does not have a gaseous form

III. The Carbon Cycle

Name two important processes in the carbon cycle:
1. Photosynthesis: Plants use CO_2, sunlight, and water to produce oxygen and glucose
2. Decomposition: The breakdown of dead organisms, returning carbon to the soil

How do human activities contribute to the carbon cycle?
Humans contribute to the carbon cycle primarily by burning fossil fuels, which releases CO_2 back into the atmosphere.

IV. The Nitrogen Cycle

List the steps of the nitrogen cycle in order:
1. Nitrogen gas in atmosphere
2. Nitrogen fixation
3. Nitrification
4. Assimilation
5. Ammonification
6. Nitrogen gas returned to atmosphere

V. The Water Cycle

Name three forms of precipitation:
1. Rain
2. Snow
3. Sleet (or Hail)

Explain the process of transpiration:
Transpiration is the process where plants release water vapor from their leaves into the atmosphere.

VI. The Phosphorus Cycle

True or False:
False Phosphorus has a gaseous form like carbon and nitrogen.
True Phosphorus is released from rocks through weathering.
False Plants absorb phosphorus from the air through their leaves.

How does phosphorus move from living organisms back to the environment?
When plants and animals die, decomposers break down their bodies, returning phosphorus to the soil.

VII. Importance of Biogeochemical Cycles

In your own words, explain why biogeochemical cycles are essential for life on Earth:
Biogeochemical cycles are essential for life on Earth because they ensure that essential nutrients and elements are continuously recycled and made available for all living organisms. Without these cycles, the supply of crucial elements would be depleted, making life as we know it impossible.

Biogeochemical Cycles

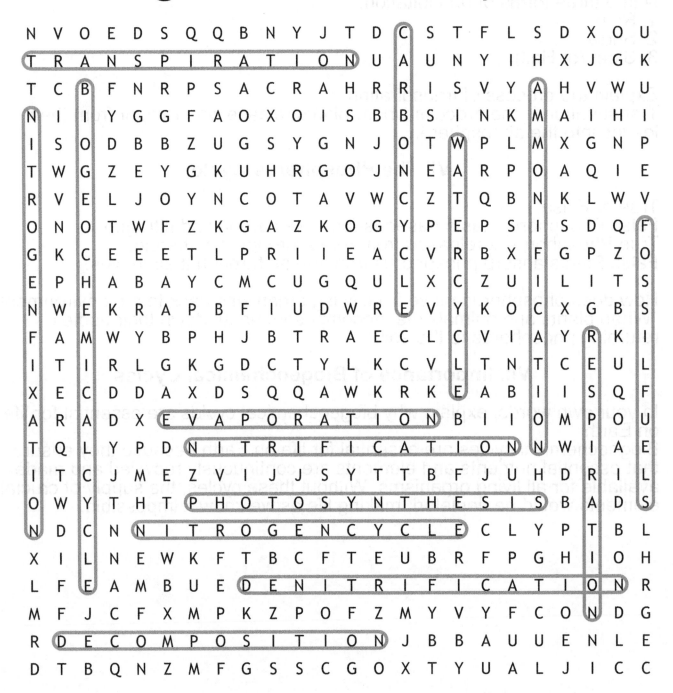

Water cycle

Fossil fuels

Transpiration

Nitrification

Respiration

Nitrogen fixation

Carbon cycle

Evaporation

Ammonification

Photosynthesis

Nitrogen cycle

Biogeochemical cycle

Denitrification

Decomposition

Biogeochemical Cycles

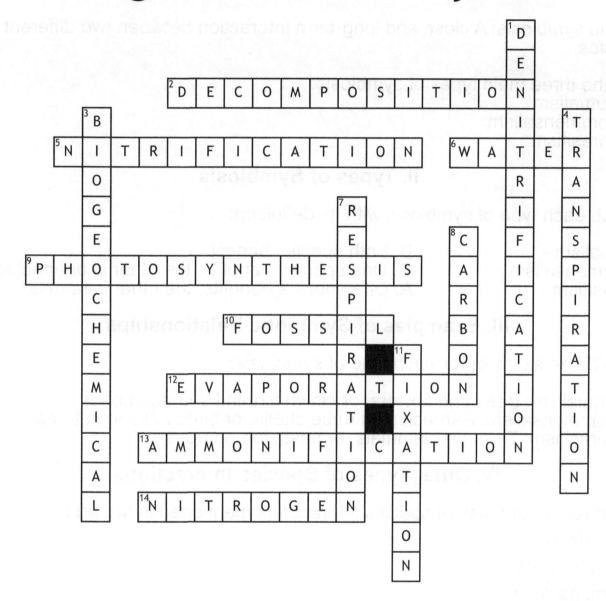

Across

2. The breakdown of dead plants and animals by decomposers like bacteria and fungi, returning essential nutrients, including carbon and nitrogen, back to the soil.

5. The process by which bacteria convert ammonium (NH_4^+) into nitrate (NO_3^-), a form of nitrogen that plants can absorb and use.

6. The continuous movement of H_2O through the Earth's atmosphere, surface, and underground, involving processes like evaporation, condensation, precipitation, and transpiration. ____ cycle

9. The process by which plants use sunlight to convert carbon dioxide and water into glucose (a type of sugar) and oxygen, playing a crucial role in the carbon cycle.

10. Natural fuels such as coal and oil formed from the remains of ancient plants and animals over millions of years, which release carbon dioxide when burned. ____ fuels

12. The process by which water changes from a liquid to a gas (water vapor) due to heat from the sun, part of the water cycle.

13. The conversion of organic nitrogen (from dead plants and animals) into ammonium (NH_4^+) by decomposers.

14. The series of processes by which nitrogen is converted into different chemical forms and moves between the atmosphere, soil, and living organisms. ____ cycle

Down

1. The process by which bacteria convert nitrate (NO_3^-) back into nitrogen gas (N_2), releasing it into the atmosphere and completing the nitrogen cycle.

3. The natural pathways by which essential elements like carbon, nitrogen, oxygen, and phosphorus move through the Earth's atmosphere, hydrosphere, lithosphere, and biosphere. ____ cycle

4. The process by which plants release water vapor from their leaves into the atmosphere, contributing to the water cycle.

7. The process by which living organisms, including plants and animals, convert glucose and oxygen into energy, releasing carbon dioxide back into the atmosphere.

8. The process by which carbon is exchanged between the atmosphere, oceans, soil, and living organisms, mainly through photosynthesis, respiration, decomposition, and combustion. ____ cycle

11. The process by which certain bacteria in the soil and water convert nitrogen gas (N_2) from the atmosphere into ammonia (NH_3), a form that plants can use. Nitrogen ____

I. What is Symbiosis?

Define symbiosis: A close and long-term interaction between two different species

List the three main types of symbiosis:
1. Mutualism
2. Commensalism
3. Parasitism

II. Types of Symbiosis

Match each type of symbiosis with its definition:

Mutualism -   B. Both species benefit
Commensalism -   C. One species benefits, the other is unaffected
Parasitism -   A. One species benefits, the other is harmed

III. Examples of Symbiotic Relationships

Provide an example for each type of symbiosis:

1. Mutualism: Bees and flowers, or clownfish and sea anemones
2. Commensalism: Barnacles on turtle shells, or birds nesting in trees
3. Parasitism: Ticks on mammals, or mistletoe on trees

IV. Other Types of Species Interactions

List three other types of species interactions mentioned in the article:

1. Predation
2. Competition
3. Amensalism

V. Definitions

Define the following terms:

1. Predation: When one species (predator) hunts and eats another species (prey)

2. Competition: When two species compete for the same resources (food, water, shelter)

3. Amensalism: When one species is harmed while the other remains unaffected

VI. True or False

False - In mutualism, only one species benefits from the relationship.
False - Parasitism always results in the immediate death of the host.
True - Competition can occur between members of the same species.
True - Biodiversity refers to the variety of life in an area.

VII. Short Answer

1. Explain why understanding species interactions is important for ecosystems:

   Understanding species interactions is essential because they shape ecosystems and affect biodiversity. These interactions can enhance the survival and reproduction of species, making ecosystems more resilient to changes.

2. Describe how coral reefs demonstrate a mutualistic relationship:

   In coral reefs, there is a mutualistic relationship between coral and algae. The algae live inside the coral and provide it with food through photosynthesis, while the coral provides the algae with a protected environment and nutrients.

VIII. Reflection

(Answers will vary. Look for responses that demonstrate understanding of symbiosis and its relevance to everyday life or the environment.)

Symbiosis & Species Interactions

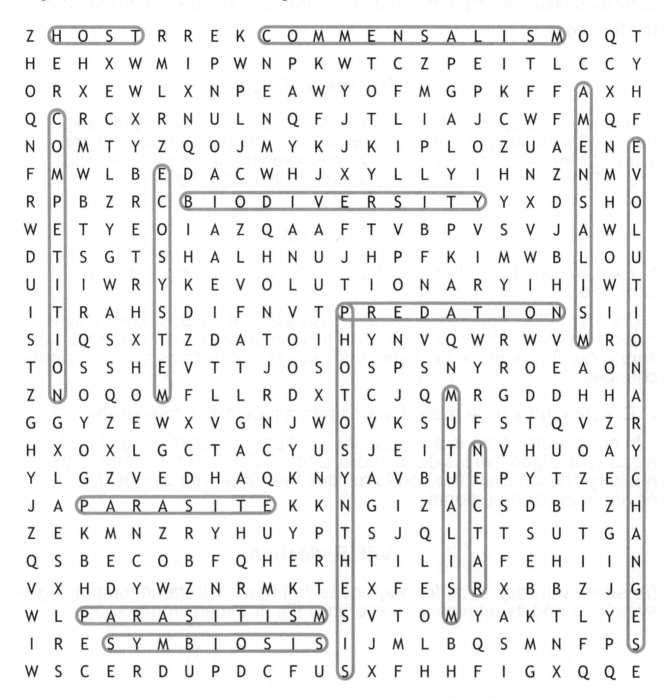

Z	H	O	S	T	R	R	E	K	C	O	M	M	E	N	S	A	L	I	S	M	O	Q	T
H	E	H	X	W	M	I	P	W	N	P	K	W	T	C	Z	P	E	I	T	L	C	C	Y
O	R	X	E	W	L	X	N	P	E	A	W	Y	O	F	M	G	P	K	F	F	A	X	H
Q	C	R	C	X	R	N	U	L	N	Q	F	J	T	L	I	A	J	C	W	F	M	Q	F
N	O	M	T	Y	Z	Q	O	J	M	Y	K	J	K	I	P	L	O	Z	U	A	E	N	E
F	M	W	L	B	E	D	A	C	W	H	J	X	Y	L	L	Y	I	H	N	Z	N	M	V
R	P	B	Z	R	C	B	I	O	D	I	V	E	R	S	I	T	Y	Y	X	D	S	H	O
W	E	T	Y	E	O	I	A	Z	Q	A	A	F	T	V	B	P	V	S	V	J	A	W	L
D	T	S	G	T	S	H	A	L	H	N	U	J	H	P	F	K	I	M	W	B	L	O	U
U	I	I	W	R	Y	K	E	V	O	L	U	T	I	O	N	A	R	Y	I	H	I	W	T
I	T	R	A	H	S	D	I	F	N	V	T	P	R	E	D	A	T	I	O	N	S	I	I
S	I	Q	S	X	T	Z	D	A	T	O	I	H	Y	N	V	Q	W	R	W	V	M	R	O
T	O	S	S	H	E	V	T	T	J	O	S	O	S	P	S	N	Y	R	O	E	A	O	N
Z	N	O	Q	O	M	F	L	L	R	D	X	T	C	J	Q	M	R	G	D	D	H	H	A
G	G	Y	Z	E	W	X	V	G	N	J	W	O	V	K	S	U	F	S	T	Q	V	Z	R
H	X	O	X	L	G	C	T	A	C	Y	U	S	J	E	I	T	N	V	H	U	O	A	Y
Y	L	G	Z	V	E	D	H	A	Q	K	N	Y	A	V	B	U	E	P	Y	T	Z	E	C
J	A	P	A	R	A	S	I	T	E	K	K	N	G	I	Z	A	C	S	D	B	I	Z	H
Z	E	K	M	N	Z	R	Y	H	U	Y	P	T	S	J	Q	L	T	T	S	U	T	G	A
Q	S	B	E	C	O	B	F	Q	H	E	R	H	T	I	L	I	A	F	E	H	I	I	N
V	X	H	D	Y	W	Z	N	R	M	K	T	E	X	F	E	S	R	X	B	B	Z	J	G
W	L	P	A	R	A	S	I	T	I	S	M	S	V	T	O	M	Y	A	K	T	L	Y	E
I	R	E	S	Y	M	B	I	O	S	I	S	I	J	M	L	B	Q	S	M	N	F	P	S
W	S	C	E	R	D	U	P	D	C	F	U	S	X	F	H	H	F	I	G	X	Q	Q	E

Evolutionary changes

Biodiversity

Host

Predation

Mutualism

Nectar

Ecosystem

Amensalism

Parasitism

Symbiosis

Photosynthesis

Parasite

Competition

Commensalism

Symbiosis & Species Interactions

Across

3. An interaction where one species is harmed while the other remains unaffected, such as a large tree blocking sunlight from smaller plants.

7. A community of interacting species and their physical environment, which can be shaped by symbiotic relationships.

10. When two species compete for the same resources, such as food, water, or shelter, which can limit the growth of species, like plants competing for sunlight in a forest.

11. An interaction where one species, the predator, hunts and eats another species, the prey, such as lions hunting zebras.

12. Adaptations that occur in species over time, often influenced by interactions like predation and competition, leading to survival and reproduction advantages. _____ changes

13. The variety of life in an area, which is crucial for the health of our planet and can be affected by species interactions.

14. A close and long-term interaction between two different species that can be beneficial, harmful, or neutral to one or both species involved.

Down

1. A symbiotic relationship where one species benefits at the expense of the other, like ticks feeding on the blood of mammals.

2. The species that benefits in a parasitic relationship, like a tick feeding on a mammal.

4. The process by which plants and some other organisms use sunlight to synthesize foods from carbon dioxide and water, important in mutualistic relationships like that between coral and algae.

5. A sugary fluid produced by flowers that attracts pollinators like bees, playing a key role in mutualistic relationships.

6. A type of symbiotic relationship where one species benefits while the other is neither helped nor harmed, such as barnacles attaching to turtles.

8. A type of symbiotic relationship where both species involved benefit from the interaction, like bees and flowers.

9. The species that is harmed in a parasitic relationship, like a mammal hosting ticks.

I. Types of Ecological Succession

1. Primary succession
2. Secondary succession

II. Primary Succession Stages

Correct order:

1. Bare Rock Stage
2. Pioneer Species
3. Soil Formation
4. Grasses and Small Plants
5. Shrubs and Fast-Growing Trees
6. Climax Community

III. Secondary Succession

1. disturbance
2. soil
3. pioneer
4. intermediate
5. climax

IV. Importance of Ecological Succession

1. B
2. C
3. D
4. A

V. Real-Life Examples

1. Primary succession
2. Secondary succession
3. Secondary succession

VI. True or False

False (Ecological succession occurs after various disturbances, not just major natural disasters)

True

False (The climax community is the final stage of ecological succession)

True (Generally, secondary succession occurs faster because soil and some organisms remain)

VII. Importance of understanding ecological succession

Answers may vary. A good response might include:

Understanding how ecosystems recover from disturbances

Appreciating the resilience and adaptability of nature

Recognizing the importance of biodiversity and ecosystem balance

Gaining insights into long-term environmental changes and conservation

VIII. Vocabulary

1. Ecological Succession: The process by which the structure of a biological community evolves over time.

2. Pioneer Species: The first organisms to colonize a barren environment, capable of surviving in harsh conditions and starting the process of ecosystem development.

3. Climax Community: A stable, mature community of plants and animals that represents the final stage of ecological succession for a given environment.

Note: For open-ended questions, answers may vary. Evaluate based on understanding of concepts and ability to explain in their own words.

Ecological Succession

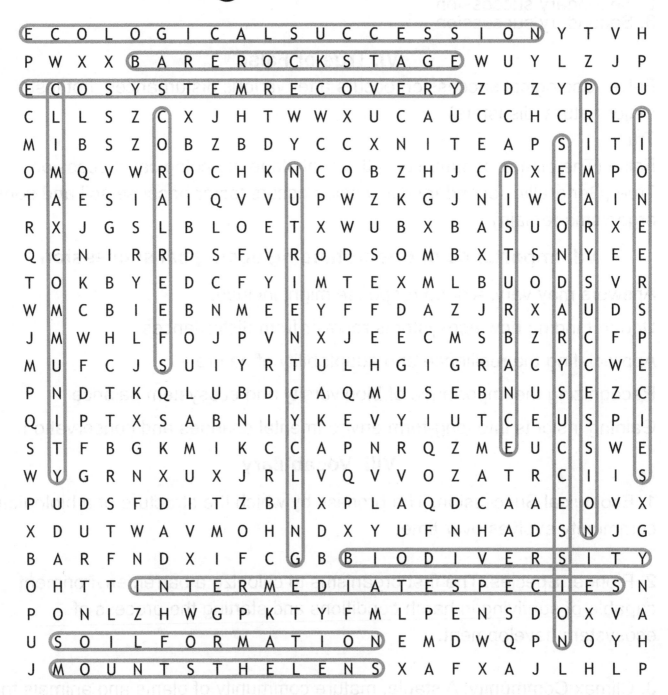

Coral reefs

Ecosystem recovery

Soil formation

Secondary succession

Biodiversity

Mount St Helens

Nutrient cycling

Bare rock stage

Primary succession

Disturbance

Intermediate species

Climax community

Pioneer species

Ecological succession

Ecological Succession

Across

2. The first organisms to colonize a barren environment in primary succession, such as lichen and moss, which help to break down rock and form soil. ____ species

4. A type of ecological succession that occurs in areas where an existing community has been disturbed but soil and some organisms still remain. ____ succession

5. A stable and mature community of plants and animals that emerges at the end of ecological succession, representing a balanced ecosystem. ____ community

9. The initial stage of primary succession where the environment consists solely of bare rock with no soil or plants. ___ ___ stage

10. An example of primary succession observed after the 1980 volcanic eruption, where scientists studied the gradual return of life to the barren landscape. Mount St. ____

12. The process by which an ecosystem regains its structure, function, and species diversity after a disturbance, often through secondary succession. Ecosystem ____

13. An event such as a fire, flood, or human activity that disrupts an existing ecosystem, often initiating secondary succession.

14. The process during primary succession where organic material from decomposing pioneer species combines with rock particles to create soil. Soil ____

Down

1. Plants and animals that colonize an area after pioneer species during succession, often including shrubs and small trees. ____ species

3. The process by which nutrients are recycled within an ecosystem, playing a vital role in maintaining the balance of nutrients in the soil during succession. Nutrient ____

6. An example of secondary succession, where new corals and marine life recolonize a reef after disturbances like hurricanes, helping the ecosystem recover. Coral ___

7. The variety of plant and animal species within an ecosystem, which increases during ecological succession as new habitats are created.

8. The process by which the structure of a biological community evolves over time, involving stages of species colonization and ecosystem development. ____ succession

11. A type of ecological succession that occurs in lifeless areas where there is no soil, starting from bare rock or other barren environments. ____ succession

INTRODUCE | REINFORCE | HOMEWORK | REMEDIATION | HOME | SPED
Introducing The 25x Series Of Workbooks For Middle & High School

Current Titles Available & Launching Now on Amazon & TPT:

25x: Biology (HS)

25x: Personal Finance (HS)

25x: Economics (HS)

25x: Foundational Life Skills (MS)

25x: Life Skills (HS)

25x: Food & Kitchen (HS)

Current Titles In Production For 2024-25

25x: Chemistry (HS)

25x: Physical Science (HS)

25x: High School Prep (MS)

25x: Soft Skills (MS & HS)

25x: Consumer Sciences (HS)

25x: Money Skills (MS & HS)

25x: Career & Technical Education

25x: Computer Literacy (MS)

Written & Produced By Award-Winning & Recognized Teachers With 20+ Years Of Classroom Experience

Current Titles In Production For 2025

High School

25x: Physics

25x: Astronomy

25x: American Government

25x: U.S. History

25x: World History

25x: Law

25x: Entrepreneurship

25x: Graphic Design

25x: Programming

25x: Web & Internet

25x: Electronics

25x: Network Security

Middle School

25x: Earth Science

25x: Biology

25x: Physical Science

25x: Civics

25x: Geography

25x: ELA-Literature

25x: Decision Making

25x: Money Matters

25x: Online Life

Mathematics Titles In Development

Inspired Educators Reflection Journal, Now Available On Amazon

Introducing - Inspired Educators K-12 Professional Development (PD Credit Available)

Empower teachers with the resources to nurture resilience and longevity.

Introducing the *Inspired Educators K-12 Professional Development Series!* Designed for educators, this unique program offers five 60-90 minute sessions that focus on nurturing teacher mental and emotional well-being.

Join us for engaging sessions delivered through Zoom, in-person, or via our convenient online course system. By completing the optional reflection journal, educators can earn one professional development credit.

The Five Sessions Are: 1. The Importance of Self-Care, 2. The Importance of Letting Go, 3. Raising Self-Awareness as an Educator, 4. Maintaining a Positive Mindset, and 5. Maintaining a Growth Mindset

Introducing - Let It Go: 7-Steps to Keeping Your Cool for High School Stu dents!

This comprehensive workbook is written specifically for grades 9-12 and contains 10 complete lessons for students looking to improve their social emotional learning.

Let It Go teaches students to take back control from their Defense Cascade (fight-flight-freeze response) and remain calm, cool, and collected when facing any situation. The program is designed with real solutions that teach students how to regulate their emotions, build self-awareness, and maintain a positive mindset. Not only does this program give students the skills they need to manage difficult situations in life but also gives them practical solutions to help them live their very best lives.

Let It Go: 7-Steps To Keeping Your Cool Workbook for High School Students. TPT & Amazon

Our Lessons On:
TeachersPayTeachers (TPT)
https://www.teacherspayteachers.com/store/3andb

Our Workbooks On:
Amazon
https://amzn.to/3ygpsvk

To learn more about our resources visit our website: 3andB.com

Made in the USA
Las Vegas, NV
17 November 2024